99

Three Plays by Kōbō Abe

MODERN

ASIAN

LITERATURE

SERIES

Three Plays by

COLUMBIA

UNIVERSITY

PRESS

New York

◆

Kōbō Abe

TRANSLATED

AND WITH

AN

INTRODUCTION

BY

Donald

Keene

Columbia University Press
New York   Chichester, West Sussex

The Press gratefully acknowledges the contributions of the Saison Foundation
and Osaka Gas Co., Ltd. toward the costs of publishing this book, which is part
of the program of the Association of 100 Japanese Books.

Library of Congress Cataloging-in-Publication Data

Abe, Kōbō, 1924–1993
    Three plays by Kōbō Abe : translated and with an introduction by
Donald Keene.
      p. cm.
    ISBN 0–231–08280–0
    PA ISBN 0–231–08281–9
    1. Abe, Kōbō, 1924–1993—Translations into English. I. Title.
PL845.B4A25 1993
895.6′25–dc20   93–36358
                                           CIP

Printed in the United States of America
c 10 9 8 7 6 5 4 3 2 1
p 10 9 8 7 6 5 4 3 2 1
All dramatic rights must be applied for to Bridget Aschenberg, ICM, Inc., 40 West
57th Street, New York, NY 10019.

The translation
is dedicated to
Tom and Laurence Rimer

◆

CONTENTS

◆

THE
PLAYS OF
KŌBŌ ABE: AN
INTRODUCTION

Kōbō Abe (1924–93) was a contemporary Japanese writer of world stature. Although he was best known as a novelist, especially for his *Woman in the Dunes* (1962), his achievements as a dramatist were almost equally important, and he published several outstanding volumes of criticism. He was frequently mentioned as a likely recipient of the Nobel Prize in literature, but his death in his sixty-ninth year, when he was still at the height of his powers, prevented him from obtaining this honor.

Ironically, Abe's career as a dramatist began as a purely temporary expedient. Late in 1954 he was under pressure to meet a magazine's deadline for the story he was writing. He was such a meticulous craftsman that if ever he felt he must change a single phrase, he generally rewrote the whole page on which the phrase appeared. It seemed impossible that such a perfectionist would meet his deadline, but it suddenly occurred to Abe that recasting the story as a play would make it easier. The editor of the magazine was not pleased to receive the play instead of the promised story, but as there was no time to ask anyone else, he had no choice but to print Abe's play. To everyone's surprise, *The Uniform* attracted favorable attention, and it was successfully staged in March 1955. Abe's career as a playwright had been launched.

Three months after the production of *The Uniform*, Abe's next play, *The Slave Hunt*,[1] a much more considerable work, was performed at the Actors' Theatre, the leading showcase for contemporary Japanese drama. It was directed by Koreya Senda, for many years a central figure in Japanese theater, especially of the left wing. During the next sixteen years—until 1971—Senda directed nine new plays by Abe, including *The Ghost is Here* (1958) and *Involuntary Homicide* (1971).[2]

In 1971 Abe announced the formation of a "studio"— a company whose distinguishing feature would be the active participation of the performers in creating the plays that were staged. *Guidebook* (1971) was the first production of Abe's studio. Although his controlling hand was apparent, he insisted that he himself had functioned merely as a "guidebook" for the actors to consult, and the play has not been included in his collected works.

The contributions of individual performers to subsequent plays staged by the studio were of less significance than the cooperative efforts they displayed under Abe's extremely careful

[1]A revised version of the play, originally called *Dorei-gari*, was produced in 1967, and in 1975 a much more thoroughly revised version, called *Oo-way* (the cry that gives the strange animals of the play their name), was produced by Abe himself.

[2]Other plays by Abe of this period included *You, Too, are Guilty* (1965), directed by Senda and translated by Ted T. Takaya in *Modern Japanese Drama*. *Friends* (1967) was directed by Masahiko Naruse, and *The Man who Turned into a Stick* (1969), by Abe himself. The latter two plays have been published in my English translations.

guidance. The members of Abe's studio were mainly young actors and actresses, most of them graduates of the theater program of Tōhō Gakuen, the leading music and drama school in Japan. Abe trained the actors in every aspect of performance, working with them day after day from early in the morning until night on basic techniques of speech and movement. The studio itself was open twenty-four hours a day, and the performers stopped by whenever they felt like it to perform calisthenics or to practice their lines. A sense of belonging to a special company developed, and word soon spread of Abe's "method." Several well-known actors, including Eiji Okada and Tatsuya Nakadai, joined the company and cheerfully accepted Abe's direction, though by this time they were already seasoned performers.[3]

The plays Abe wrote after 1976 reveal his increasing preoccupation with nonliterary theater. *The Little Elephant is Dead* (1979) pushed this concept to its logical development: it is virtually without dialogue and depends on the movements of the performers, the lighting, and the music to arouse responses in the audience that Abe believed to be the true function of theater. In 1979 his company performed this work not only in Japan but throughout the United States; in fact, it relied so little on dialogue that there was virtually no language barrier to separate it from American audiences, and the response was overwhelmingly favorable.

Abe wrote a brief statement concerning the objectives of his company after it had completed its successful American tour with *The Little Elephant is Dead* and was again performing the play for Tokyo audiences. It opened, "This work represents the end results achieved during the seven years since I first began to participate in all aspects of theatrical activity. At the same time, it is a point of departure." Abe expressed his conviction that literature had usurped the original purpose of theater, and that critics who insist that a play must have a "meaning" that they can analyze are an anachronism in a world where "meaning" is not required of literary works. He pointed out that an actor's performance, because it can never be exactly the same twice, is always in a present, progressive state, and is not subject to cate-

---

[3]Okada appeared in *The Green Stockings* as the doctor, and Nakadai in the revised version of *Friends* as the victim.

Introduction ◆

gorization and being disposed of with analytical judgments. ("The true actor is always a cause; he cannot be a conclusion.") Abe ended his remarks with these words addressed to the audience: "I would like to share with you, here and now, a world that you could never have experienced or even imagined before you first encountered this work."

Although Abe believed when he wrote these words that *The Little Elephant is Dead* was not only a summation of what he had achieved theatrically but a beginning for further exploration in nonliterary theater, it was his last play. He returned to being a novelist—a man of words, rather than a director of actors on a stage. Perhaps he found that he had actually reached the limit of what could be achieved without dialogue or a plot. He had been successful but at a cost of sacrificing his most precious asset, his marvelous skill with words.

The plays contained in this volume, far from being nonliterary, are written in language of consummate skill. But even if a play was an unqualified success when performed according to the original text, Abe generally did not leave it unchanged when the play was revived. Sometimes the changes were dictated by the available performers: for this reason, the grandmother in *Friends* became a grandfather when the play was revived. Or his attitude toward his material sometimes changed: for another revival of *Friends* he added a character, the third son, in order to establish a link between the family and the outside world, a matter that had previously not seemed essential. On the other hand, one fairly important character in the original text of *The Ghost is Here* was eliminated in later performances, after Abe had decided he was unnecessary, and his lines were assigned to another character. Apart from such major changes, passages of dialogue were altered repeatedly, always in an effort to further refine his message.

Abe did not consider any text of his plays to be definitive. Although he did not disavow earlier versions, each was considered a work-in-progress. For this reason, I have chosen to translate the most recent text available to me.

The plays all present problems of translation. The most difficult was *Involuntary Homicide*. I know what the title (*mihitsu no koi* in Japanese) means, but I could not find a lawyer who was able to supply the English equivalent, and I had no choice but to use the dictionary translation. Yet that was the least of my problems. The dialogue of *Involuntary Homicide* is written in two distinct varieties of Japanese. The first is a dialect fairly close to the one spoken on an island off the coast of Kyūshū, the setting Abe had in mind. The second is the formal, rather stilted standard Japanese spoken by the characters of the play when making a deposition before an imagined magistrate. Abe suggested that I model the English of my translation of these sections on the language a New York policeman might use in court in reporting a crime, but this, alas, was beyond my powers. I hope that at least some of the differences between the two spoken styles of Japanese will be felt even in my English version.

The other two plays posed lesser problems of translation. One I never surmounted in *The Ghost is Here* was the song the model sings toward the close of the play. For the refrain of "I love *yūrei*" (*yūrei* meaning a "ghost"), I simply could not come up with a pun that worked in both languages. In *The Green Stockings*, I translated the term *sōshoku ningen* as "herbivorous human being," though I realized this was rather too much of a mouthful. But "grass-eating human" seemed even worse. Such problems, faced by every translator, are particularly troublesome when translating dialogue that must flow naturally from the mouths of actors and actresses. I hope that if these plays are performed in English the actors will modify the words to accord most easily with their own speech.

The modern Japanese theater originated at the beginning of the twentieth century but its development was slow because of the competition both from native forms of drama, notably Kabuki, and, later, from film. It has only been since 1945 that it can be said to have achieved maturity. The plays of Kōbō Abe, together with those by Yukio Mishima, were the first to be performed widely outside Japan. It is hoped that the plays represented in this volume will find an audience not only among Abe's many admirers but among all interested in the state of world theater.

◆

NOTE

ON THE

PLAYS

Involuntary Homicide (*Mihitsu no koi*) was first performed in 1971.

The Green Stockings (*Midori-iro no sutokkingu*) was first performed in 1974. It was directed by Abe himself.

The Ghost is Here (*Yūrei wa koko ni iru*) was first performed in 1958. It has been revived several times, most recently with music by Tōru Takemitsu.

Other plays by Kōbō Abe that have been published in English include *Friends*, *The Man Who Turned into a Stick*, and *You, Too, Are Guilty*.

Three Plays by Kōbō Abe

Involuntary Homicide
A Play in Eleven Scenes

Hisashi Igawa as
FIRE CHIEF
(center) in a
scene from
*Involuntary
Homicide.*

■

SCENE 1

(*Intermittent lightning flashes. A group of people have surrounded and are beating with sticks a man lying on the ground* [EGUCHI]. *Their movements are deliberate, creating an impression of a film in slow motion. The attackers all wear black rubber boots, black rubberized raincoats, and black parka hoods. The heavy, dull sound, resembling that of beating against a sandbag, continues intensely and without letup.*)

EGUCHI'S VOICE (*brokenly, gasping for breath*): Let me go . . . Ohh . . . You're hurting me . . . Let me go . . .

FIRE CHIEF: You've all hit him? One whack's enough, but everybody's got to join in.

EGUCHI'S VOICE (*becoming fainter, groaning*): It's enough . . . let me go, won't you? I apologize. Let me go . . . it hurts . . .

FIRE CHIEF: We're all together in this. No shirking, now.

(*The sounds stop. The people of the island all freeze into pale silhouettes.* ISLANDER A *emerges from the dark, illuminated by a spotlight.*)

ISLANDER A (*awkwardly, as if reciting by rote a text he does not understand*): With respect to the beating to death with clubs, by myself and other people of the island, of Eguchi Itaru, aged thirty-eight years, the manager of a bar, a pachinko parlor, and a movie theater, and the distributor of popsicles on this island, Kiku Island, I will respond as precisely as possible to the questions. The night of the incident was not absolutely dark. You could see the road clearly and make out people's movements. However, unless you got up real close and took a good look, you couldn't tell one face from another. I and my friends had been hiding for a while in a clump of bamboos, but I suppose it wasn't until about half past eleven that Eguchi finished toting up his sales for the day, and showed himself from behind the movie theater. He looked in at the pachinko parlor next door, and he said in a loud voice, to nobody in particular, "Damn it! Not a customer all day. Again! These islanders are stingy as hell." The machines in Eguchi's pachinko parlor are fixed, and nobody's ever won a thing, so people all stay away. But I knew Eguchi from way back was a hoodlum, and he always had a terrible temper, so when he showed himself, I was afraid and I hid behind a garbage can. It was then that some of the others, who had come from the opposite direction, gathered around Eguchi, and began to question him peacefully. All of a sudden, Eguchi took off his geta, and holding them in his hands, began hitting somebody. Before I knew what was happening, it had developed into a free-for-all. I was some distance away and it was dark, so I don't know exactly who was first surrounding Eguchi. Before long everybody started

4

■ *Involuntary Homicide*

moving toward the square. I and the others followed along hesitantly. I somehow didn't feel like jumping out right away and hitting Eguchi, so I sat down on the steps of the public toilet in front of the shrine. I smoked a cigarette and watched for a while as they fought it out. I wasn't the only one watching. There were lots of other people, but it was dark and I don't know exactly who they were. The people involved in the fight moved back and forth, over and over, between the torii and the gingko tree, and each time I looked Eguchi was either falling down or else getting to his feet. It was then that somebody called out, "Nobody's excused from hitting him! Don't forget we promised to maintain solidarity!"

(FIRE CHIEF *steps forward from the background. One can see the self-possession and composure that stems from his awareness that the trust of the islanders is centered on him.*)

FIRE CHIEF (*removes his hood. Reprovingly*): No, that's not it . . . You've got it wrong.

ISLANDER A: There was nothing wrong in what I said. I memorized the words, exactly the way they were written down for me.

FIRE CHIEF: Surely, nobody gave you any instructions. Right?

ISLANDER A: . . . All the same, I learned the whole thing by heart. I wouldn't know otherwise what to say.

FIRE CHIEF (*takes some handwritten papers from under his raincoat, and moistening his finger with saliva, runs through them quickly*): That's funny . . . Ah, here it is . . . (*Reads.*) It was then that somebody . . .

ISLANDER A: That's what I said, wasn't it? "It was then that somebody . . ."

FIRE CHIEF: Something's been left out here. It should be—it's just past "somebody called out"—(*he reads ahead*) "Nobody's excused from hitting him."

ISLANDER A (*following him*): Don't forget we promised to maintain solidarity.

FIRE CHIEF: This is where the correction comes. (*Thinks awhile.*) Prompted by the voice of conscience . . .

ISLANDER A: Prompted by . . .

FIRE CHIEF: the voice of conscience . . .

5

ISLANDER A: the voice of conscience . . .

FIRE CHIEF: The rest is OK as it stands. (*Continues to read*) I finally went to where the fighting was going on . . .

ISLANDER A (*stammering*) . . . Prompted by the voice of conscience, I finally went to where the fighting was going on.

FIRE CHIEF (*with a note of appreciation in his voice*): That's it. Now it all matches up. And it's the truth, what's more.

ISLANDER A (*reverting to recitation by rote*): Eguchi was sitting there, his head in his hands, and he was screaming, "Forgive me . . . forgive me, please." But we were afraid of what he might do later on if we let him off, and we all knew that if we didn't at least break his arms so he couldn't hold a knife anymore, there wouldn't be any peace on the island. People were shouting, "Damn the bastard! This'll teach you a lesson!" and things like that, and they went on hitting him by turns. This was when I stepped out from the ranks of the spectators. I gave Eguchi two fairly hard blows to his back. A little while later, somebody called out, "How about stopping?" and with that almost everybody stopped. Just then it started to rain. We felt sorry for him, and a number of people turned Eguchi over face-up and carried him by the hands and feet to the entrance to the movie theater, where the rain wouldn't wet him, and left him lying there.

(*At this point in the testimony figures in the background begin to move. They pick up* EGUCHI *and carry him offstage.*)

While they were carrying Eguchi, I was so intent in watching him as he was being taken away that I didn't get a good look at who was actually carrying him. Afterward, some people, a couple at a time, passed me going along the main street, but I went directly home. I put the stick I'd used to beat Eguchi in the wood pile back of the house, spread out my bedding and went to sleep. The next morning, when I heard Eguchi was dead, I was surprised and I also felt sorry for him. I deeply regretted what had happened. There was no need to beat him so hard he died of it.

(*Dark change, leaving only* FIRE CHIEF.)

6

■ *Involuntary Homicide*

SCENE 2

(During the dark change there are sounds of a wooden door being kicked open and of breaking glass. A sound of a shelf full of bottles falling over. A sound of a chair being slammed against a wall. Similar noises. Two young men, GIMPY *and* ONE EYE, *are picked out from the obscurity by spotlights. They are dressed like two very ordinary young men.* GIMPY *is standing. He moves about quite freely despite his artificial leg. Once in a while he makes use of a cherry branch that serves as a cane, but that is all.* ONE EYE *is sitting down. He wears an eye patch, and he tends to look down. He has spread open on his knees the same papers as the* FIRE CHIEF. *The sounds become shorter and intermittent, and after a time, the intervals lengthen.)*

GIMPY *(he also speaks in the awkward tones of a recitation by rote, brandishing a stick in his hands, as if performing a sword dance)*: With respect to the incident in which Eguchi Itaru, the manager of a bar and movie theater on this island, was indiscriminately beaten until he died of his injuries at the hands of persons who assaulted him by way of revenge for his intolerable acts of violence, we, the young men of the island, bear absolutely no responsibility, but we bear a heavy sense of responsibility for having created the impetus for this action, and we feel deeply ashamed of our criminal acts of violence and disorder at the Bar Kewpie, which resulted in such damage as to make it impossible to carry on business there any longer. For this reason, of my own free will, I have turned myself in. Again, beating Eguchi to death was undoubtedly excessive, but if one examines the causes, it will become evident that this action was taken by way of retaliation for the violence to which we young people had been subjected, and for this reason, I would like to request the authorities to favor us with humane judgment and their lenience.

FIRE CHIEF *(in the manner of a prosecutor)*: Are you saying, then, that it was fair and proper for Eguchi to be killed?

GIMPY: No, I don't think it was proper.

FIRE CHIEF: But don't you consider that, in view of what Eguchi did, it was fitting that he should be killed?

7

Involuntary Homicide ∎

GIMPY: No matter what a man may do, it surely is never fitting to be killed for it.

FIRE CHIEF: Then why are you testifying on behalf of the islanders who in fact employed violence?

GIMPY: In the final analysis, it's because they've always showed us young people parental affection.

FIRE CHIEF: Do you consider it's permissible to kill someone, providing it's inspired by parental affection?

GIMPY: I'm not saying anything of the kind. But for him to have made peaceful, unsophisticated islanders . . .

ONE EYE (*correcting him*): Diligent islanders . . .

GIMPY: Diligent islanders . . . (*He hesitates.*)

ONE EYE: resort to such violence . . .

GIMPY: resort to such violence, was an act of provocation on Eguchi's part which I heartily detest.

FIRE CHIEF: Then do you consider killing Eguchi was unavoidable, in view of such acts of provocation?

GIMPY: No, I do not. Regardless of the reasons, surely it is not possible to say that killing him was unavoidable.

FIRE CHIEF: But you do feel, don't you, in terms of the result, that it was a good thing he died?

GIMPY: No matter how great the provocation, I can't possibly imagine feeling glad that any human being is dead.

FIRE CHIEF: Then, please describe to us in the order that the events took place and in detail the nature of the violence that occurred at the Bar Kewpie.

(ONE EYE, *putting down the papers, stands. Whipping out the cherry branch he had stuck into his belt, he starts to slash at* GIMPY. *The two of them fence playfully, rather like puppies frolicking together. However, their manner of speech remains awkward and suggestive of rote memorization. When one of them while talking exposes himself to attack, the other thrusts in on him.*)

ONE EYE: I shall respond in detail with respect to the matter about which you inquire. I have been informed that I need not testify concerning anything about which I prefer not to speak, and I am fully aware of this . . .

GIMPY: I am eager to confess the truth, without concealing anything.

ONE EYE: Concerning Eguchi's violence . . .

GIMPY: As I stated at the time of the previous investigation . . .

ONE EYE: If such incidents were to continue, we could not . . .

GIMPY: Remain on the island.

ONE EYE: Eguchi seemed to have considered us young men as his particular enemies, so we thought that if we were to leave . . .

GIMPY: Peace might return to the island . . .

ONE EYE: The three of us belonging to the Fire Brigade, discussed this and reported our conclusion to the Fire Chief.

(ONE EYE, *hit by* GIMPY, *falls with a thud.*)

FIRE CHIEF: That's exactly what happened. When I heard their complaint, I was flabbergasted. If the young men, who carry the burden of the island's future, deserted it, what kind of peace could there be? What kind of progress could there be on the island?

GIMPY (*having straddled the fallen* ONE EYE *and administered the coup de grace, he suddenly shifts his attack to* FIRE CHIEF): I would like to ask the witness what relations exist between the young men of the island and the Fire Brigade.

FIRE CHIEF: As Fire Chief, I have under me three members of the brigade.

GIMPY: In other words, the Fire Brigade consists entirely of young men?

FIRE CHIEF: That is correct.

ONE EYE (*lifting his head*): And two of them are defendants in the present case?

FIRE CHIEF: That is correct.

(ONE EYE *gets up and brushes the dust from his clothes. He and* GIMPY *exchange glances and snicker. The two young men do nothing in particular to indicate that they have now assumed a stance of attack against the* FIRE CHIEF, *but one begins to sense a vague tension in the air.*)

GIMPY: What was the third member doing?

FIRE CHIEF: He was on duty that night. He was standing guard at the observation post.

ONE EYE: Have you ever noticed anything special in the relations between the members of the Fire Brigade and the young men who are not members?

9

Involuntary Homicide ■

FIRE CHIEF: I do not understand the meaning of the question.

ONE EYE: It appears that there were frequent altercations between the young men belonging to the Fire Brigade and Eguchi. Were there not similar incidents in the case of the other young men?

FIRE CHIEF: There aren't any other young men.

GIMPY: You mean that there are only three young men on the island?

FIRE CHIEF: That's right. Only three young men.

GIMPY: Have the words "young men" some special sense on Kiku Island?

(GIMPY *and* ONE EYE *burst out laughing.*)

FIRE CHIEF: No, nothing like that. But surely it would not be proper to refer to people who are not actually living on the island as "young men of the island."

GIMPY: It would seem that the members of the Fire Brigade under the witness's command all share some special characteristics. Could you explain how this has come about?

FIRE CHIEF: The hopes of the entire population of the island hang on these three young men.

GIMPY: My question concerns physical characteristics. If the witness finds the question objectionable, he is not obliged to respond.

FIRE CHIEF (*hotly*): What could be objectionable about it? To think of it as objectionable is in itself much more objectionable. Yes, it's true, the three young men are all what people call cripples—one of them has a bad leg, another has only one eye, and the third is deaf. In general people try to show special consideration toward cripples, but on this island nobody shows them any consideration. Nobody hesitates to call them One Eye, Deafy, Gimpy!

GIMPY: Hey, One Eye!

ONE EYE: What do you want, Gimpy?

(*They glare at each other, their hands clenched around their sticks.*)

FIRE CHIEF: . . . They're only speaking the plain truth. There's absolutely no contempt behind the words. The young men are the pillars of the island, the object of our hopes—there's no need to pity them. As long as they remain on the island, there's no chance of their ever developing an inferiority complex or a persecution complex.

(GIMPY *and* ONE EYE *begin to circle around, each looking for an opening in the other's defenses.*)

ONE EYE: Gimpy!

GIMPY: One Eye!

FIRE CHIEF: If anyone suffered from paranoia, it would have been Eguchi, wouldn't you say?

GIMPY: Was there any reason for Eguchi to feel paranoia?

FIRE CHIEF: As long as they go on living on the island, the young men have nothing to worry about.

(GIMPY *and* ONE EYE *clash once, only to jump back and resume their mutual glaring.*)

GIMPY: You one-eyed bastard!

ONE EYE: You lousy one-leg!

FIRE CHIEF (*making an effort to maintain his calm, insofar as possible, he returns to rote recitation*): I would like to take this opportunity to mention that I myself am by no means free of physical infirmities. I formerly worked as a bus and truck driver in the Kansai region, but I suffered from epilepsy, though I did not notice it myself because the seizures were momentary. But before I knew it I had piled up a record of fifty-three accidents, and in the end I suffered the tragic misfortune of having my driving license rescinded. I came back to the island heartbroken. Happily for me, I received the warm support of the people of the island, and I have been elected three times as a member of the town council. I know from my own experience . . .

(*Suddenly,* GIMPY *and* ONE EYE *groan and begin to flail with the sticks they hold up over their heads. They are not aiming at each other in particular, but seem to be trying to knock to the ground an invisible enemy. Presently the invisible enemy falls. The two groan and continue to slash wildly, only for the strength to drain from them all of a sudden. They put down their weapons and stand there looking dazed.*)

Involuntary Homicide ∎

SCENE 3

(*The whole stage becomes light. It is a room in the community center that serves both as an office and a place to sleep. An office desk and several chairs. A wood-burning stove converted from a gasoline drum. On top of it a kettle from which steam rises. At the back of the room two rows of built-in three-tiered bunk beds. Higher up, an observation post equipped with large-size binoculars. On the wall rubberized raincoats, lanterns, etc. The others maintain the same positions and attitudes as in the previous scene.* DEAFY *can be seen in the observation post looking through the binoculars.*)

FIRE CHIEF (*approaches the two who look dazed by their fight, and taps them encouragingly on the shoulders. He takes their sticks.*): You did just fine . . . I appreciate the trouble you took . . . Nobody's going to bother you now, so stretch out and take it easy.

(FIRE CHIEF *holds sticks up to the light and examines them. He then thrusts them into the stove. The two young men, exhausted, sit on the edge of the bed.* DEAFY *turns momentarily in their direction but returns at once to his binoculars.*)

DEAFY (*gloomily*): It looks as if there's still blood sticking to them.

FIRE CHIEF: When you put it in the fire, it doesn't make any difference if it's blood or shit, it all turns to ashes.

ONE EYE (*rubbing his hands as with the cold*): At first there was solid resistance from his body . . .

GIMPY: Mmm.

ONE EYE: But somewhere along the line I suddenly felt him grow limp . . .

GIMPY (*with the gestures of savagely battering someone with a stick*): Bang! Bang! Bang!

FIRE CHIEF: That's the way it is with everything. As long as they're alive and kicking, you can feel their resistance. But once you've hit a vital part, they all turn limp, even dolphins or no matter what. It's just as if their bones'd melted.

GIMPY: Dolphins?

ONE EYE: Does that mean they're dead?

GIMPY: It looks that way.

■ *Involuntary Homicide*

ONE EYE: It seemed to happen just after we'd given it to him. All the resistance suddenly went out of him and he became limp . . .

GIMPY: Even his nose began to run.

FIRE CHIEF (*laughs before he realizes it, but his expression at once becomes serious again*): Are you guys talking in your sleep? Of all the stupid things. Nobody here laid a finger on Eguchi. You'd finished wrecking the Kewpie, and you just got back here, right? That was when you heard what had happened from the man on duty, and you were completely taken aback. That's the line we're following. Now, Deafy, it's your turn.

DEAFY: During the twenty-four minutes between eleven thirty-four and eleven fifty-eight . . .

FIRE CHIEF: What happened in those twenty-four minutes?

DEAFY: There seems to have been a free-for-all in the square in front of the shrine.

FIRE CHIEF (*his eyes seem to be sparkling with anticipation*): Oh, there was a free-for-all? Then what happened?

DEAFY (*he seems to find the question bothersome*): Don't you know without my saying?

(*An unpleasant pause.*)

ONE EYE: Wasn't going to the Kewpie premeditated?

FIRE CHIEF: It's not the same thing as attacking a person. You've nothing to worry about.

DEAFY: It won't be so long before a report comes . . .

FIRE CHIEF: Even if it doesn't, we know what happened.

(*An even more unpleasant pause.*)

GIMPY: There wasn't much blood.

ONE EYE: That's right. There wasn't.

DEAFY: You know, it's just like dolphins. If you first beat the daylights out of them, they don't bleed much even if you cut them afterward.

FIRE CHIEF (*irritated*): Of all the stupid . . . How about dropping the subject of Eguchi?

DEAFY (*calmly*): Why couldn't you let us leave the island?

FIRE CHIEF (*turns on him*): Why couldn't I let you leave the island? . . . I'm glad you asked . . . That hearing aid you're wearing— they're still quite a few installments to pay on it, if I'm not mistaken.

DEAFY (*with a bitter smile*): Is that so? Bought on the installment plan, was it? (*He removes the hearing aid.*)

FIRE CHIEF: Another seventeen months to go. It's a new model, approved by IC, and the price was pretty high.

GIMPY: That reminds me—my artificial leg was also bought on the installment plan.

FIRE CHIEF: There're still nine months to go on that. It was made to order, and it seems to fit you.

GIMPY: You can't swim across the sea when you're wearing leg irons. Any way you look at it, we're all birds in a cage.

ONE EYE: We're birds in a cage even without the installments to pay. We're already prime suspects. No matter how much we kick and struggle, we won't escape.

FIRE CHIEF: You needn't be so sarcastic. You don't seem to understand. Everything I did was for you guys. What've you got to complaint about? Now that Eguchi's dead, the island's yours. You can do anything you please. Tell me, what do you want that you haven't got?

ONE EYE: I want a woman.

FIRE CHIEF: I understand. I assure you, I understand. That's already in my plans. Pretty soon I'll be bringing you a girl from the Kewpie. Women like that'll do anything for money. Now that Eguchi isn't around any more, they're ours.

DEAFY: I want a woman of my own, not somebody I have to share with other people.

FIRE CHIEF: You're just making things difficult for me if you insist on talking about the distant future. One step at a time is the way to do things. You just leave everything to me. As long as you remain on the island, I'll see to it you won't want for anything. I'm not the only one who's made up his mind to this. Everybody on the island feels the same way. Surely you must have felt this yourselves a couple of hours ago.

(*Sudden dark change, leaving only* FIRE CHIEF.)

■ *Involuntary Homicide*

(*Stage is dark.* FIRE CHIEF *steps forward. His movements suggest that he is at a public meeting where he is addressing an investigator to stage left at the rear.*)

FIRE CHIEF (*in rote delivery manner*): At this point somebody who was evidently quite overwrought said, "The island can't survive if we're deserted by the young people. Let's not lose any time in sending somebody to negotiate with Eguchi." I gave my opinion, "I don't mind going myself to negotiate with Eguchi, but the most he'll do is let me talk. There's no chance of his having any second thoughts. Besides, a guy like that always carries a knife. If he draws his knife before we reach a settlement, what am I supposed to do then?" Then somebody suggested, "In that case, wouldn't the best thing be to give him a poke?" But one of the young men said, "That won't do any good. There's no telling what Eguchi might do to get even if we gave him a poke. Forget it." Then a lot of people, all at once, said, "We can't let things go on this way. If we cut some branches and give him a sound whipping, he's not likely to do anything bad afterward." The young men, taking into consideration the feelings of the people of the island who've worried so much about them, decided they couldn't oppose them any further, and agreed with the rest.

(GIMPY *and* ONE EYE *appear in a spotlight to stage rear. They slowly put on high rubber boots, raincoats, and hoods.*)

Well, then, the discussion proceeded as to what we should do. I gave them careful warning, "We mustn't beat his head or his internal organs. All we want to do is make sure he won't be carrying a knife anymore. We should concentrate on breaking his arms." Then somebody said, "He's carrying a knife. Wouldn't it be better to attack with six-foot poles?" But somebody else said, "Six-footers are too long. If you miss just once, he can drill a hole in you. A handier size stick'd be better." And that's what we decided. Then we all got into high rubber boots, raincoats, and hoods, picked up sticks of firewood that were lying in the yard of the community center, and went outside. Everyone was pretty worked up at the

15

Involuntary Homicide ∎

time, but I believe that there was not one person who intended to beat Eguchi to death.

(GIMPY *and* ONE EYE, *having dressed as prescribed, each select a branch of cherrywood from a pile of firewood in a wing of the stage, and come forward.*)

GIMPY: Everything's ready.

ONE EYE: Well, isn't it about time we got moving?

FIRE CHIEF (*lights a cigarette. In high spirits*): No need to be in such a rush. Your job is to administer the finishing touches. Wait until the others have laid the groundwork sufficiently, and then you can start off, taking your time. (*To* ONE EYE.) Branches with knotholes are no good. Your aim'll go wild, and the branch'll break in no time.

(ONE EYE *puts the branch back in the pile of firewood and searches for another stick.*)

GIMPY (*swinging down his stick with fury*): Damn you, Eguchi!

FIRE CHIEF: You seem to be shaking.

GIMPY: I don't know anything about it. I'm not the one who picked the quarrel.

FIRE CHIEF: That's right. You don't know about anything. And One Eye doesn't know anything either. (*Looks at his wristwatch.*) Eleven thirty-three. According to the deposition I'll have to write one of these days, right now the two of you are supposed to be breaking in at the Kewpie. It doesn't matter what you do to Eguchi— you've got an iron-clad alibi.

(*Cries of people in the distance:* "What d'you think you're doing?" "Damned louse!" "Trying to run away?" *etc. This is followed by the sounds of a door being smashed and of window glass shattering.*)

ONE EYE: It's started.

FIRE CHIEF: Well, shall we be weighing our anchors?

(ONE EYE, *squaring himself for a fight, starts outside.* GIMPY *follows behind, thumping with his wooden leg.*)

FIRE CHIEF (*calls them back. He speaks in the role of an examining officer*): At this time, I take it, the two of you had already arrived at the Bar Kewpie?

GIMPY (*in rote tones*): That is correct. We decided we didn't want to cause the people of the island any further worry, so we ran on ahead of the others. We cut across a wheat field,

16

and when we got to the Kewpie, we were the only two people there, maybe because we'd taken a short cut.

FIRE CHIEF: There were absolutely no signs of anyone else?

GIMPY: Nobody at all. We figured Eguchi was in the bar, so we thought we'd wait a bit longer until there were a few more of us, and we stood for a while outside the back door of the Kewpie. Just then, all of a sudden, we heard shouting at the front entrance, and the sound of the glass door being smashed. "That's it," I thought, and I started in, with a stick in my right hand. But as bad luck would have it, it was so dark I didn't see the drainage ditch. I stuck my right leg in it, and my artificial leg snapped off at the knee.

FIRE CHIEF: Does it often happen that an artificial leg snaps off? Was it because it was badly attached?

GIMPY: It was not because it was badly attached. My artificial leg, like the new-model skis, is so made that it detaches itself automatically when excessive force is applied from an unnatural angle, and in this way it protects the other joints.

FIRE CHIEF: I understand. Please continue.

ONE EYE: I helped him, and between us we pulled his artificial leg out of the ditch, and reattached it to his leg, without wasting much time. In the meanwhile, about ten minutes had passed, I'd say. Then, we thought we shouldn't let the others do all the work. We went into the Kewpie as quickly as we could, to join in the break-in, but the others had already left, and neither Eguchi nor the waitresses were to be seen. Inside was a shambles. Every last bottle of whiskey and beer had been broken. The smell was enough to make you drunk.

(*Dark change.*)

SCENE 5

(*In the dark, the only light is from the red glow of the fire in the stove.*)

YOUNG WOMAN'S VOICE (*her voice is low and sounds rather frightened*): Nobody here? . . . Nobody here? . . . Come on, there must be somebody . . . (*Her figure can be seen as she*

17

Involuntary Homicide ∎

comes closer to the stove.) It looks as if somebody has just put wood on the fire . . .

DEAFY'S VOICE: Who is it?

YOUNG WOMAN'S VOICE: I'm sorry. It's Kumiko. You know, from the Kewpie.

(*The lights are switched on.* DEAFY *stands by the entrance to the observation post, his hand on the light switch.* YOUNG WOMAN *holds in her arms a Kewpie doll about the size of a baby. She stands before the stove. She is a waitress at the Bar Kewpie.*)

DEAFY: What do you want?

YOUNG WOMAN: Something terrible's happened. A customer went on a rampage and wrecked the whole place.

DEAFY: A customer?

YOUNG WOMAN (*nods*): Somebody I'd never seen before. He didn't look like anybody from the island.

DEAFY: How long had he been there?

YOUNG WOMAN: About an hour.

DEAFY (*without thinking*): That messes up everything!

YOUNG WOMAN (*nods*): Yes, it's a real mess. Would you mind helping me out?

DEAFY: Are you sure he's the one who made all the rumpus?

YOUNG WOMAN: An absolutely blank face—it gave me the creeps. Drunken frenzy is what it was.

DEAFY: Are you absolutely sure this man did it? Did you see him do it with your own eyes?

YOUNG WOMAN (*shakes her head*): It happened just after I left the table where I was sitting. The maid called me over and said the manager wanted to see me.

DEAFY: I see. Up to then everything was all right.

YOUNG WOMAN: Yes, up to then everything was all right. I thought the manager must be in the pachinko parlor and I started off in that direction, when suddenly I heard this terrific noise. Hardly had I turned my head for a look than the front window glass came crashing down, and then there were three beer bottles, bang, bang, bang. I was stunned, what with the terrific noise and the beer bottles and the explosions . . .

DEAFY: What's that you've got there?

YOUNG WOMAN: This? (*She makes a gesture for money by form-*

■ *Involuntary Homicide*

ing a circle with her fingers above the head of the Kewpie doll.)
My savings bank.

DEAFY: Savings bank?

YOUNG WOMAN: I had a suspicion something would happen. It's a good thing I took this with me. Sometimes, you know, I get premonitions, right here. (*She presses her finger against her left temple.*)

DEAFY: You might've gone back to make sure what'd happened.

YOUNG WOMAN (*shaking her head*): The next minute it became pitch dark. The lights'd been smashed, and the maid leaped out, screaming, "Run for your life!" . . . (*As if she had remembered why she came.*) Please, I'm begging you, come with me right away . . . (*She holds out her arm as if to draw him with her.*)

DEAFY (*perplexed, he pulls back his arm*): You put me on the spot. You come here, telling me what's happened . . . Why don't you go to the police substation?

YOUNG WOMAN: I've already been there. The place is empty. There's nobody there.

DEAFY: What's happened to the manager? Where is he?

YOUNG WOMAN (*puzzled*): It's funny—after going to the trouble of sending for me . . . I thought I'd stop by the movie theater and look for him there, but there were some sinister-looking men in raincoats loitering around the place, and I got frightened . . .

DEAFY: What do you mean, sinister-looking?

YOUNG WOMAN (*holding up her Kewpie doll*): I'm not taking any chances.

DEAFY: Is there a lot in it?

YOUNG WOMAN (*laughs happily*): It only takes one-yen coins . . . But it's not the amount that counts. It's now only up to a little over the groin . . .

DEAFY: Over the what?

YOUNG WOMAN (*points to a part of the doll*): The groin, here . . . He's promised to marry me when the whole thing's full.

DEAFY: Who has?

YOUNG WOMAN: The manager.

DEAFY: The manager? You mean Eguchi?

YOUNG WOMAN (*raising her voice*): You know him?

19

Involuntary Homicide ■

DEAFY: Of course I know him.

YOUNG WOMAN: Are you friendly with him?

DEAFY: Not exactly.

YOUNG WOMAN: That's right. The manager's not the type who can make friends. But this *is* a branch of the town office, isn't it?

DEAFY: What time do you think it is? It's the middle of the night.

YOUNG WOMAN: Then, what do you do here?

DEAFY: I'm the watch officer for the fire brigade.

YOUNG WOMAN: A fireman's fine with me.

DEAFY: But there's no fire, is there?

YOUNG WOMAN: It's something like a fire. Please.

DEAFY: But I can't neglect my official duties.

YOUNG WOMAN: Now, what am I going to do? . . . Even as we stand talking this way, he may be breaking up the whole place, one thing after another . . .

DEAFY: In my opinion, you have nothing to worry about, in the long run, anyway.

YOUNG WOMAN: You mean, it's none of my business, right? (*Removing her raincoat.*) It's hot . . . (*She wears a gaudy blouse with a low neck and an extremely short skirt.*)

DEAFY: The important thing is that you yourself didn't see anything.

YOUNG WOMAN: Look how I'm sweating. Here, under my brassiere . . .

DEAFY: No, you did see something. You saw the customer who made all the trouble.

YOUNG WOMAN (*with a sigh*): Well, I suppose I should go back to look for the manager.

DEAFY: If there's ever a fire or a shipwreck, don't hesitate to call again.

(YOUNG WOMAN, *bunching together the Kewpie doll and her raincoat, starts to exit, with a show of reluctance.*)

YOUNG WOMAN (*turning back*): Did you hear a funny noise just now?

DEAFY: What kind of funny noise?

YOUNG WOMAN: Pretending to be deaf, are you? (*Starts to leave.*)

■ *Involuntary Homicide*

DEAFY: Wait. Maybe it'd be better if you didn't leave . . . The scenario seems to have got a little mixed up, thanks to that customer . . . Even if they've sealed *his* mouth, it'll be awkward if you're still around to talk . . . Stay here. I'll see what's going on.

YOUNG WOMAN: I tell you it's all right. If only I can find the manager, everything will work out somehow.

DEAFY: It's best for you not to go out by yourself. I'm giving you good advice.

YOUNG WOMAN (*flashes a smile in return*): Do I look so fragile?

DEAFY: Are you in love with Eguchi?

YOUNG WOMAN: What a funny thing to say! (*Puts her hand on the door.*)

DEAFY: You'll never see Eguchi again.

(YOUNG WOMAN *clutches the doll closer to her without realizing it.*)

DEAFY: Right now, they've just started beating him to death.

YOUNG WOMAN: Why?

DEAFY: You saw them, didn't you—those men in black raincoats loitering around . . .

YOUNG WOMAN (*for the first time, a look of fear crosses her face*): You mean that customer was one of them?

DEAFY: I don't know about the customer. But it's too bad you saw his face. Tonight I'll hide you somehow, but tomorrow morning you've got to take the first boat from the island.

YOUNG WOMAN: Was that what the noise was?

DEAFY: Maybe.

YOUNG WOMAN: How come you know so much about it?

DEAFY (*gestures with his chin at the binoculars in the observation post*): Because I'm on watch duty.

YOUNG WOMAN: How about ringing the fire alarm?

(DEAFY *shakes his head.*)

YOUNG WOMAN: Will you let me look through the binoculars?

(DEAFY *nods.* YOUNG WOMAN *climbs up to the observation post.*)

DEAFY: It's hard to see unless the room's dark. Shall I turn off the lights?

YOUNG WOMAN (*looking through the binoculars*): Mmm.

(DEAFY *places his hand on the switch. Dark change.*)

Involuntary Homicide ∎

SCENE 6

(*In the pale light* GIMPY *and* ONE EYE *appear as silhouettes, beating down toward the ground with all their strength. They pant heavily for breath. A dull sound as of beating against sandbags. Some ingenuity is essential in the use of the sticks to suggest that the object of the beating is a human body. A regular rhythm should be avoided.* ISLANDER B *is picked out by a spotlight.*)

ISLANDER B (*in tones of rote recitation*): The people of the island hated Eguchi. He was as repulsive to them as a caterpillar, and everybody thought the best way to deal with such a monster was to stay clear of him and to patiently put up with his ways, but when he took to harassing the young men, who are really good boys, this finally set off the anger of the people of the island. That night I stopped off at my house to leave the change I got after buying some cigarettes, so I arrived on the scene a little later than the others. By the time I reached the square Eguchi was already more dead than alive. I felt embarrassed about being late, so I wasted no time in breaking through the wall of people around Eguchi. I hit him twice on his rear, and he blubbered at me, "I'm sorry. Let me off." This frightened me and I shrank back. It's surprising, considering how big I am, that I've always been timid, ever since I was a kid, and—you may not believe it—this was the first fight I ever got involved in. All the same, I'd hit him twice, and that meant I had done my share. I heaved a sigh of relief, and then my only thought was that I wished the whole thing was over with so I could go back home. I sat down on the concrete base of the torii. By this time almost everybody was exhausted with the beating, but two men, I don't know who they were, went on hitting him. I watched what was going on, smoking and squatting there. It was dark and I have no idea who was hitting him. Then somebody said, "How about laying off? If you hit him any more, it'll kill him." I didn't feel like killing anybody, so I left for home without waiting. The others all started to leave about the same time. This made me think that nobody was any more eager than I was to kill him. I threw the stick I had used to beat him into the

■ *Involuntary Homicide*

yard of the community center, the way the others did, so I can't be sure whether or not there were any bloodstains on mine. I thought I wasn't doing anything special, just what everybody else was doing, but when I heard this was the cause of Eguchi's death, I thought I had done a shameful thing even though people said he was the bloodsucker of the island. I regretted what I had done from the bottom of my heart, and I thought I never wanted to get involved in a fight again. I humbly request your lenience. (*He remains where he is.*)

(GIMPY *and* ONE EYE *repeat their beating motions with even greater intensity. In between the blows they deliver with their sticks, they occasionally poke or kick their victim. For a time one hears the words exchanged between* YOUNG WOMAN *and* DEAFY *in the dark.*)

YOUNG WOMAN'S VOICE (*in very matter-of-fact, calm tones*): Does the fire brigade keep you busy? There can't be all that many fires or shipwrecks. What do you do when there aren't any?

DEAFY'S VOICE: Let me see, when there aren't any . . . There's liaison with the town office on the mainland, mimeographing copies of circulars, patrol of harbor facilities. Collection for the Red Cross and insurance. Instruction about garbage disposal. Disinfection of night-soil pots and sewers. Airing of the portable shrine, help with festivals, athletic meets, and funerals. Replacement of bulbs in street lighting, reception of petitions, cleaning of spider webs and soot from the shrine. And, in addition, help with the Respect for the Aged Society, distribution of blood donations, night watch, and in the swimming season, life guard at the beach . . .

(ISLANDER C, *a woman, appears in spotlight.*)

ISLANDER C (*in tones of rote recitation*): I hear people are gossiping behind my back. They say that, even though I'm a woman, I took part in violence, but my husband was lying in bed with a cold, and when word got around that the head of every household was ordered to appear, I thought I had responsibilities as somebody who lives on the island, so after discussing it with my husband, I decided to attend the meeting, since these days men and women have equal rights, and

23

Involuntary Homicide ■

it isn't fair to make excuses because I'm a woman. I had a pretty good idea of the kind of man Eguchi was because my husband would always complain to me when he came back broke after been caught by Eguchi on the way home from the union meeting and made to play pachinko. I had my own grudge against him from way back. My house is near the Bar Kewpie, so I was often forced to do the laundry for the Kewpie and to help clean the drains and do other things like that, and they wouldn't take no for an answer, and I was never paid, so I could tell that my husband wasn't lying. But no matter how much he forced me to do the laundry or my husband to play pachinko, I don't think that makes it all right to kill a man. I hadn't the least such intention, and I hit him only about five times, but I didn't know anything about hitting people, and one time, by mistake, I hit in the back a man standing next to me, and he slammed me back, so I don't know how many of the five times I hit at Eguchi I actually struck him. It's just that, even though it wasn't my intention to beat him so hard it killed him, all the anger I had felt for a long time put strength into my arms, and when I hit him it was with everything I had, thinking it'd teach him a lesson, and I hurt one finger on my right hand. In the meantime, the crowd of people around him grew thicker, and I was pushed back, too far to reach him with my stick. But I felt relieved to think that I had done what I could to repay the people of the island who've always been so kind to us, and I returned straight to my house to my husband who was lying sick to give him his medicine. Later on, I heard Eguchi had died, and I was so surprised I couldn't believe it, and I remembered the proverb, "Little drops of water can split a mighty boulder," and I repented from the heart, resolved I would never do anything like that again. (*She remains where she is.*)

(GIMPY *and* ONE EYE *beat even more furiously. In the dark once again there is a brief conversation between* YOUNG WOMAN *and* DEAFY.)

DEAFY'S VOICE: You know where Foggy Heights is, don't you? They've put through a skyline drive . . .

YOUNG WOMAN'S VOICE: I'm crazy about fog.

■ *Involuntary Homicide*

DEAFY'S VOICE: My brother has a little auto repair shop near the entrance to the old road up the mountain.

YOUNG WOMAN'S VOICE: Then, you can take drives, can't you?

DEAFY'S VOICE: My brother, instead of spending a lot of money getting together all the necessary repair tools, bought only a secondhand tow car. You know why?

YOUNG WOMAN'S VOICE (*her voice is lively*): Why?

DEAFY'S VOICE: He's clever, my brother is . . . It's just like the name, it gets terrifically foggy at Foggy Heights.

YOUNG WOMAN'S VOICE: How beautiful—fog.

DEAFY'S VOICE: The fogs get thickest along about July, during the tourist season. That's when my brother goes to a good place, as far downwind as possible, and he waits there, straining his ears. What do you think he hears?

YOUNG WOMAN'S VOICE (*as if she is being tickled*): Hee-hee-hee.

DEAFY'S VOICE: Crash! Bang!—That's a collision. Wa-wow-wa-wow, wa-wa-wa, woh . . . That's a car that's fallen into a ditch racing its engine and the tires slipping.

YOUNG WOMAN'S VOICE: Thick fog . . .

DEAFY'S VOICE: Something's fallen into the trap!

YOUNG WOMAN'S VOICE: Everything looks beautiful in the fog. That's because you can't see the garbage or the picnic leftovers . . .

DEAFY'S VOICE: It costs a minimum of 5,000 yen to repair a car. I've been thinking that when I finish paying the installments on my hearing aid I might go to work for him. (*Abruptly.*) I wonder if he's dead . . .

YOUNG WOMAN'S VOICE: What?

(GIMPY *and* ONE EYE, *breathing very heavily, stop their beating. They go through various gestures of ascertaining that* EGUCHI *is dead, kicking lightly at the body with the point of their shoes, turning it over, peering down on the face.* GIMPY *strikes his lighter three times, then touches the flame to a cigarette.* ONE EYE *wipes the sweat from his forehead and neck.*)

DEAFY'S VOICE: The lighter flashed once, twice, three times.

YOUNG WOMAN'S VOICE: Show me.

DEAFY'S VOICE: It's eleven fifty-eight . . . In two minutes it'll be tomorrow.

Involuntary Homicide ■

YOUNG WOMAN'S VOICE (*sadly*): My Kewpie doll was too big from the start . . .

(ISLANDER A *appears in the spotlight.*)

ISLANDER A (*in tones of rote recitation*): For someone like myself, who grew up on this island, which was so peaceful I never heard any rumors even of a sneak thief, it seemed most unfortunate a quarrel of this sort should have occurred. As I recall, I hit Eguchi at most five or six times, but it tired me, emotionally anyway, and when I struck my lighter, thinking I'd have a smoke, I saw the blood oozing out of his nostrils, the corners of his eyes, and his forehead, and I immediately regretted what I had done. But I can't say for sure whether or not the blood was caused by my stick. Cherrywood bark is a reddish brown anyway, and there was oil on it, so I couldn't see blood with nothing more than the flame from a lighter. I threw the stick into the yard at the community center, where it got mixed in with the sticks of the other people, and I'm really sorry but I'm unable now to pick out which one it was.

ISLANDER B (*in tones of rote recitation*): No matter what he may have done, it was too bad he died.

ISLANDER C (*in tones of rote recitation*): I feel sorry for him, to think so many people beat him. I regret it from the bottom of my heart.

ISLANDER A (*in tones of rote recitation*): You ask whether it's true, as people generally say, that fishermen are violent by nature. Let me say that Eguchi was far more violent. Even when he hadn't had a thing to drink, he would poke and kick people, and everybody feared and hated him.

ISLANDER B (*in tones of rote recitation*): You ask about things that used to happen in the past—how people of the island would attack ships from other places at night and drill holes in the ships' bottoms or rip up the nets—but that is a very serious question involving fishing rights and is an entirely different matter from the case of Eguchi who, for no reason at all, opened holes in other people's daughters and tore up their clothes.

ISLANDER C (*in tones of rote recitation*): You ask if we thought that if we didn't kill Eguchi, he'd kill us. But nobody seri-

■ *Involuntary Homicide*

ously thought of killing Eguchi, so I have no way of replying to your question.

(*A pulsing sound of rain fiercely beating down. In the dark a brief conversation once again between* YOUNG WOMAN *and* DEAFY.)

DEAFY'S VOICE: The weather forecast was right for a change.

YOUNG WOMAN'S VOICE: It's not like the city—we seem to have more customers than usual when it rains. They say it's because the ships don't go out.

DEAFY'S VOICE: But I wonder who he could have been, that customer you mentioned.

YOUNG WOMAN'S VOICE: I always think it's a good sign if we haven't a single customer while it's still light. I wonder why.

DEAFY'S VOICE: Does it give you a good feeling when you have your monthlies?

YOUNG WOMAN'S VOICE: It hurts, that's all.

DEAFY'S VOICE: Oh, they seem to be carrying the body somewhere.

YOUNG WOMAN'S VOICE: They'll throw him into the ocean, I'm sure of it.

DEAFY'S VOICE: It's already tomorrow.

YOUNG WOMAN'S VOICE: If I get caught, they'll kill me too. I saw too many things, all sorts of things.

DEAFY'S VOICE (*trying to cheer her*): You'll be all right, if you just stay where you are.

(*Strong illumination on* GIMPY *and* ONE EYE. *Their expressions are tense. They stand erect and seem to be looking up at something diagonally across to stage rear.* [*The particular direction faced by the witnesses who have been picked out by spotlights is not as important as that of the young men's, but it is essential that each one face in a different direction.*] *The sound of rain moves off into the distance.*)

GIMPY (*in tones of rote recitation*): You ask how we can be so sure we were in the Bar Kewpie just as Eguchi was being beaten to death, and I would like to explain. As I stood there, smelling the spilled beer and saké and looking at the scattered bits of broken bottles with my flashlight, I was thinking what a waste it was—I could have gone on drinking for five days running on what had been spilled. Just then I heard a voice coming from the back room near where I was. It was the last television weather report of the day, the one that begins at eleven-fifty. But when I looked in, I saw that the picture tube had been broken, and the hibachi next to it was turned over. There were ashes all over the place. I figured somebody must have thrown the hibachi against the television. As members of the fire brigade, we know that television is high voltage and dangerous, so I at once cut off the power. In addition, while I was investigating the ashes, I discovered many live bits of charcoal, and I thought that if they were left lying there it might turn into a fire, so each of us brought in water in teapots and washbasins, and set about putting out the fire. There were bits of charcoal scattered all over, but we carefully extinguished every last one. In the meantime the rain started to fall heavily. Only when we were satisfied that the fire was completely out did we relax and decide we could leave.

ONE EYE (*in tones of rote recitation*): You ask how we can be so sure we were in the Bar Kewpie just as Eguchi was being beaten to death, and I would like to explain. I've heard they carried Eguchi's body to the front entrance of the movie theater because it had started to rain, and it was while we were in the back room of the Bar Kewpie, putting out the fire that the rain started. Anyone who belongs to the fire brigade knows, as a part of his basic training, that during the dry season carelessness with live charcoal on the tatami must be avoided at all costs, so I have a particularly distinct memory of feeling relieved when I heard the sound of the rain. But since I'd brought a stick with me, I thought as I was leaving that I'd have a little fun with it, and I broke a glass door about a yard square and a couple of other things. I believe that the total damage came to about 1,000 yen, figuring a pane of glass at 200 yen, and taking into account the cost of other materials and labor. In any case, it is deplorable that I should have broken other people's property, and I now deeply regret it. I felt so ashamed of what I had done that I turned myself in, and I ask that you deal with me as you see fit.

■ *Involuntary Homicide*

SCENE 7

(The stage suddenly becomes bright. It is a room in the community center, as in Scene 3. The people who have been spotlighted remain in the same positions and attitudes. DEAFY *is alone in the observation post;* YOUNG WOMAN *cannot be seen. In a corner of the room, in addition to the* FIRE CHIEF, *there is a person who appears for the first time. He is the* TEACHER *at the island school.* TEACHER *is dressed rather sloppily. His necktie is twisted to one side, and he wears sandals instead of shoes on his bare feet. He seems to be under the lingering influence of liquor: his eyes are bleary and he is unsteady on his feet. He is picking his back teeth with a matchstick. Once in a while a sneeze shakes his whole body.* DEAFY *looks as if he is glued to the binoculars. Apart from* TEACHER *and* DEAFY, *the others still wear their black raincoats.)*

TEACHER *(walking around the stage)*: I see . . . Yes, I understand . . .

(The others stare at TEACHER *with tense expressions.)*

I mean *(sneezes, tweaks his nose with his fingers and rubs it)* the position in which I find myself seems to be extremely complicated and delicate.

FIRE CHIEF: Our position is even more complicated and delicate.

TEACHER: In short . . . as I understand it . . . *(pause)* . . . in other words, you are asking me to commit perjury.

FIRE CHIEF: We thought, in any case, we'd like you to understand in what a difficult position we have been placed—that's about it.

(The islanders nod and lean forward in their seats, as if to lend emphasis to FIRE CHIEF'S *words; their gestures suggest they are pleading with* TEACHER.)

TEACHER *(with a wry smile)*: But that's not my responsibility, after all.

FIRE CHIEF: Of course. What possible responsibility would you have? But in view of all that has happened, we've had no choice but to make a clean breast of things and hope for your understanding and cooperation.

TEACHER: And what if I say I don't want to?

Involuntary Homicide ∎

FIRE CHIEF: There's no need to rush to conclusions . . .

TEACHER: If I refuse, will I get the same sort of treatment as Eguchi?

FIRE CHIEF (*his voice suggests exasperation*): You needn't say such disagreeable . . .

TEACHER: You've spilled the works to keep me from backing out afterward, right? I didn't want to hear anything. (*Pointing to* ISLANDERS A AND B.) Look at the two of them standing there, to keep me from leaving. In short, this is imprisonment in everything but name. You dragged me here, against my will . . . My cooperation—that's a good one . . . Damn it. My throat stings me. The whiskey I drank at that place seems to have gone to my head.

ISLANDER B (*not to* TEACHER *but to* FIRE CHIEF) Some water?

FIRE CHIEF: Yes, water.

ISLANDER B (*to* ISLANDER C) He said to get some water.

(ISLANDER C *exits to fetch some water.*)

TEACHER (*with sighs*): Perjury, is it?

FIRE CHIEF: Perjury doesn't sound too good.

TEACHER: How it sounds is hardly the question at this point. You've certainly got yourself into a fine mess . . . Even I have some principles . . . as an educator.

FIRE CHIEF: We, the people of the island, have the duty to protect our young men. We can't stand by without doing anything when these young men, who have their whole lives before them, are sacrificed to a skunk like Eguchi.

TEACHER: I understand all that! Your intentions are admirable. For that matter, I'm under no particular obligation to Eguchi. But you put me in a fix . . . What a crazy mess to get involved in! . . . (*Suddenly.*) No, it's no good . . . I can't go through with it . . . It'd be physically impossible—my false testimony wouldn't hold water . . . That woman . . . that waitress in the bar . . . you forgot about her. No matter how much I try to cover up what happened, if she doesn't back my story, it's hopeless.

FIRE CHIEF: We haven't forgotten about her. There's nothing to worry about.

TEACHER (*with a shocked expression*): You wouldn't . . .

FIRE CHIEF: With a woman like that, money'll settle anything.

■ *Involuntary Homicide*

(ISLANDER C *returns with a glass of water.*)

TEACHER (*drinking*): You're sure it's all right? . . . Can you really trust her that far?

FIRE CHIEF: If you're so worried, try discussing it with her yourself.

TEACHER: Where is she?

FIRE CHIEF: She'll be coming here, by and by.

TEACHER: By and by? (*Drinks the rest of the water.*) This water stinks.

FIRE CHIEF: The place where she worked was destroyed. Eguchi didn't come back. The police substation was the first place she'd think of taking shelter. However, the officer was away. Then, where would she go? This is the only place she can go, isn't it?

ONE EYE (*without warning, slashes at* GIMPY): Attack!

GIMPY: Parry! (*Stops* ONE EYE'S *stick with his own.*)

TEACHER: Why?

ISLANDER A: He's the fire chief. He's on duty all night long . . .

ISLANDER B: The beacon on the roof can be seen in every part of the island.

TEACHER: But your "by and by" is not exactly reassuring. What if the police arrive here first—you're finished, right?

FIRE CHIEF: And that's why the officer happens to be away, just tonight, most unfortunately.

TEACHER (*dubiously, looking at the young men*) But the two of you turned yourselves in, didn't you? Now that you've turned yourselves in, even if the officer isn't here . . . it doesn't take twenty minutes for the police launch to get from the pier on the mainland to the island.

FIRE CHIEF: Don't insist on rushing things. They're both ready for their punishment, and they're calmly awaiting whatever may come.

ISLANDER C: That's right. The people of the island are all so thankful to our officer for his help over the years. How could we be so ungrateful as to give the credit for the arrest to the police somewhere else?

TEACHER: So now all you're doing is waiting with folded arms.

FIRE CHIEF: We've made all the arrangements.

ISLANDER A: Twenty minutes ago a boat left to pick him up.

FIRE CHIEF: He went to do some night fishing. Once the autumn festival was safely behind us, we of the island thought, well, as an expression of our appreciation to the officer, we'd arrange a boat for him with everything he needed, and have him enjoy a pleasant evening with his family . . . We never dreamed that anything like this would happen.

ISLANDER A: The boatman is from the island, and he's got a pretty good idea where the fishing grounds are. At best it'll take an hour, at worst about two hours, to get him.

ISLANDER B: The rain seems to have let up. It won't be long before they head for shore.

ONE EYE (*to observation post*): Still no sign of anything?

DEAFY: I can't see a thing.

(TEACHER *gives a long sigh. Pause.*)

TEACHER (*nods*) I understand . . . It's OK . . . You don't suppose I went drinking in a place like that because I enjoyed it . . . All I feel now is shame and regret . . . To tell the truth, at my previous school I also committed a little indiscretion while I was drunk . . . (*Laughs weakly.*) I volunteered to teach here. I thought the air would be clean, the sky blue, the fish fresh, the vegetables right from the ground, the people simple and unaffected—a life in the sun . . . I thought I'd wash away the impurities from my mind and body. And that's how I happen to be teaching at a village school on an island like this . . . (*Hits his head hard three times with his fist.*) Damn it! It's all a matter of making up my mind to it! . . . (*Sneezes and holds his nose with his fingers.*) Yes, it's best for me too . . . I've got to think of how I look in the eyes of the children . . . I'll say I was in my room all night long. As a matter of fact, I have a stack of examination papers I promised to return by tomorrow.

FIRE CHIEF (*as if he has difficulty in pronouncing the words*): I'm afraid that won't do. The woman actually sat at your table . . .

TEACHER: You were the one who said she could be bought.

FIRE CHIEF: But a story like that is too implausible. A woman like that, who's made up of nothing but weaknesses, is likely to spill everything.

TEACHER: Then what's the point of giving her money?

■ *Involuntary Homicide*

FIRE CHIEF: If they start asking questions about this and that, quite apart from what she saw, it could be unpleasant. Some people, when they're called before the police, like nothing better than to spill everything, fact and fiction alike, hoping to create a good impression.

TEACHER: I don't understand. What *do* you want me to do?

FIRE CHIEF (*slapping his hand against his neck*): Mosquitoes. This time of year, they're really stubborn.

TEACHER: If I'm going to admit I was in the bar, what's the point . . .

FIRE CHIEF: The closer you stick to the truth, the less likely you are to have a bad conscience. (*Suddenly addresses* ISLANDER C *in the role of an investigating officer.*) Then, am I correct in thinking that the witness observed everything, from beginning to end, that occurred during the period in question?

ISLANDER C (*confused, and at a loss for words*): But, you don't mean . . . (*Unable to express herself, looks at* FIRE CHIEF *as if seeking help.*)

FIRE CHIEF (*unperturbed*): Then the witness, as she had frequently been obliged by Eguchi, was washing plates and glasses at the sink behind the counter, but she was at the same time observing the interior of the bar through a peephole in the wall?

ISLANDER C (*at last regaining the tone of rote recitation*): Yes, that is quite correct.

FIRE CHIEF (*rubbing the place on his neck stung by the mosquito*): Was it also by request of Eguchi that you were looking through the peephole?

ISLANDER C (*in tones of rote recitation*): Yes, that is quite correct. (*Begins to scratch her side through her raincoat.*) Eguchi was extremely suspicious, and even though he'd put the waitress Kumiko in charge of the bar, he suspected her of cheating on the number of drinks the customers had, or on the chits, or of pilfering the cash receipts. As a matter of fact, Kumiko used to make a whiskey and water with a lot more water than whiskey, and she diluted the saké before heating it. She did a lot of things like that, but all the same, Eguchi was a terrible man, and I felt sorry for Kumiko, and I never once told on her.

33

Involuntary Homicide ∎

FIRE CHIEF: Did Kumiko seem to be aware that she was being spied on?

ISLANDER C (*in the same rote tones*): I am unable to say.

FIRE CHIEF: Then, on the day of the incident the witness was, I take it, observing the interior of the bar through the peephole?

ISLANDER C (*in the same tones*): Yes, that is correct.

(DEAFY *takes the binoculars from his eyes and begins to listen attentively.*)

FIRE CHIEF: Then what did the witness see? Please tell me the facts truthfully—exactly what you saw.

ISLANDER C (*an expression of confusion plainly apparent*): What I saw? . . . You mean the teacher?

FIRE CHIEF (*unperturbed*): Is the witness quite sure that the customer she saw was one and the same person as this man (*pointing at* TEACHER)?

ISLANDER C (*in her natural voice*): Yes, there's no mistaking it. It was the teacher.

FIRE CHIEF: Can you describe what Kumiko and the teacher were doing up until the time when the mob broke in and smashed the lights so you couldn't see any more?

ISLANDER C (*in her natural voice*): First, the teacher emptied two bottles of saké. He didn't say much until he'd had his second whiskey. On his third whiskey he gave a couple of sneezes one after the other. It was while the girl was wiping his nose with a kleenex that his tongue suddenly began to loosen, and he said he'd like her to wipe a better place . . .

(*The young men sniff.* ISLANDERS A AND B *laugh to themselves.*) Then he paid with two thousand-yen bills, and went off to sit in the booth in the corner.

TEACHER: Enough is enough! (*Barely controlling an explosion of emotion.*) I see. That's what you mean by the truth! Now I'd like you to hear my version of what happened . . . I'm sorry to tell you, but the real culprits, the men who vandalized the Kewpie, from beginning to end, were these two gentlemen and nobody else. (*He points a shaking finger at* ISLANDERS A AND B.)

(ISLANDER A *averts his eyes, as if the light was too bright.* ISLANDER B *pursues a mosquito. The two young men, with half-*

34

■ *Involuntary Homicide*

smiles on their faces, begin to play poker in the lower deck of a bunk bed.)

FIRE CHIEF: But it's easy to make a mistake when everybody's wearing the same kind of clothes.

TEACHER: Don't try to worm out of it. (*To* ISLANDER A.) Look—the armhole of that raincoat is torn.

FIRE CHIEF: That's the easiest place to get torn. (*With gestures of inspecting the armholes of his own raincoat.*)

TEACHER (*to* ISLANDER B): And you're bow-legged.

(ISLANDER B, *startled, stops chasing mosquitoes. They all start comparing, out of the corners of their eyes, one another's legs. Of course,* TEACHER *is also examined. At this point* DEAFY *returns to the binoculars.*)

FIRE CHIEF: Surely you know, bow-legs are a characteristic of the Japanese.

(*Pause.*)

TEACHER (*with feigned calm, trying to regain the upper hand*): Very clever of you . . . Well, all right . . . It doesn't seem there's much room left for me to cooperate with you. (*Suppresses a belch.*) I feel nauseous. The wind from the sea has a fishy smell.

FIRE CHIEF (*hesitantly*): None of us has your kind of brains, sir . . . How am I going to explain? . . . Please don't get angry . . . Unless the two of us manage to put together a story that sticks as closely as possible to the truth—just as it happened— the others won't be able to remember it all.

ISLANDER C: (*shakes her head repeatedly and exaggeratedly*): We can't remember it all. We just can't.

FIRE CHIEF (*again in the role of an investigator*): Then, it was after the customer and Kumiko moved to the booth in the back that Eguchi asked the witness to transmit a message to Kumiko?

ISLANDER C (*forlornly*): If you're going to keep asking me so many questions, I really won't be able to remember it all.

GIMPY: Should I take notes for her?

FIRE CHIEF: It's only a little bit more. Even a monkey could remember that much. (*Resuming the tones of an investigator.*) Has the witness any idea why Eguchi himself did not directly inform Kumiko?

35

Involuntary Homicide ■

ISLANDER C (*in tones of rote recitation*): Whenever Eguchi came into the bar, it put a damper on almost all the customers. People stopped drinking, and they held onto their money.

FIRE CHIEF: Does the witness know why Eguchi wanted to see Kumiko?

ISLANDER C (*in tones of rote recitation*): I was told nothing about it.

FIRE CHIEF: After Kumiko left her place beside the customer, did he remain in the bar?

ISLANDER C (*perplexed, in her natural voice*): It happened all of a sudden . . . After the girl left the bar . . . there wasn't even time to drink a glass of water before I heard shouting and some wild men with sticks smashed the glass door in front . . .

TEACHER (*interrupts immediately, imitating* FIRE CHIEF'S *manner of speech*): I would like to verify something for my information. When the witness was asked to transmit a message to Kumiko, did she actually see Eguchi's face?

ISLANDER C (*more and more confused*): I'm not sure . . . (*With movements suggesting she is chasing after a butterfly, she steals a look at* FIRE CHIEF.)

(*A prickly silence overtakes everyone.* DEAFY *leans forward in expectation.* FIRE CHIEF, *as one might expect, is the first to recover.*)

FIRE CHIEF (*imitates* ISLANDER C'S *manner of speech, but not so closely as to become humorous*): I didn't see his face. He was on the other side of the blinds on the window over the sink, and I couldn't see him.

TEACHER: In other words, there is no proof, is there, that the man the witness thought was Eguchi was in fact Eguchi. It is not impossible that it was a charade arranged by one of the hoodlums who were planning to break in, so as to lure Kumiko outside.

FIRE CHIEF (*imitating* ISLANDER C): I remember Eguchi's voice very well. It's hardly likely I would mistake it.

(*The tension suddenly drains from* TEACHER. *He gives a little laugh, then teeters forward as if on the verge of collapse. He sits on the bottom bunk of a bunk bed [not the same one as the young* men], *removes his sandals, and claps them together a couple of times to shake off the sand.*)

TEACHER (*scraping the sand from between his toes*): I thought sand sticking to your toes was supposed to cure athlete's foot, but it was just the opposite . . . (*Self-mockingly.*) Physical therapy, was it? . . . To wash my insides, that were covered with mold, in the sun and the salt breezes . . . Nature—simple, unaffected, healthy, innocent as a freshly dug potato . . . (*Puts on his sandals. Breathes a sigh.*)

(*Pause.*)

ONE EYE (*calls to* DEAFY *in observation post as if he has just remembered something*): You still can't see anything?

DEAFY (*returning to the binoculars*): Not a thing. In this rain, the distance lens doesn't work too well.

TEACHER: Yes, there's no sense in being obstinate . . . Even if the others don't treat you like one of the bunch, that's no reason to be sulky . . . (*Turning toward* FIRE CHIEF, *he waves one hand.*) Please don't get upset. I didn't mean to be disagreeable. I had a pretty good idea of the kind of bastard Eguchi was, even without asking. I'm sure that unless there was some very good reason an incident like this would never have occurred. Considered from that point of view, there's no need for me to hesitate any longer. (*Holding his nose, he shakes it strongly to left and right.*) Then . . . what is it I'm supposed to have witnessed?

FIRE CHIEF (*slowly, carefully choosing his words*): After Kumiko left your table, you went on drinking for a while by yourself. Is this correct?

GIMPY: Wasn't the television blasting away?

TEACHER: That's right, it was sure making a lot of noise. But, it was . . .

GIMPY (*hurriedly, urging* ONE EYE): The program–get the newspaper . . . (*He points up at the observation post.*)

(*The next moment a newspaper is thrown down from the observation post.* DEAFY *is hiding* YOUNG WOMAN *and doesn't want anybody else to come close.* TEACHER *picks up the newspaper.*)

DEAFY: It was near the end of "An Invitation Just for You."

37

Involuntary Homicide ∎

TEACHER (*running his eyes over the newspaper*): Is that the program with Kariya Junko?

FIRE CHIEF: You don't say? Was Kariya Junko in it?

DEAFY: It's one of this week's best three. She's the star. "I hate it, I hate it . . ."

GIMPY AND ONE EYE: "I hate it when you say goodbye."

TEACHER: Wasn't that the song she sang in bed at the end of the program?

FIRE CHIEF: Then it must've been "Make me cry some more." That's real mood music.

TEACHER: It's got more of the feeling.

FIRE CHIEF (*changing his tone*): Just then a group of men who'd long been deeply resentful of Eguchi, smashed the glass door out in front and broke in with sticks in their hands. They made a commotion and demanded to see Eguchi.

TEACHER: Stop. It's a small matter, but there's a little correction I'd like to make at this point. They should come into the bar without making any fuss. Your story won't work unless you have them smash the glass door from the inside—quite apart from the matter of respecting the truth. You can't lie about such a thing as which direction the glass fragments landed . . . The police are pretty shrewd when it comes to this sort of thing.

FIRE CHIEF (*darting a glance at the* ISLANDERS): There's something to that. Well, then, shall we have them just push the door open and walk in?

TEACHER (*doing his best to make it sound like a joke*): I don't mean to fish for compliments, but I was hoping you'd at least say "Thank you."

FIRE CHIEF: Thank you.

TEACHER: Next, how many people broke in?

FIRE CHIEF: You were startled by the noise, but before you could turn around to get a good look, the lights were smashed, and the place was thrown into darkness.

TEACHER: I had a feeling there were two of them, both of them pretty unsteady on their legs, and they came crawling up from behind the counter . . . I suppose it was just my imagination.

38

FIRE CHIEF: When they couldn't find Eguchi, it went to their heads, and some of them started breaking up everything in sight. But after four or five minutes of rampaging, the whole lot of them left.

TEACHER: Is that all?

FIRE CHIEF: Fortunately, you weren't hurt, and there was nobody who could possibly blame you for what happened. I believe you returned without incident to your lodgings.

TEACHER: Clear and simple, isn't it?

FIRE CHIEF (*concentrating his thoughts and tracing back his line of reasoning*): Now everything's consistent . . . The girl from the Kewpie knew that you had come for a drink, but not when you left.

TEACHER: And I was present only for the first half of the rumpus, and . . . (*he winks at* GIMPY *and* ONE EYE) I have absolutely no idea what happened afterward.

GIMPY: It all hangs together, doesn't it?

ISLANDER A (*impressed*): It takes *him* to think of something like that.

ISLANDER B (*flatters* FIRE CHIEF *with a smile*): For a time I was wondering how it would turn out. I was worried.

ONE EYE (*in a whisper*): How can we be sure Kumiko won't come here?

TEACHER: That would be awful! It'd ruin everything if she came here now. I'm not supposed to be here. If she catches sight of me, we're in trouble. Where would you hide me if she came in now?

GIMPY (*gesturing with his chin at the observation post*): Up there'd be safe.

DEAFY (*with greater emphasis than intended*): You can't do that. It'd distract me from my work.

(*An awkward pause.*)

ONE EYE (*to* DEAFY): Isn't it about time somebody else took a turn at the lookout?

DEAFY (*emphatically*): I'm fine. I'm not in the least tired.

ISLANDER C (*approaching the observation post casually*): You mustn't neglect your duties. How about my helping you? A hussy like that is more than a young fellow can handle.

39

DEAFY: I'm all right, I tell you.

ISLANDER A: You mustn't make fun of her just because she's old.

ISLANDER B: She's had experience keeping watch at the Kewpie.

DEAFY (*hardly knowing what he is doing, stands at the top of the stairs, and blocks the way up. He shouts*): Stop bothering me! I won't take any interference from you.

(ISLANDER C, *taken aback, looks around towards the others as if seeking their support.*)

FIRE CHIEF (*jokingly*): Don't make such a commotion! . . . How about a smoke, ma'am? (*He offers her a cigarette.*)

ISLANDER C (*taking the cigarette*): Terrible, the young people these days. Like mad dogs.

DEAFY: If I'm a mad dog, what does that make you? A rotten pig?

FIRE CHIEF: Come off it, why don't you?

DEAFY: I don't like that kind of dirty, lying old hag.

ISLANDER C: What's that, you little imp?

DEAFY: You took hush money from the girl, didn't you?

ISLANDER C: Hush money?

DEAFY (*facing the others*): This sweet old lady was squeezing 2,000 yen every month from Kumiko. Otherwise, she said, she'd tell Eguchi.

FIRE CHIEF: How come you know such things?

DEAFY: I've heard it.

FIRE CHIEF: From who?

DEAFY: I don't want to say.

(*An awkward pause.*)

TEACHER: In general, the payment of hush money presupposes the performance of acts that require the sealing of somebody's mouth. The question is, who did what . . .

FIRE CHIEF (*to DEAFY in a peaceable manner*): Very well, I see. Telling lies is contemptible. I understand what you mean. Go back to your post. I'm sure you'll feel better for having got that off your chest.

DEAFY: I won't. Why, even you've said nasty things about Kumiko.

FIRE CHIEF: I have?

DEAFY: Yes, you have.

■ *Involuntary Homicide*

FIRE CHIEF (*in soothing tones*): OK, OK. How about coming down and having a cup of tea? If you've something to say for yourself, I'll listen. One Eye, you take his place up there.

ONE EYE: Right! (*He slams down his cards and stands.*)

GIMPY (*clicks his tongue*): Of all the bad luck!

DEAFY: I don't want you here. Don't come up.

(*The glances of all of them converge once more on* DEAFY.)

FIRE CHIEF (*as if feeling him out*): Why not? What makes you so unreasonable? You're no longer a kid at the rebellious age. Come on down, won't you? (*He moves toward the observation post.*)

DEAFY (*he picks up a small anchor. He seems to have prepared it for an emergency*): Don't come any closer!

FIRE CHIEF (*stares up at* DEAFY. *The amiablility gradually fades from his face*): He's out of his mind.

DEAFY: I've had enough. I'm sick of the whole thing . . . Even without Eguchi, we were all fed up with this miserable little island. (*Seeks confirmation from the other young men below.*) Right?

(ONE EYE *and* GIMPY *remain silent.*)

DEAFY (*to his two pals*): Why don't you answer me?

FIRE CHIEF (*shrewdly sizing up the situation*): Drag that deaf bastard down here!

(*However,* ONE EYE *and* GIMPY *remain where they are.*)

DEAFY: Why don't the two of you say something?

(ONE EYE *and* GIMPY *keep silent.*)

FIRE CHIEF: Come on down!

DEAFY (*to the two young men*): Shall I tell you? Do you want to know why Eguchi picked a fight with us yesterday?

(ONE EYE *and* GIMPY *keep silent.*)

DEAFY: OK, then, I'll tell you.

FIRE CHIEF: We know without having to listen to you. He came to get the three of you to help out at his movie theater and pachinko parlor.

ONE EYE: He had a dagger in his belly band.

GIMPY (*showing the length with his hands*): The dagger was like this. The blade must've been six inches long.

TEACHER: Was that all there was by way of direct motive for killing him?

41

FIRE CHIEF (*irritated*): Nobody intended to kill him. I thought I'd told you nobody had any intention of killing him. (*To* DEAFY.) Come on down. This is an order. Forget about such things.

DEAFY (*mockingly*): An order?

FIRE CHIEF (*confused*): No, it's not an order. It's a request. Please come down. I'm asking you.

DEAFY: Who's going to fall for a trap like that?

FIRE CHIEF: OK, then. If you've made up your mind to disobey me, how about returning the hearing aid? According to Fire Department regulations, nobody has the right to order anybody else, but the hearing aid is different. I personally advanced the money. Now that you've trampled on my good will, I'd like the hearing aid back. You're acting like a thief. How about it? Are you going to do what I say, or . . .

DEAFY (*removing the earphone from his ear*): Now I can't hear a thing. I don't care, even if I can't. (*He takes the main body of the hearing aid from his pocket, and holding it up, as if making an offering, starts down the stairs.*) I don't want to hear. I don't want to hear anything . . . (*To* FIRE CHIEF, *who has stepped forward.*) Don't come any closer!

(FIRE CHIEF *stops in his tracks.* DEAFY *places the hearing aid on the steps, about halfway down, then returns to the place he was before, maintaining a defensive posture.* FIRE CHIEF *watches* DEAFY *for a while, then slowly goes up the stairs and picks up the hearing aid. He also returns to where he was previously.*)

FIRE CHIEF: Damn fool! Gets carried away like that . . . You think it takes nothing more than emotions to make your way through life?

DEAFY (*exultantly*): He seems to be saying something. I can't hear him. Can't hear a thing. When you can't hear sounds, the whole world looks white, as if a fog hung over it. I'm glad I can't hear. Up to now, I've always felt horribly afraid when nothing made any sounds, but now, for the first time, I'm glad not to hear. It's as if a load's been lifted from my chest. Shout your head off, I can't hear a thing. (*Turns around, picks up the radio, and switches it on. It blares forth rock music. He laughs.*) Even the radio doesn't make a sound.

■ *Involuntary Homicide*

(*Turns the dial. Static, then a melody by Mozart.*) It's so quiet . . . perfectly white . . .

(FIRE CHIEF *with extremely casual, unruffled movements places the hearing aid on the floor, and slowly but very precisely grinds it to pieces.* DEAFY'S *expression is taut with fear. The others are also unable to conceal their fright. The piece by Mozart goes on.*)

FIRE CHIEF: If you change your mind, it'll mean another twenty months on the installment plan.

DEAFY (*comes down the stairs. His feet move as if in a trance*): What made you do such a thing . . . It feels as if my head is being crushed . . . Stop . . . (*He sits on the bottom step and holds his head in his hands.*) I'm sick of being deaf.

FIRE CHIEF (*he kicks the hearing aid, which is now completely crushed, toward* DEAFY): Here are your ears. Would you like them as a souvenir?

DEAFY (*picks up the broken hearing aid tenderly as if condoling with it*): I don't suppose I'll ever hear another thing . . . (*His face crumples and sobs well up. He begins to cry in a low voice. His voice is unmodulated, like the winter wind.*)

(FIRE CHIEF, *seizing the chance, gives* GIMPY *and* ONE EYE *a signal to occupy the observation post. The two young men are so intimidated they seem to have lost the power to act on their own volition, but they obey the signal and start up the stairs.* DEAFY, *despite his tears, shifts with surprising alacrity and assumes a defensive posture. The other two young men, taken aback by this show of spirit, stop in their tracks.* DEAFY *goes on weeping and the music of Mozart also continues. At this point a stark pause of about 12 seconds. Quietly, so quietly that almost nobody is aware of it,* YOUNG WOMAN *appears at the top of the stairs with the savings bank in the shape of a Kewpie doll in her arms.*)

YOUNG WOMAN (*she calls to* DEAFY *timidly*): Use this toward a new hearing aid. I don't suppose it'll be of much help—it's nothing but one yen coins . . . Anyway, I won't need it any more myself . . . Oh, you can't hear me, can you? . . . I'm sorry . . .

(DEAFY, *of course, shows no reaction. The others are taken aback. They stare at* YOUNG WOMAN *as if showering on her the arrows of their wordless gaze.*)

43

Involuntary Homicide ∎

FIRE CHIEF (*groans*): I had a feeling it might be something like this.

ISLANDER C (*in dull tones that suggest this is too much for her*): Shameless hussy!

(GIMPY *and* ONE EYE *stand immobile as if frozen, but they, even more than the others, look as if they are about to explode with inarticulate reactions.*)

YOUNG WOMAN: You can't hear, can you? (*She turns the dial of the radio. Noise . . . a snatch of a popular song . . . then, once again, the boisterous, sweet sounds of rock.*)

(DEAFY *finally becomes aware that something has happened. He turns around and looks up the stairs.* YOUNG WOMAN *holds up the Kewpie doll and, with an expression full of expectancy, awaits* DEAFY'S *reaction.*)

DEAFY (*stares at* YOUNG WOMAN): It doesn't matter what you say, it's too late . . . I can't hear . . . Half of the world's been ripped off from me . . . The relations between the two of us are finished. There's no hope now of getting a job at my brother's place . . . (*With rising anger.*) It's partly your fault. Somebody who was on the side of those who get pitied stepped out of character and went over to the side of those who pity . . . I'm sick of being deaf! Damn it! What makes you like fog? I'm sitting in the midst of a fog that will absolutely never lift, and I feel a chill creeping over my ass . . . I wish you'd just once try being deaf yourself.

(YOUNG WOMAN *disappears to the rear, seeming to melt into the darkness.* DEAFY *begins to cry quietly once more. At a signal from* FIRE CHIEF, *the other two young men try to break through* DEAFY'S *defenses and rush upstairs, but he is instantly back on his guard. He turns and withdraws to the observation post. At the top of the stairs he grabs the anchor and brandishes it against any possible attack from below. He switches off the radio. Pause of about thirty seconds.*)

SCENE 8

(*After the long silence. The scene is a continuation of the previous one.*)

TEACHER (*as if he has remembered something, gets up from the*

44

bed, rubbing his stomach): Now, I'd appreciate it if by and by you'd let me go wherever I'm supposed to be at this time.

FIRE CHIEF (*to nobody in particular*): That's all right, I suppose . . . Misunderstandings arise from the emotions . . . You can't get by only on emotions . . . He doesn't realize how lucky he is to be able to talk in that completely irresponsible way, and that's what makes him so hard to handle . . .

TEACHER (*pours hot water into a glass from the kettle on top of the stove and drinks*): That's the way of the world. I'm used to that sort of thing, maybe because my business is looking after kids in school.

DEAFY (*with a moan*): What are you saying? I can't hear you . . . But it doesn't make any difference even if I can't hear you. It's not likely you're saying anything worth hearing.

FIRE CHIEF (*gloomily*): I've always done what I've done, regardless of the cost to myself, because I thought it was for the sake of all of us. And then to have everything backfire on me this way! I've got to think this over carefully. I wonder if I made a mistake somewhere.

TEACHER (*sipping slowly as if it is very hot*): It doesn't become someone who's conceived such a grand undertaking to sound so discouraged. (*Darts a glance up at the observation post.*) But I'm uneasy. I wonder if that girl doesn't know a bit too much.

FIRE CHIEF (*in a low voice*): I'll arrange things with her somehow.

ISLANDER C: She's the kind if you beat her the dust'll come out.

FIRE CHIEF: You know, the only thing I've ever thought about was the happiness of the young fellows . . . The construction of the ferry pier, the expansion of facilities on the bathing beach in preparation for the leisure boom, the disinfection of the sewers, the promotion of deep wells, the purchase of film equipment for the community center, and then, yes, the opening of a school on the island, and being able to invite you here as the teacher . . . And what was the situation six years ago? . . . The specialities of the island were trachoma and amoebic dysentery . . . Six years I've spent working for young people who don't know how bad the rice used to taste with sand in it, or how the tea made from shallow wells used to stink . . . Once they get a taste of the world outside the island, the men generally don't come back . . . That leaves only widows, old people, half-human simpletons . . . It was a pitiful situation . . . The weak people huddled together like mice in a hole . . .

GIMPY (*blurts out*): Laughing and crying as they writhed against the odds . . .

FIRE CHIEF: But do you suppose, then, that those who left the island found happiness? Not on your life. The homeless stay homeless, no matter where they go. They can't find decent employment, and after wearing themselves out with wandering from one place to another, they drop dead like dogs.

ONE EYE (*blurts out*): Why don't they come back, then?

FIRE CHIEF (*stealing a glance in* DEAFY'S *direction*): It's because they lack backbone. The worm will turn, they say, but once vagrancy comes to be a way of life, a man's soul falls asleep, and he can't wake up any more.

GIMPY: Some guys must find it better to live like stray dogs, rather than be fed and chained.

FIRE CHIEF: As a matter of fact, here I am, as proof that some do come back.

GIMPY (*as gently as possible*): But you were suffering from epilepsy . . .

FIRE CHIEF (*stung, but immediately recovering*): Do you think it was because I had epilepsy that I turned tail and ran back here? Don't be a fool! Epilepsy is what woke me up—it was a case of good coming out of evil. At any rate, it became my mission to turn this island into a good place to live. Anybody—even an epileptic—would be only too glad to live here if the island was a good place to live. And it was only natural for you fellows, who are cripples, just like me, should share my way of thinking.

ONE EYE: I've heard that Deafy's brother has opened an auto repair shop on the mainland somewhere and made a success of it.

FIRE CHIEF: Those who've deserted the island all say the same sort of thing. Success, success, success . . . If they can manage to afford a glass of gin before they go to bed, they talk as

■ *Involuntary Homicide*

if they'd made a tremendous success, even if they work as shoeshine boys or as touts at the bicycle races.

(YOUNG WOMAN *suddenly shows herself behind* DEAFY.)

YOUNG WOMAN (*with perfect innocence, but hesitantly, as if she was rather afraid of hurting* DEAFY'S *feelings*): It's true. He has a wrecking car on Foggy Heights at the entrance to the road up the mountain. (*Suddenly fear seems to overtake her, and she stammers.*) When the fog is really thick, cars fall into the ditches . . . If he thinks his brother's place is where we should go, I haven't anywhere else . . . And I wouldn't enjoy being questioned by the police . . . If you'll put up with us a bit longer, we'll leave by the first boat, and then take the first bus, and we'll go as far as we can tomorrow. We've got nothing to pack . . .

FIRE CHIEF: You can't do that. You're a key witness. For the time being you can't leave the island.

TEACHER: That's right. If you leave the island, all it'll do is make people suspect you.

DEAFY (*supposing that he is being addressed*): Talk all you like, it won't do you any good. Like a fish, gasping for breath. No, a lot uglier than a fish. (*Suddenly annoyed.*) I can't hear . . . If only I could forget, the sooner the better, what I heard while I still could hear, I would never want to hear anything else. (*Sticks his fingers into his ears. An expression of pain.*)

FIRE CHIEF (*to* YOUNG WOMAN): Do you want us to forgive you?

YOUNG WOMAN (*hopefully*): Yes, forgive me.

FIRE CHIEF: Well then, come down here.

(YOUNG WOMAN *hesitates.* DEAFY, *sensing something in the air, turns round.*)

DEAFY (*suddenly overcome by a paroxysm of rage*): So it's you! What were you bargaining over?

YOUNG WOMAN: I wasn't bargaining.

DEAFY: You're making fun of me because I'm deaf. That's right, I'm deaf. No matter what you say to me, I can't hear a thing. All the same, it baffles me how all of you can keep chattering on without ever getting your fill of it. When will you have enough of your endless gabbing about stupid things? I've had

47

Involuntary Homicide ■

enough. (*He stands aside to let* YOUNG WOMAN *pass.*) OK, go on. Your mouth and ears are craving to stick to his, like a cat in heat. Go ahead, I tell you!

FIRE CHIEF: Now's your chance.

(*But* YOUNG WOMAN *steps back instead and disappears into the darkness.*)

TEACHER (*with a coaxing voice*): It's better for you if you come down here. Wouldn't you rather dispose of your problem as soon as possible?

DEAFY (*to the invisible darkness*): Eh? Did you say something? (*Weakly.*) I can't hear. (*Looks from one to another of the people downstairs, then turns back once again to the observation post.*) I can't hear you . . . Are you afraid of me? Sometimes, because I can't hear, I let out a loud voice, but there's nothing to be afraid of . . . Anyway, considering you're a professional, there was nothing for you to get so sore about. (*Slumps down onto the step. Looks at* FIRE CHIEF.) You also seem to enjoy bullying people weaker than yourself . . . (*Suddenly he cups his hands behind his ears, and listens intently as if he was expecting to hear something from the distance, only to sink back haplessly.*) The rumbling of the sea and the ringing in my ears sound about the same.

FIRE CHIEF (*to the young men down below*): When did I ever bully the weak?

GIMPY: I've never thought so.

FIRE CHIEF: No matter what I do, I do it democratically. I've never once done anything to keep you under my control. It's not the same thing as the way Eguchi used to put you up to mischief.

ONE EYE: How can we go on associating with a guy like that, who's in favor of violence?

FIRE CHIEF: I believe in you. I really believe in both of you. And even Deafy, though now he's being so unreasonable, if the crunch comes, I know he won't betray us. I know him. (*To* TEACHER.) That's right, isn't it—wouldn't you say being unreasonable is a kind of self-indulgence?

TEACHER: I think so, too. Every child knows it can take advantage of its parent's love, but it doesn't work with a stranger.

48

■ *Involuntary Homicide*

Well, isn't it about time we left? It'd be awkward if the resident constable's boat came back and found us here.

FIRE CHIEF (*nods*): I'm sure I said many things that offended you, but I was terribly wrought up . . .

TEACHER: It was mutual.

FIRE CHIEF (*shakes the shoulder of* ISLANDER A *who at some point has dozed off*): How about lending him a light?

(ISLANDER A *confusedly starts to take a flashlight from the wall.*)

ONE EYE: No answer yet from the marriage bureau?

GIMPY: Not yet.

ONE EYE: It's funny, but there doesn't seem to be all that much difference in the number of men and the number of women.

(*In the meantime,* TEACHER *seems to have become fascinated with some sticks of firewood that have been left lying by the stove. Instead of taking the flashlight from* ISLANDER A, *he picks up a piece of firewood. He turns around with a rather tense expression.*)

TEACHER: This firewood . . .

FIRE CHIEF: Yes, what about it?

TEACHER: If I were a police officer, I think I might be rather interested in it. When did you lay in this firewood and where did it come from? And about how many sticks were there?

ISLANDER A: I guess they came from Yamaichi's. It must have been at the beginning of the fall last year.

TEACHER: In other words, the plans to murder Eguchi must have been underway as far back as the fall of last year at the latest.

FIRE CHIEF (*his expression hardening*): It puts me in an awkward position when you make a crazy, false accusation like that.

TEACHER: False accusation? This is no joke. Now that I've committed myself to being your partner, I'm the one who'll suffer if you make a blunder. They'll revoke my teaching license if they find out I've committed perjury. And then how am I to make a living?

FIRE CHIEF: There was never anybody on this island who thought of killing Eguchi.

TEACHER: After all we've been through, why not stop pretending? (*Brandishes a stick of firewood.*) What a handy size this cherry branch is . . . A souvenir of a mountain-climbing

49

trip, I suppose? . . . It wouldn't be easy to get together enough sticks like this for everybody, at the drop of a hat . . . Are you sure all these branches are nothing more than firewood?

FIRE CHIEF (*motioning to the two young men*): Burn the lot of them right away. (*To* ISLANDERS.) How about taking another good look at the vacant lot in front?

TEACHER: All of them, even broken pieces.

(GIMPY *and* ONE EYE *begin feeding the firewood into the stove, with no apparent interest.* ISLANDER A *shakes* B *and* C, *who have begun to doze off.*)

ISLANDER A: Wake up! We've got to inspect the vacant lot again.

FIRE CHIEF: There'll be hell to pay if any sticks are left behind.

TEACHER: They're not sticks, they're firewood.

DEAFY (*all of a sudden, in a voice like a bassoon*): Bohhh. (*Responding to the astonished looks in the others' faces.*) People with ears are all the same. (*Leans his forehead on his clenched fist, and shuts his eyes.*)

(ISLANDERS, *flashlights in their hands, rush outside as if someone were chasing them. The two young men resume their burning of the firewood.*)

TEACHER: I ask you to be more careful. One careless slip like that one and the consequences for everybody can be frightening. (*He notices a bundle of documents on the desk.*) What's this?

FIRE CHIEF (*as if recalling something, he picks up the mock investigation reports from the beds on which the young men have been lying, and takes them to the stove*): Those are records of the damages suffered by the people of the island at Eguchi's hands. I thought they might be necessary if something came up . . .

TEACHER: If something came up?

FIRE CHIEF: There're all kinds of possibilities. (*He tosses the bundle of documents over the shoulders of the young men into the stove.*)

TEACHER (*accusingly*): What were those?

(*Cries of alarm outside. Sounds of people running.* ISLANDERS *rush back in confusion.*)

50

■ *Involuntary Homicide*

ISLANDER C: Somebody's jumped in the water. (*She points, but her finger is unsteady.*)

ISLANDER A: She threw herself in. It was that girl. (*Even those who have been in the room, finally understand from his look, directed at the observation post, what has happened.*)

FIRE CHIEF (*glances up at the observation post. His voice is constricted*): She jumped?

ISLANDER B: Was she was wearing a red dress before? It's a bright red now. She's at the edge of the water under the cliff. The sides of the cliff are sharp as a razor—maybe it's blood.

(*They have all turned their gazes to* DEAFY, *but he is still not aware of this.*)

ISLANDER C: What a terrible thing to have done! She needn't have killed herself that way.

TEACHER: Maybe she was only trying to escape and missed her footing.

GIMPY: No, there's a sheer drop from under that window all the way down to the bottom of the cliff.

ISLANDER A (*lowering a rope from the cliff*): There's a stretcher in the shed, isn't there?

FIRE CHIEF: She mustn't be touched until the police officer arrives.

ISLANDER A: But we can't be sure she's dead.

GIMPY: It's a twenty-meter drop over jagged rocks. It'd kill even a cat.

ISLANDER B: She seems to be wrapped in something like a red cloth, from the bottom of her feet to the top of her head.

(DEAFY *suddenly lifts his head.*)

DEAFY: What's happened?

ONE EYE (*with pity*): It wouldn't do any good even if I told you. A deaf man's harder to handle than a blind one.

ISLANDER C: Nobody said anything that'd make her want to kill herself.

TEACHER: If that boy had known, he'd never have made such a fuss. As far as I could see, he seemed a bit too sympathetic to the woman from the Kewpie.

ONE EYE: It really hurt her when Deafy called her a professional.

ISLANDER C: What a thing to say!

51

ISLANDER B: It was plain nastiness.

ISLANDER A: If we don't bring her back here in a sailcloth, it'll be on our conscience.

TEACHER (*irritated*): Anyway, it's a lousy thing to have happened.

FIRE CHIEF: If you need sailcloth, there's some in the shed.

DEAFY (*he looks rather anxious*): What're you all chattering about? (*Suddenly turns around. He looks about uneasily.*) Where's she gone, I wonder? . . . Hey, where've you gone? . . . (*Stands up. In a loud voice.*) Where are you? . . . (*With apprehension in his voice.*) The window's open!

(ISLANDER A, *a rope over his shoulder, motions to* ISLANDER B *to follow him. They exit.* DEAFY *disappears into the darkness.* B *follows* A *off.*)

FIRE CHIEF (*to young men below*): Leave two or three sticks.

TEACHER: Firewood, you mean.

(DEAFY *appears. His expression is tense. He holds the Kewpie doll in his arms.* GIMPY *picks up a stick.*)

DEAFY: The window's open, and she's not anywhere . . .

TEACHER (*relieved*): He seems comparatively calm.

DEAFY: Nobody's surprised . . . You must've known . . . I couldn't hear a thing . . .

ONE EYE (*defensively*): I didn't hear anything either. I'm not lying.

DEAFY: When was it?

TEACHER (*to* FIRE CHIEF): Why don't you try communicating with him in writing? He's perfectly calm. You've got all the time to discuss it with him.

DEAFY (*suddenly, stamping noisily down several steps of the staircase, begins to shout*): Why didn't you stop her? You've got ears, haven't you? You must've heard. If you heard and didn't stop her, it's the same as having killed her.

TEACHER (*disgusted*): He's raving, after all.

ONE EYE: And he couldn't even hear anything . . .

DEAFY: This makes the second victim. Whose turn is it next? You can kill people who have ears with only your mouth, but I haven't got ears, so your mouth isn't enough. (*Abruptly lowers his voice.*) What did you say to threaten her? Your tongues are sharper than a fighting cock's claws. (*Weakly sits*

52

down on the step alongside the Kewpie doll.) It's all right even
if I can't hear . . . I've had all I want of human words . . .
I'd prefer not to hear any more . . . Being deaf is fine with
me. (*He sits with his arms around his knees, looking as if he
is frozen to the spot.*)

(*They all breathe a sigh of relief.*)

GIMPY (*drops the stick he was holding*): Two dead. Who's next?

ONE EYE: Cut it!

ISLANDER C: It's bad luck.

TEACHER (*to* FIRE CHIEF, *in tones that suggest he is trying to
pick a quarrel*): I think it would be appropriate at this point to
make it perfectly clear that I can't be expected to keep any
promises if things continue in this vein. I'm under no obligation to keep you company in walking over thin ice.

FIRE CHIEF: Thin ice?

TEACHER: Doesn't it seem to you that your hard-of-hearing
sidekick is a lot more likely to talk than the dead woman from
the Kewpie?

FIRE CHIEF: The situation is entirely different. This is like a
quarrel among brothers. It's ridiculous to think he'd betray
one of his own because of some stranger . . .

DEAFY (*his voice is strained*): I can't hear you. I can't hear a
thing.

FIRE CHIEF: I'll buy you another hearing aid. As long as you
understand my feelings, that's all I ask.

(DEAFY *looks at the Kewpie doll. He pushes it gently to one end
of the step and he moves to the opposite end. After this he begins
to cry calmly and monotonously in a loud voice like wind crossing
over the sea.*)

TEACHER: His mental state is completely abnormal. I wish you'd
do something instead of just watching him without saying a
word.

FIRE CHIEF: The best thing is to let him cry his fill. Once he's
cried all he can, he'll feel better.

(ISLANDER C *with a sigh sits herself down on the floor.*)

ONE EYE: Somebody's got to go up and man the observation
post.

GIMPY. It's your turn.

ONE EYE: As a favor, go with me.

53

GIMPY: Not me.

ONE EYE: I don't want to go up there alone.

FIRE CHIEF (*trying to make a joke of it*): That's not like you! Go on up there! (*He pats* ONE EYE *on the behind.*)

ONE EYE (*brushes off* FIRE CHIEF'S *hand. Unyielding*): No, I won't go.

TEACHER (*becoming irritated*): This incident was planned for a whole year back. It was premeditated murder, and whoever was the mastermind will have quite a lot to answer for.

FIRE CHIEF: I think you've said enough, teacher.

TEACHER: No matter what kind of monster Eguchi may have been, compared to a calculated murder, he was innocence itself.

FIRE CHIEF: I gather, then, you consider this has nothing to do with you . . .

TEACHER: You're asking too much of me. I refuse to be an accomplice to a brutal crime.

FIRE CHIEF: That's overstating it. You have no evidence.

TEACHER: Do you really feel confident you can carry this off without giving yourself away? If you do, that's fine. I'm not a prosecutor and not a judge either, and I don't give a damn what the truth may be. Can't you do something about that wailing? It gets on my nerves.

FIRE CHIEF: The best thing is to let him cry. He's crying because the island is calling to him. If he cries, his heart will come back to the island.

TEACHER (*abruptly, in the manner of a prosecutor*): According to the testimony we have just heard from the accused, they decided to use firewood, rather than six-foot poles, because it's actually dangerous if one misses the mark when using a pole. Is it the custom on the island to use for firewood cherry branches that might equally well serve as walking sticks?

FIRE CHIEF: No, there's no custom of that kind especially.

TEACHER (*in the manner of a prosecutor*): I imagine that cherry branches must be fairly expensive. Why should they have been used for firewood?

FIRE CHIEF (*with a suggestion of having been driven into a corner*): I don't remember exactly . . .

TEACHER (*in the role of defense counsel, with an air of being

54

pleased with himself): Would it be proper to interpret your testimony as meaning that, although it was fairly cold that day, it just so happened that the firewood you had ordered wasn't delivered on time, and you had no choice but to make do with some cherry branches you had put aside?

FIRE CHIEF: Yes, I believe that was the case.

TEACHER (*switching back to being a prosecutor*): Those cherry branches were purchased a whole year ago. Please explain your original purpose in buying them.

FIRE CHIEF: It happened such a long time ago . . .

TEACHER (*from the standpoint of defense counsel*): Have you no recollection of having bought them for use in a sword dance— or possibly a mock cavalry battle—at the island festival or at an athletic meeting of the island school?

FIRE CHIEF (*meaninglessly scratching the back of his hand*): I do seem to have some such recollection.

TEACHER (*resuming his normal voice*): I've no particular desire to make an enemy out of you. All I'm saying is that it makes things awkward for me when you're so unsystematic. The police are sure to focus their investigation on whether or not there was a conspiracy . . . Can't you really do anything about that howling?

FIRE CHIEF (*motions to young men with a kind of hysteria induced by his feeling of defeat*): Hey, you guys, how about coming a little closer?

(GIMPY, *a rather cynical smile on his face, looks at* ONE EYE *out of the corner of his eye, and tilts his head to one side to express his doubts.* ONE EYE, *responding, performs a similar gesture.*)

TEACHER: Insubordination, is it?

(FIRE CHIEF *walks to the foot of the stairs.*)

FIRE CHIEF: If I stop him crying, will that satisfy you?

TEACHER: As a first step . . .

(FIRE CHIEF *looks up into* DEAFY'S *face. There is no reaction. He motions to* GIMPY *to pick up the stick on the floor and bring it to him.* GIMPY *hesitates.* TEACHER *instead picks up the stick and hands it to him.* ONE EYE *starts to prevent him, but stops.* FIRE CHIEF *grasps the stick and, walking with a catlike tread, starts up the stairs. After he has climbed several steps, he straightens. Suddenly he swings the stick sideways and smashes the Kew-*

55

Involuntary Homicide ∎

pie doll. *The broken Kewpie doll rolls to the floor scattering one-yen coins all over the place.* DEAFY, *taken by surprise, stands up in astonishment, and stops crying. Anger bends his whole body like a spring. The next moment* FIRE CHIEF *stretches out toward* DEAFY *a banknote [its denomination is not clear] and places it on the step below him. He hurries back to his previous position.*)

DEAFY (*staring at the broken Kewpie doll, he mutters*): The promise was a lie, anyway . . . I don't suppose you even feel any sympathy. (*Without so much as a glance at the bill left by* FIRE CHIEF, *he returns to the observation post.*)

(*As he leaves,* ISLANDERS A AND B *slip into the room like shadows. They are startled to see the one-yen coins. They stand behind* ISLANDER C *as if rooted to the spot. Several seconds elapse in this manner.*)

SCENE 9

ISLANDER A (*in a whisper*): She was dead.

ISLANDER B (*in a whisper*): Her dress wasn't red any more. She'd been exposed to the rain and it turned white.

ISLANDER C (*looking around to* ISLANDERS A AND B): About how much did she have on her?

ISLANDER A: About 300 yen, I guess.

ISLANDER B: Closer to 5,000 yen, I'd say.

ISLANDER C: Who's going to get it?

ISLANDER B: How should I know?

ISLANDER A: Dead men tell no tales, they say.

FIRE CHIEF (*holds out the stick to nobody in particular. He turns to* TEACHER): He's stopped crying.

(TEACHER, *apparently worried about something, continues to stare at the observation post. He nods.* GIMPY *takes the stick from* FIRE CHIEF'S *hands.*)

GIMPY (*holds the stick in readiness. All of a sudden*): Two are dead. Who'll be the third? (*He closes in on* ONE EYE.)

ONE EYE (*nimbly circles around* FIRE CHIEF *toward stove. He picks up one of the remaining sticks*): Who's next? The third time is the decisive one. (*He confronts* GIMPY.)

56

■ *Involuntary Homicide*

(GIMPY *and* ONE EYE *circle halfway round the stage with* FIRE CHIEF *in between them.*)

TEACHER (*in the manner of a prosecutor, but not looking directly at the young men*): According to his deposition, the defendant claims that he was in the Bar Kewpie at the time that Eguchi was clubbed to death. Is this correct?

(FIRE CHIEF *steps out of the range of the sticks of the two young men. They stay where they are in the same postures. The lights gradually dim.*)

FIRE CHIEF (*imitating* GIMPY'S *manner of speech*): That's quite correct. I've been told that it started to rain just as they were carrying Eguchi to the entrance of the movie theater, and I remember quite vividly that the rain started just as we were putting out the fire at the Kewpie, and that I felt relieved that this meant there wasn't much danger of a real conflagration.

TEACHER (*in the manner of a prosecutor*): From whom did the defendant hear that it started to rain just after Eguchi had been clubbed to death?

(*At this point the whole stage becomes dark, leaving* TEACHER *and* FIRE CHIEF *in spotlights and* GIMPY *and* ONE EYE *as silhouettes.*)

FIRE CHIEF (*takes another step forward. Speaks in his own person*): I relayed this to the two of them. I was one of those who carried Eguchi, so I remember it clearly.

TEACHER: And for that reason, I take it, you believe that the two young men have an alibi with respect to the murder of Eguchi.

FIRE CHIEF: I do.

TEACHER: Will the witness inform us why he carried Eguchi to the movie theater?

FIRE CHIEF: As I have already explained, I have always been in the position of having to serve as the leader for the islanders, and although I myself did not once use a stick on Eguchi, when I thought of Eguchi's usual behavior and the feelings of the islanders, I could not flatly order them to stop.

(*The two young men shorten the distance between them. They begin to thrash at the floor with their sticks, as if* EGUCHI *were lying there, shouting by turns. An expression of brute force, rather*

57

Involuntary Homicide ■

than of speed, is needed here. A heavy sound like beating against a sandbag.)

I wasn't particularly worried. I thought Eguchi, once he saw the determination of the islanders, would take fright and apologize before it came to blows. That is why I was somewhat late in joining them. But when I got to the scene, Eguchi was already more dead than alive. I thought they mustn't beat him any worse—it would kill him—and I quieted them down. Just then it started to rain pitchforks, and I felt sorry to expose a hurt man to the rain. With the help of some people close by, I carried Eguchi to the entrance of the Kiku Theater.

TEACHER (*sardonically*): Isn't there a mistake in the testimony the witness has just given us?

FIRE CHIEF (*guardedly*): I don't believe there is . . .

TEACHER: In other words, Eguchi was still alive?

FIRE CHIEF: Yes, and that's why I felt sorry for him getting wet in the rain.

TEACHER: In what sense does the witness normally use the words "club to death"?

FIRE CHIEF: To hit and kill someone.

TEACHER: Then someone who has been clubbed to death is dead, correct?

FIRE CHIEF: Of course.

TEACHER (*sharply*): Then why did the witness, when testifying with respect to the confession made by the two men about the incident at the Bar Kewpie, lie by using the expression "clubbed to death" to describe Eguchi's condition at that time?

(FIRE CHIEF *is at a loss for words.* GIMPY *and* ONE EYE *stop their fencing and look at* FIRE CHIEF *as if trying to read his expression.*)

(*Maliciously.*) If by that time Eguchi had definitely been clubbed to death, the alibi of the two young men can be accepted as definite. But if he was still alive, it's a different story. The young men harbored feelings of hatred against Eguchi. It is possible, therefore, they stopped by the movie theater on their way home, and, without anyone seeing it, dealt Eguchi the final blow.

58

FIRE CHIEF (*painfully, stammering*): That's inconceivable.

TEACHER: Am I correct in inferring that the contradiction in the witness's testimony is the result of his having been requested or perhaps coerced into making this statement by the two young men?

(*The young men huddle together. They resemble two stray dogs that, frightened as they are, prepare to counterattack.*)

FIRE CHIEF: Nothing of the sort took place. It is absolutely untrue to infer that I was either requested or coerced.

TEACHER (*pounding it in*): But you must have had some aim in attempting to attract the attention of the court with such a transparently false declaration. Please tell the truth. Was it your aim to avoid the stigma of being a secret informer by forcing the court to pass judgment on them?

(FIRE CHIEF *unable to answer*)

ONE EYE (*in a low voice, looking at the place on the floor that he was beating until a few moments earlier*): It looks as if he's dead.

GIMPY (*shining his flashlight on the supposed corpse*): Turn him face up.

ONE EYE (*makes the gestures, using his stick and his feet, of turning the corpse face up*): He's dead, all right.

GIMPY (*looking into the face of the corpse*): His nose is running.

ONE EYE: At first, his body was tough and made a sharp crack when we hit it, didn't it?

GIMPY: Mmm.

ONE EYE: But somewhere along the line, all at once, I seemed to feel a change in the resistance . . .

GIMPY (*stands and switches off his flashlight*) He's dead.

FIRE CHIEF (*forced into a corner*): My memory may have been mistaken . . . he may already have been dead.

TEACHER: Are you withdrawing your previous testimony?

FIRE CHIEF: I don't recall exactly.

TEACHER (*with the confidence of the victor*): One would suppose, as a matter of common sense, that you, as the person in charge of the fire department, would have to possess a general familiarity with first aid measures, confirmation of life or death, processing bodies of persons who have met violent deaths and so on.

59

Involuntary Homicide ■

FIRE CHIEF (*weakly*): I think he was probably dead.

TEACHER (*as if passing sentence*): Perjury! Abandonment of a dead body! Destruction of evidence! If falsely implicating the young men was not the witness's aim, he must be protecting someone. Probably the witness himself.

(FIRE CHIEF *stands there, bewildered.* TEACHER *shows a smile of triumph. He self-satisfiedly throws out his chest, and shifts his position expansively. Even as he does so, however, he changes to the role of the defense attorney.*)

TEACHER (*in the role of the attorney*): I object. It is improper and lacking in common sense to ask leading questions of this sort of someone without medical knowledge. As is clear from the question of heart transplants, it is by no means easy to determine whether a person is alive or dead even with expert knowledge. (*To* FIRE CHIEF.) Has the witness ever had the experience of looking after someone who was dead drunk?

FIRE CHIEF: I have.

TEACHER: Has the witness also had the occasion to carry a drowned person?

FIRE CHIEF: I have.

TEACHER: Are you confident you could distinguish by the feel, even in the dark, whether you were carrying a drunken or a drowned man?

FIRE CHIEF (*inclining his head in doubt*): . . . It would probably be impossible.

TEACHER: It started to rain just as the witness was lifting up Eguchi. I presume, of course, it must have been dark. All that the witness can clearly remember is the sensation of having carried Eguchi. Is this correct?

FIRE CHIEF: I believe so.

TEACHER: While the witness was sympathizing with Eguchi, he felt he was carrying a man who had been hurt. Later on, after he learned that the victim was dead, he remembered it as a feeling of carrying a corpse. Is this correct?

FIRE CHIEF: Yes, I believe it is.

TEACHER (*pleased with himself*): It would seem, then, that there is no particular contradiction in the witness's testimony. All it shows is that, although the witness had only one experience, it is difficult to sum up in a single expression the nature

■ *Involuntary Homicide*

of this experience, whether the man was hurt or he had met a violent death.

(*Dark change.*)

SCENE 1 O

(ISLANDER B *in spotlight.*)

ISLANDER B (*in rote tones interspersed with miming*): . . . At the time I was passing in front of Eguchi's pachinko parlor. I just happened to look in to see what was going on. Eguchi's pachinko parlor had a bad reputation. People said the machines were fixed, and you were sure to lose your money, so there were almost no customers except for tourists. Of course, I was not in the least inclined to play the pachinko machines, but, as bad luck would have it, Eguchi caught sight of me, and he insisted that my having looked in was proof I really wanted to play, and he forced me to, and wouldn't take no for an answer. I begged off, saying I had urgent business, but then he suddenly got angry and said, "I want a word with you." I was startled, but he dragged me into the place and, opening the front of his jacket, he pulled a dagger from his cotton cloth bellyband. He threatened me, "Do you know what this is? Try asking yourself again whether you want or you don't want to play pachinko." I was afraid of his dagger, so much against my will I lost a thousand yen. But I don't think that because that happened it was a good thing that Eguchi got killed. No matter what the reasons may be, one can't help feeling sorry for someone who's dead, can one?

(ISLANDER B *disappears, and in his place* ISLANDER A *appears.*)

ISLANDER A (*in rote tones. He stands perfectly erect*): To start at the beginning, I have a relative who drills wells, and we were playing cards with the usual gang, when somebody suddenly stuck in his head at the window. We looked up and saw it was Eguchi. Eguchi was angry from the start. I couldn't figure out why and asked him. He screamed at me, "Tell the truth—which is more interesting, cards or pachinko?" I answered politely that cards suited me better. At which Eguchi suddenly burst into the house and kicked the cards we had

61

Involuntary Homicide ■

started to play in all directions. He screamed at my friends, "It's because people like you go around saying such things that I have so few customers in my pachinko parlor. Take this for interfering with my business!" And he went on a rampage. The frame of my glasses got broken and it cost me 370 yen to have it repaired. But I never thought of killing Eguchi, not even after having had such an experience. No matter what the cause may be, it's a crime to kill a person, isn't it?

(ISLANDER A *disappears, and in his place* ISLANDER C *appears.*)

ISLANDER C (*in rote tones with some miming*): I never thought I wanted to have anything to do with him, but unfortunately my house is in his neighborhood, and sometimes I met him in the street. One day he accosted me and said, "There're a lot of dishes at my place that need washing." I thought if I refused he would get even with me, so, much against my wishes, I was forced to work for nothing in the kitchen of the Bar Kewpie. But one day my husband was lying sick in bed with a cold, so I asked to be allowed to return early, since I couldn't leave him all alone, only for Eguchi to threaten me—"What do you mean talking that way? I'll teach you a lesson for trying to disobey me." He made me hold a metal basin full of cold water and stand there like a post, without moving, for a whole day. My knees began to shake and I spilled some water, so next he sent for my husband who was lying in bed with a cold, and he made him wipe up the water. Even so, we thought it best to let sleeping dogs lie, and we continued to put up with this treatment. But you asked me if Eguchi deserved to get killed for having done such a thing. I couldn't answer that I thought so. Surely everybody feels sorry for someone who gets killed.

(ISLANDER C *disappears, and in her place* ISLANDER A *appears.*)

ISLANDER A (*in rote tones*): It was at the end of last year, when we had live performances by Miura Tenko at the Community Center, the movie theater—the Kiku—was empty and Eguchi was jealous. He tried to disturb the performance at the Community Center by throwing stones, and he broke three panes of window glass. But I feel only sympathy with Eguchi, from the bottom of my heart, for having got killed.

■ *Involuntary Homicide*

(ISLANDER A *disappears and in his place* ISLANDER B *appears.*)

ISLANDER B (*in rote tones, with some miming*): Eguchi was a frightening man. About five years ago, along when he first came to the island, Eguchi's business was still small-scale, just selling popsicles. One day I was selling popsicles at the beach when he muscled in and without any warning turned my box of popsicles upside down. On top of that, he punched holes in the tires of my bicycle. The kids got frightened and started to run away, but he grabbed them, and he went through their pockets, took their money, and made them buy his popsicles. After that, nobody on the island dared to sell popsicles, and Eguchi came to monopolize sales. That was how he made money in everything he did. But I don't think it's a good thing Eguchi is dead. One can't say about anybody that he deserved to die.

SCENE 11

(*The stage suddenly becomes light. Near the middle of the stage an office desk.* TEACHER *sits facing desk. At some distance away,* FIRE CHIEF, *along with* ISLANDERS A AND B. GIMPY *is sitting on the lower bunk of one of the beds.* ISLANDER C *is nowhere to be seen. They are all gazing fixedly at the top of the stairs.* ONE EYE *has crawled up the stairs and is peering into the observation post.*)

FIRE CHIEF: What do you see?

(ONE EYE *mutters something that is almost inaudible.*)

FIRE CHIEF: Why don't you speak up plainly? You won't bother him—he's deaf.

ONE EYE: He's sleeping.

FIRE CHIEF: Sleeping?

TEACHER (*laughs*): Can you beat that? After making people worry that way . . .

ONE EYE: Maybe he's thinking. Concentrating hard . . .

ISLANDER A: Are his eyes open?

ONE EYE: I can't tell. He's lying under the window facing the other way. He's curled up with his head on his elbow . . .

ISLANDER B: He must be in a state of shock.

ISLANDER A: I wonder if he was really interested in that girl.

63

Involuntary Homicide ∎

(GIMPY *averts his eyes rebelliously. He is flailing fiercely with the stick in his hand at nothing in particular.*)

TEACHER (*in a humorous manner*): Do me a favor, and hurry up.

FIRE CHIEF (*urging* ONE EYE): Don't be so nervous. He can't hear you, you know.

(ONE EYE *cautiously enters the observation post.*)

TEACHER (*looking around him*): Well, then . . .

FIRE CHIEF (*uneasily, thumbing through the bundle of papers in his hands*): Here're some more. There're quite a lot of reports of damage.

TEACHER (*interrupting him*): That's enough. (*Darting a glance in the direction of the observation post.*) If I may be so bold as to offer my own personal conclusion . . . In short, there is only one remaining course of action . . . (*Takes another look at the observation post.*) But at the moment the question is how much time we've got left . . . It worries me there's nobody manning the lookout. When the police officer's boat gets back, will there be some sort of signal—blowing a whistle or maybe a messenger?

FIRE CHIEF (*calling*): Hey, One Eye!

ONE EYE (*in a stifled voice*): I'm coming!

FIRE CHIEF (*calling*): How about taking over the observation post in place of Deafy?

ONE EYE (*sticking out his head only, hurriedly*): I don't want to. I've had enough. (*Withdraws.*)

GIMPY (*avoiding the eyes of* FIRE CHIEF): I also refuse.

TEACHER: It'll be extremely awkward if the police officer unexpectedly arrives and finds me here.

FIRE CHIEF (*to* ISLANDER A): Would you mind running over to the place where the community antenna is and having a look?

ISLANDER A: With all this rain, the road's probably turned to mud.

FIRE CHIEF: It's for the peace of the island.

(ISLANDER A, *muttering something or other, pulls the hood of his raincoat over his head and exits reluctantly.*)

TEACHER: To state in brief my conclusion : . . The question is

64

■ *Involuntary Homicide*

how a third party—of course, I include the police—examining the evidence—the confessions of the young men, the testimonies of the islanders and similar materials—would interpret it . . . In short, I think they would probably consider it a carefully contrived, mass premeditated murder . . .

FIRE CHIEF (*flaring up before he realizes it*): But that's exactly why I asked for your advice. After going to all the trouble, thinking of every possibility . . . What is the point of the advice you're giving me, anyway? That's no advice, it's a false accusation, isn't it?

TEACHER (*glancing up at the observation post*): He seems to have found something.

(ONE EYE, *comes down the stairs, making as little noise as possible. He carries two bottles of beer in his right hand, and another one under his right arm. In his left hand he is carrying the anchor.* ISLANDER B *hurries to the foot of the stairs to take them.*)

ISLANDER B: Didn't he notice anything?

ONE EYE: It took some doing. I was sweating, I tell you.

(ISLANDER B *reaches up to take the anchor, but* ONE EYE *passes him the beer bottles instead.*)

TEACHER (*joyfully*): That's what I was waiting for.

(ISLANDER B *lines up the beer bottles on the desk.* ONE EYE *stows away the anchor in some suitable place.*)

ONE EYE: If somebody started brandishing a thing like this at you, you wouldn't forget it.

TEACHER: A glass and a bottle opener.

(ISLANDER B *picks up a bottle, and removes the cap with his teeth.*)

FIRE CHIEF (*to* GIMPY): A glass . . .

(GIMPY *ignores him.* FIRE CHIEF, *at a loss what else to do, heads for the back of the room to get a glass.*)

ISLANDER B (*takes a teacup from the shelf beside the stove*): How'll this do as a substitute?

TEACHER (*grabs it, pours a cupful with a trembling hand, and drains it in one gulp. Sighs as he pours a second cup*): It's to get the taste of the liquor I drank at the Kewpie out of my mouth . . . (*Drains second cup. While pouring the third.*) My

65

throat's parched . . . But leaving my throat out of this, I've got to clear my wits . . . (*He drinks half the third cup, puts it on the table, and wipes his mouth.*) I feel like a new man!

FIRE CHIEF: Then, in your opinion . . .

TEACHER: Yes, your story hangs together. But it's no good, no matter how well it hangs together.

FIRE CHIEF: That's what I'm trying to find out. What upsets you so much?

TEACHER: Mmm. For example . . . there's the resident policeman somebody's gone to get . . . If you say his being away was just a coincidence, there's nothing more to be said, but it *is* fairly suspicious . . . (*Drains rest of cup. Pours another cup.*)

FIRE CHIEF: I don't understand very well what you're driving at.

TEACHER (*deliberately, in the manner of a prosecuting attorney*): Even supposing that the present incident was, as the witness claims, unforeseeable violence on the part of simple, hardworking islanders . . .

FIRE CHIEF: That's exactly what it was.

TEACHER: Even if one accepts it as unforeseeable violence, this unexpected act naturally must have been inspired by an appropriate . . . what do you call it?

GIMPY: You mean motive?

FIRE CHIEF: There was a motive. How many times have I told you . . .

TEACHER (*shifting slightly in his seat*): The young men who had been brutally treated indicated they wished to leave the island. (*Drinks the last cupful.*)

(*He holds out a new bottle, and* ISLANDER B *again opens it with his teeth. He licks the beer that spills over.*)

FIRE CHIEF: Maybe it's not possible for someone who wasn't born on the island to understand. Why should the entire population of the island, people who normally are very peaceful, have created such a disturbance if that was all there was to it?

TEACHER: No, I suppose I don't understand. Who would?

FIRE CHIEF (*his anger rising*): Yes, I'm afraid even you, Mr. Teacher, are an outsider . . .

■ *Involuntary Homicide*

TEACHER (*calmly, resuming the manner of a prosecuting attorney*): It would seem that the color of the ink on the reports of injury submitted by the witness has changed remarkably. (*Sips some beer.*) What comment would the witness like to make concerning the opinion of experts that it takes a minimum of six months for ink to change this much in color?

(FIRE CHIEF *runs his eyes over the documents he holds in his hands. With a rigid expression on his face, he goes to the stove, and, without a word, throws in the documents.* ISLANDER C *enters, a basket in her hands.*)

ISLANDER C: It was quite a struggle . . . (*She shakes her raincoat and brushes off the raindrops.*)

TEACHER: Thank you for your trouble.

ISLANDER C: There wasn't anything decent. Canned whale-meat, salted beans, dried cuttlefish, bean-jam cakes . . . (*She spreads them out on the table.*)

TEACHER: Bean-jam cakes?

ISLANDER C: They'd been offered at the altar in the temple, so they smell a little of incense.

TEACHER: I'll take the whalemeat. I don't care what it tastes like. It's canned, so it'll be sanitary. (*He starts to open the can.*)

FIRE CHIEF (*to* ISLANDER C, *pointing at the stove*): How about raking the ashes? (*To* TEACHER, *circling behind him.*) It beats me why I ever thought I could depend on you.

TEACHER (*absorbed in opening the can*): It's not all that mysterious. If I weren't here, there'd be only one course you could choose . . .

FIRE CHIEF: What makes the motivation inadequate?

TEACHER (*finishes opening the can*): It's not that there isn't enough—there's too much . . . (*Takes a slice of whalemeat and stuffs it in his mouth.*) Up to now, there'd been any number of possibilities for an explosion . . . (*Washes it down with beer.*)

FIRE CHIEF (*to* ONE EYE): It was the first time I'd ever listened to any such proposal, and it came from you guys.

ONE EYE: Yes, it was the first time we'd ever been subjected to anything quite that brutal.

TEACHER (*resumes the manner of a prosecuting attorney*): The

67

Involuntary Homicide ∎

essential thing is why this particular day, today, was chosen . . . (*Chews noisily on the salted beans.*) The defendants had all been waiting a long time for an opportunity, but I suppose they simply weren't favored with the chance to lure the resident constable into accepting an invitation to go night fishing.

FIRE CHIEF: I'm too disgusted to say a thing.

TEACHER: In that case, we might try asking the constable directly. Whose statement will make the best sense? I'm willing to lay about 10,000 yen on that.

(FIRE CHIEF *stares at* TEACHER, *murder in his eyes.* TEACHER *does not notice this because he is intent on scraping the bottom of the can of whalemeat. After a brief pause,* DEAFY *comes slowly down from the observation post.*)

DEAFY (*quietly*): Who took my anchor? Give it back.

(*They all remain silent.*)

ISLANDER C (*in a low voice*): What'll we do?

DEAFY: I need it. My anchor . . .

(DEAFY, *after looking around, discovers where the anchor was hidden. He goes up to it.*)

TEACHER: Don't let him! You're putting a knife in the hands of a lunatic.

(ONE EYE *tries to stop* DEAFY.)

DEAFY (*quietly*): I'm not going to do anything violent. I've had enough violence. Out of my way! Kumiko's asked me to. She's sleeping under the cliff. She says she doesn't want anybody touching her any more. And she says I should tie the anchor to myself and sink to the bottom of the sea. I can't hear the voices of living people, but I've started to hear the voices of the dead. Get out of my way! (*He pushes* ONE EYE *aside, and picks up the anchor.*) The responsibility is entirely my own. You've nothing to worry about.

(DEAFY *quietly exits, carrying the anchor. He does not look at anyone's face. During the long pause that ensues, one hears a protracted sigh, but it is not clear from whom.*)

FIRE CHIEF (*faces* TEACHER *again*): Let's hear it now . . . You were saying there was only one course we could follow . . .

TEACHER (*seriously*): The blood went to your head. Understand? The blood went to your head.

68

FIRE CHIEF: To whose head?

TEACHER (*suppressing a belch, in the tones of a defendant*): At that time the blood went to my head. I can't remember why I ever did anything like that. (*Passes a fresh bottle of beer to* ISLANDER B.) Hey, defendant!

FIRE CHIEF (*knocking the bottle from his hand*): I'm asking you seriously.

TEACHER: Hmm.

FIRE CHIEF: I'm in a position where I can even get you dismissed.

TEACHER (*his drunkenness gradually becomes conspicuous*): You don't seem to understand . . . Your feelings of love for the island are, in the final analysis, an example of blood going to your head. Nobody blames you for loving the island. I'm not the type to have blood go to my head, and that's actually why I understand you so well. (*Suddenly changes his tone.*) What do you mean? I'm not exactly defenseless. Do you suppose you can get me dismissed so easily?

(TEACHER *picks up beer bottle from the floor, and holds it out to* ISLANDER B, *gesturing for him to open it. But* FIRE CHIEF *suddenly snatches it from him. Holding the bottle by the neck, he swings it hard against the back of* TEACHER'S *head.* TEACHER *immediately slumps over.*)

FIRE CHIEF (*looking around at the others. In a voice that suggests he will not take no for an answer*): All of you, hit him! Everything that happens on this island is the joint responsibility of all of us. Hurry up! Don't be afraid!

(*Two* ISLANDERS, *in response to his command, pick up sticks lying beside the stove, and begin to beat the prostrate* TEACHER. *Their manner of beating suggests discomfort and reluctance, but gradually they begin to put strength into it. Fear has aroused them. A heavy sound, like a sandbag being beaten. Next,* ONE EYE *gets to his feet.*)

FIRE CHIEF (*repeats, as if intoning a prayer*): The blood went to our heads . . . All of us—the blood went to our heads . . . Don't forget, we lost our heads . . . We all lost our heads . . .

(Suddenly GIMPY, *a stick in his hand, circles round* FIRE CHIEF *and is about to bring the stick down on him, but at that instant,*

69

ONE EYE *notices him, and pushes* GIMPY *away.* GIMPY *falls back heavily. His artificial leg is twisted off with the recoil.* FIRE CHIEF, *dodging the blow, turns to confronts him.* ISLANDERS, *not knowing what else to do, stand rooted to the spot.*)

FIRE CHIEF (*muttering*): So, that's the way things are, are they?

(TEACHER *groans.* FIRE CHIEF *picks up the wooden leg and brings it down with full force on* TEACHER'S *head.* TEACHER *gives a final spasm, then stops moving.* GIMPY *tries to stand up, but falls over.* ONE EYE *helps him over to the bed, lending him his shoulder to lean on.* FIRE CHIEF *kneels beside* TEACHER, *turns back his eyelids and inspects the pupils. He nods and stands. He motions to* ISLANDERS *to dispose of the body. With a show of reluctance, they shoulder* TEACHER. *But he is too heavy for* ISLANDER C. ONE EYE, *unable to stand by indifferently, goes to help the others.*)

ISLANDER C (*unsteadily*): Where are we taking him?

FIRE CHIEF: Lay him down next to Eguchi.

(ISLANDER A *comes rushing in. He bumps against the group carrying* TEACHER'S *body, and stands transfixed.*)

ISLANDER A: The constable's come!

(*The group carrying* TEACHER'S *body, change directions in alarm.* ISLANDER A *joins in the group carrying the body. They leave by the back door.* FIRE CHIEF *turns toward* GIMPY. GIMPY *averts his glance. He crawls forward, picks up the crutches at the side of the bed, and silently follows behind the group of* ISLANDERS. FIRE CHIEF, *left alone, stares at the others as they go, the wooden leg still in his hand. He deliberately walks to the stove and pushes the wooden leg in. He turns around and stares at the door through which the police officer is to come.*)

Curtain.

■ *Involuntary Homicide*

The Green Stockings

Kunie Tanaka as the
HERBIVOROUS HUMAN
BEING in a scene
from *The Green
Stocking*.

●

Man *(the Herbivorous Human Being)*

His Wife

His Son

Son's Fiancée

Doctor

Doctor's Assistant (a student)

Nurse

Old Woman (appears only in slide projections)

Cameraman/Stagehand A

Interviewer/Stagehand B

Patient/Stagehand C

Patient's Wife/Stagehand D

Stagehand E

Stagehand F

SCENE 1

Music. (A series of weird, rumbling sounds that serve as the theme music for the play. In fact, these are the enormously magnified

Translator's Note: The text of *The Green Stockings (Midori-iro no Sutokkingu)* I have translated is as revised by the author for the production in 1974. This version differs at a number of points from the original text written earlier in the same year that is found in the Shinchō Bunko edition (1989). With the exception of some added material in the last scene, however, the differences consist mainly of minor changes of expression, made no doubt in response to his experience directing the performance. When consulted on the matter, Mr. Abe said that no text of any of his plays was definitive. I have chosen the version I like best.

sounds of the human digestive process. When the curtain rises, only the center of the stage is illuminated, but as the action progresses, this circle of light changes in shape or character in response to the circumstances, until it finally fills the whole of what is in fact a large room. The room is divided into a number of compartments. The backdrop is a painting [or photographic panel] depicting a grassy meadow. If possible, the picture should cover the entire wall surface.

MAN, *dressed in pajamas, stands in the center of the circle of light. On the periphery of the circle are several white objects. These objects are actually characters of the play, draped with large white sheets. At first glance they resemble articles of furniture or perhaps sculpture that have been covered with dust protectors.*)

MAN: . . . I'm beginning to understand something. I can see something. (*An expression of fierce concentration.*) A color mixed of anger and love. The color of stone burnt by green flames. What I need is some adrenalin. I'll douse the muscles of my arms and legs with an adrenalin spray and then try making a break for it. (*His tone becomes introspective.*) Are you happy? Of course—or at least that's what I keep telling myself, but I wonder . . . Isn't it simply I'm afraid to think I'm unhappy? The minute you begin to have doubts, the floor under your feet starts to shake. (*Staggers.*) The trouble is, I know exactly how this floor is rigged up. (MAN *walks around the room, touching the walls. He pulls from the floor a cube about a foot and a half on all sides, removes the cover, and peers down inside.*) A bottomless pit. I'd like to take a little peek. Curiosity killed the cat, they say. (*Turns his face away.*) Ugh! What a stink! A mouldy-smelling wind hit me in the nose. But I suppose there're times when having a bad tooth can give a special flavor to a meal . . .

It was in the year 1900 and . . . What year was it, anyway? Let's say it was about three years ago that an old woman died. (*Rests one hand on a corner of the cube, which has gradually risen from the floor to the height of a grave-stone.*) She was a poor, lonely old woman without a soul in the world she could turn to. But she left behind a little farm. (MAN, *leaving the cube, walks to one of the white objects on the periphery of the circle of light.*) A doctor bought her farm.

74

(MAN *flips the sheet from the object, revealing* DOCTOR, *in a white coat. He is sitting on a chair, but rises to his feet as if he has been observing something. He begins to speak, half to* MAN *and half to the audience.*)

DOCTOR (*with an embarrassed smile*): A farm! I never thought of it in those terms. That's a surprise! I bought it as an ordinary little piece of property . . . It's right next to the hospital, and the poor old lady living there had just lost her husband. At first, the only thing I felt was sympathy. Her husband was a carpenter who'd lost an arm in the war, and they couldn't have had any savings worth mentioning. Well, then, as you might expect, not three months had passed after the husband's death than the owner of the property began to pressure the old lady into moving away. She seems to have had trouble even putting together the rent money, and on top of everything else, it wasn't long before they cut off the gas and electricity. Pretty hopeless, I think you'll agree. I couldn't stand by just watching, so I bought the property.

MAN: All that meant was that the landlord changed—right?

DOCTOR: No. I never pressured her. I offered her terms and tried to negotiate along lines that were considerably more generous than what common sense would dictate, but she turned me down flat. There were various complications, but I'll skip the details. In any case, I decided to wait patiently. Sooner or later, without any money, she was bound to run into difficulties and, excuse me for saying so, she hadn't much longer to live.

MAN: All the same, she kept you waiting three years.

DOCTOR: Yes, three whole years.

MAN: The doctor couldn't figure it out. How did she manage to find enough to live on? Once he started to worry about this, it preyed on his mind. One day he finally decided to hire a student and have him investigate.

(MAN *snatches the sheet from a second object, revealing* STU-DENT [*later,* DOCTOR'S ASSISTANT]. STUDENT *holds a slide projector in his arms.*)

STUDENT: Screen, please.

(DOCTOR *smooths the wrinkles on the sheet hanging on the wall panel to the rear, in preparation for its being used as a screen.*

75

The Green Stockings ●

STUDENT *signals for the lights to be turned off. Stage becomes dark. The projector begins to operate, flashing a series of strange pictures on the screen. First, there is a full-length shot of the* OLD WOMAN, *her elbows held up before her face and her whole body expressing violent refusal.*)

DOCTOR: Did you say something to make her angry?

STUDENT: I just startled her a bit.

DOCTOR: And did you find out anything?

STUDENT: You see what's she got in her right hand? What do you call it— the thing you use to make popped corn.

DOCTOR: A parching pan.

STUDENT: That's right, a parching pan.

DOCTOR: What was she parching?

STUDENT: It had quite a fragrant smell. Sort of sweet, like corn mush that's been scorched a little.

DOCTOR: And what was it?

STUDENT: I tried asking her straight out. When you don't know something, the best thing is to ask. (As *if addressing* OLD WOMAN.) We . . . I mean, the doctor and I, are really worried about you. Are you eating properly? How do you manage to get enough to eat? Every morning, very early, you always go out for a walk for half an hour or so. You pick up a couple of broken pieces of wood at some lumberyard in the neighborhood, and then for the rest of the day you shut yourself up here. There's no sign you ever go out shopping and, of course, nobody ever comes to visit you. How do you manage to keep eating? Living the way you do, there's not much chance of getting any food.

DOCTOR: What did she say to that?

(*Slide shifts to one of* OLD WOMAN *smiling and point to the floor.*)

STUDENT: Look! She's laughing! As much as to say she doesn't need us worrying about her.

DOCTOR: (*irritably*): But how *did* she manage?

STUDENT: She said she had grazing land.

DOCTOR: Grazing land?

STUDENT: She's pointing at a hole cut in the floor. She seems to be growing something down there.

DOCTOR: What could she possibly grow in such a place?

76

(*The slide shifts again. The next shot is of the hole cut into the tattered matting on the floor, taken from above. All one can see of the* OLD WOMAN *are her feet.*)

STUDENT: She resisted me for all she was worth. She didn't seem to want to show me, but there definitely were insects down there. If not insects, grubs or larvae.

DOCTOR (*peers intently at the picture*): Insects . . . ?

STUDENT: "Grazing land" was a nice way to put it. Exactly like *Gulliver's Travels*.

DOCTOR: What kind of insects could they be?

STUDENT: Maggots, wouldn't you say?

DOCTOR: You can't be serious!

(STUDENT *switches off the projector and stands. He gives a signal to turn on the lights in the room.*)

STUDENT: I picked one up as a sample. Here . . . (*He spreads open a crumpled piece of paper and holds it out to* DOCTOR.) This one's already been roasted, but you can still make out what it was . . .

DOCTOR: It certainly looks like some kind of bug.

STUDENT (*putting away the sheet that has served as a screen*): You don't think it's a maggot?

DOCTOR: You know, I wonder if it isn't a termite . . .

STUDENT: A termite? I get the picture now—those sticks of wood she picked up every morning were fodder for her livestock.

DOCTOR: What a repulsive thought!

STUDENT: Termites are more sanitary than maggots!

DOCTOR (*in a formal manner*): Wouldn't you like to extend your contract? On the same terms as before? It won't take much more to get to the bottom of this. I'd like to lay my hands on some firm evidence. If they really were termites, it's an incredible story.

STUDENT (*speaks casually, to hide his joy*): I'm sure it can be arranged. Your laboratory is reinforced concrete, so there's no danger from termites.

DOCTOR: Breeding termites in a residential area is an out-and-out misdemeanor!

STUDENT: But, you know, I wonder if a study of termites might not lead to some surprisingly interesting results. I have a kind

77

The Green Stockings •

of intuition. For instance, if we could succeed in domesticating termites it might solve the world food crisis.

DOCTOR: Don't make me laugh. Who ever heard of domesticating insects?

STUDENT: How about bees? They're a kind of domestic animal, aren't they?

DOCTOR: Well, yes . . .

STUDENT (*waxes impassioned*): Of course, there are all kinds of problems. The ability of termites to break down cellulose. Their value as a source of protein. Their powers of propagation. In other words, their economic efficiency. And, most important of all, their influence on the human body. But we can't stop now, when we've been provided, right before our eyes, with the results of an experiment performed on a living subject. I'm fascinated, I admit. Please let me stay on this job until we reach a solution. That's all right with you, isn't it?

(*They freeze for a moment, still looking at each other. Then* STUDENT *goes on tiptoes to a third object, and turns up the hems of the sheet.* NURSE *sticks out her head.*)

NURSE (*in a low voice*): How did it go?

STUDENT: As of today, I've been officially taken on as his assistant.

NURSE: Marvelous!

STUDENT: But that's still not enough to get married on.

(STUDENT *crawls under sheet with* NURSE. *He is henceforth referred to as* ASSISTANT.)

SCENE 2

(*A sound resembling that of hundreds of eggshells being slowly trampled underfoot.* ASSISTANT *and* NURSE *stand, throwing off the sheet.* DOCTOR, *coming to himself, assumes a tense expression. The three of them look around the room as if searching for something. They exchange glances.*)

MAN: . . . One morning, in the third year, the old woman's house collapsed without warning. Probably the broken bits of lumber she was able to carry home did not satisfy the termites—the whole house was eaten away until it was nothing

78

more than a paper cut-out. The old woman, buried under-neath, died in the debris.

ASSISTANT: No—she died of shock. The house was so flimsy there was no weight to it.

NURSE: That's right. She wasn't even scratched.

DOCTOR: Her nutritive condition was satisfactory. Of course, one couldn't say it was perfect. It's quite true there were imbalances. But the fact remains that she lived close to three years on nothing but termites and water. Three whole years. Entirely on termites. Epoch-making, that's what it is. It wouldn't be going too far to consider termites to be a perfect food.

MAN: Soon afterward a clinic and a laboratory were added to the hospital on the site of the collapsed building. (STAGEHANDS *appear and make simple changes in the props. The stage turns into one large room. The remaining sheets are removed to reveal a bed and reception-room furniture.*) But the termite farm left by the old woman is still, as you can see . . . (*Points at the cube.*) preserved intact in its original position.

DOCTOR: It's not *exactly* the same.

ASSISTANT: That's right. We completely reinforced the circum-ference with concrete. There is absolutely no danger of creat-ing a nuisance for other people with the termites. This is the only passage between the termite farm and the outside world. (*With an air of self-satisfaction.*) As you can see, it is strictly supervised, and there is literally not so much as a crack an ant could crawl out from. Moreover, the scale of the farm has been enlarged to approximately 8.2 times its original size, when it was left to nature. The interior is divided into five concrete blocks, each block capable of accommodating enough ants to feed five people weighing 140 pounds each for a full year. Five times five makes twenty-five people . . . This corresponds to about 100 head of cattle on a grazing area of 48 acres, or about 200,000 square yards. Do you have any idea how big this is? (*With a sweeping gesture that takes in the whole scene of grassy fields depicted on the walls.*) An area extending as far as the eye can see, and an equivalent of all this land lies dormant in the insignificant hole that has been excavated here.

79

The Green Stockings •

(*The lighting, which has grown steadily brighter, now illuminates the landscape on the walls so intensely as to make it glitter.* DOCTOR, ASSISTANT *and* NURSE *gaze with a reverent expression at the cube projecting from the floor. The atmosphere recalls that of Millet's* The Angelus.)

DOCTOR (*his shoulders suddenly slump. He speaks dejectedly*): But the sad part is that this treasure is doing nobody any good. Time and time again I've sent data to the National Food Agency and to the United Nations, but I've never had a word in reply. And the newspapers—completely irresponsible! They play up the food crisis, or whatever they call it, for all it's worth, and . . . You know what the reporter who came here the other day said? "Then, why don't you try eating it yourself?"

ASSISTANT: It's just plain conservatism. People are unbelievably conservative when it comes to their stomachs. No matter how conservative they may be in their sexual preferences, it doesn't bear comparison with their conservatism in food. (*Something suddenly makes his expression tense. He points at* MAN.) Doctor, that man over there . . .

(*Stage becomes dark except for* MAN.)

SCENE 3

MAN: . . . High-heel shoes run down at the heels, stockings like twisted membranes, panties with flower patterns looking like frayed handkerchiefs, elastic bands with metal fittings of some kind attached, brassieres with the sponge rubber spilling out, corsets spread out like squid drying on a line . . . Yes, I prefer those that are old and worn to new ones. I'm a coward. That's why I specialized in clotheslines. And even clotheslines are a lot of trouble, I can assure you. Women always dry their laundry in broad daylight when the weather is good—just when you're most likely to be noticed. A terrible time. And try to imagine what it's like when you're caught in the act. (*Cringes in shame.*) It's the bottom! There's no worming your way out of it, is there? And to make things worse, I'm a school teacher by profession. The times I am free and the distances I can cover in the daytime are limited, just inside the two circles described . . . (*Makes gesture of drawing circles with a compass.*) with my house and the school at the center. At first it wasn't so bad. The radius was big, and I could afford to pick and choose. But gradually the radius of my activity has shrunk. The scenes of the crimes have started to be concentrated around my house and the school. I can't be too particular any more. One of these days I'm going to lay my hands on some very ordinary item, only this time I'll get caught. But, if it's true that I can't give it up, I'll have to meet my fate, a spider's web with the spider waiting for me. I'm fully aware it's a dead-end street, and I know what's waiting at the end, but there's no possibility of backtracking now. (*He pulls a green stocking from his pocket, gazes at it, then fondles it affectionately.*) This is my number one favorite . . . Panty-stockings! What an abomination! In the first place, they show a total disregard of the aesthetics of self-completeness that, in general, each part of the body possesses. If they're to be panties, let them be panties. If they're to be stockings, let them be stockings . . . All the same, I wonder who had the idea of making green nylon stockings? He must have been quite something. The color, the feel, the contradiction between the two—it's indescribable . . . Always trembling like a leaf, but never resisting, fearful as a blade of grass, but never trying to escape . . .

SCENE 4

(WIFE *and* SON *appear.*)

WIFE (*very matter-of-fact*): Have you heard? They say there's a panty thief in the neighborhood.

SON (*paring his toenails*): You don't say . . .

WIFE (*letting out the ends of* SON'S *trousers*): He seems to come right on schedule every week. Mondays and Fridays.

SON: What're the police doing about it?

WIFE: I hear they've been making the rounds, asking questions. Not that it does any good.

SON: You don't have to take such trouble with my pants.

WIFE: What do you think?

SON: About what?

WIFE: The panty thief.

(MAN *stuffs the green stocking in his pocket and comes forward.*)

MAN: I wish you'd drop the subject. It's dirty.

WIFE: The police seem to be more interested in the criminal than in what's been stolen. I wonder if they suspect anyone from this neighborhood.

SON: It's all the same to me.

WIFE: Do you suppose the criminal is actually living nearby?

MAN (*irritated*): Why are you so fascinated by the subject?

WIFE: Today's Sunday. Tomorrow's Monday . . . (MAN *and* SON *look at* WIFE *in disgust.*) If he's on schedule, he'll make an appearance somewhere tomorrow.

SON: If it worries you, you should leave off doing the laundry.

WIFE: Just suppose the criminal was somebody we knew—I wonder how we would feel about him? For instance, if it was one of the teachers at school, or somebody equally close?

MAN: I would absolutely refuse to have anything further to do with him . . . It's no laughing matter.

WIFE: You wouldn't give him the benefit of your advice?

MAN: I'd urge him to kill himself. That'd be the best advice I could give. Isn't there a cigarette somewhere?

WIFE: I simply don't understand . . . I wonder how the people in his family must feel.

MAN: They hate him. They hate him so much they wish he was dead! (*Surprised by his own vehemence, he falls silent.*)

(*Pause.*)

SON: Aren't my pants ready yet?

WIFE: In a minute. But don't they say that many of them, if anything, have very delicate feelings?

SON: Who?

WIFE: Panty thieves.

SON: You've been reading too many women's magazines, Ma.

WIFE: You know, they say it's one form fear of women takes.

MAN: Haven't you said about enough on the subject?

SON: It's not a fit topic for parlor conversation.

WIFE: But isn't it wrong to blame him without hearing his side of the story?

MAN (*groans*): What's so wrong about it? He should commit suicide. What other course has he?

82

SON (*stretches out his hand for the trousers*): I've got to be going.

WIFE: I wonder if I might borrow that bag you keep on top of the bookcase for my odds and ends.

MAN (*cries out, without realizing it. He blocks her way*): No, you can't!

(SON *stares at* MAN *in dumb amazement.* WIFE *keeps her eyes fixed on* MAN, *as if appealing to him. They gradually begin to take in the situation.* SON's *expression hardens. During the unbearable pause that follows, the atmosphere becomes more and more oppressive.*)

WIFE: But I don't think it's too late, even now.

MAN: It's too late.

SON (*nods*): Maybe it *is* too late.

WIFE (*sharply*): Don't talk about things you don't understand.

SON: Suicide's not a bad idea, but it'd just be compounding the disgrace.

WIFE: Wait just one moment.

MAN: Don't worry. I'll go somewhere a long ways from here before I do it.

WIFE: It's not all that serious. It was just underwear . . .

SON: Doesn't that make it all the more contemptible? (*He grabs his trousers and pulls them on.*)

MAN (*heavily*): That's right. It's too late now.

(*Blackout, leaving only* MAN *illuminated.*)

SCENE 5

MAN: I killed myself. I said goodbye even to the underwear I had taken such trouble to collect. I committed suicide without leaving even a farewell note. I changed subways twice, then came all the way to the last stop in the opposite direction. There was a power generator that made the signal blink at a road construction. I attached a rubber tube to the exhaust pipe, and put the tube in my mouth. Then I covered my head with a plastic bag and lay down in an excavation they had dug in the asphalt. The last thing I can remember was a smell of soap coming at me from a long ways off. A smell of freshly laundered underwear . . . I don't like it when the smell is *too* vivid.

SCENE 6

(*The room becomes light again.* DOCTOR, ASSISTANT, *and* NURSE *enter briskly, carrying variously an oxygen respirator, equipment for a blood transfusion, and a set of injecting needles. They set up the equipment with no wasted motions, and begin treating* MAN. *The results are immediately apparent.*)

DOCTOR: He seems to have come to.

NURSE (*restraining* MAN): Lie still!

MAN: Where am I?

ASSISTANT: He seems to be fully conscious.

MAN (*groans*): Damn it. Why couldn't you have let me be?

DOCTOR: Can you remember your name? Your family?

MAN: Hmmm.

ASSISTANT: But you're sorry now you did it, aren't you? Most people who try to commit suicide regret it afterward. Once they've been rescued, they never seem to want to try it again. It must be a one-time impulse.

MAN: I haven't got a cent. Saving me won't bring you a thing.

DOCTOR: But you want to be saved, don't you?

MAN: I haven't the least desire to be saved. (*Tries to sit up.*) Let me go!

NURSE: You're not strong enough.

DOCTOR: You'll have to rest quietly for a couple of days.

ASSISTANT: What made you do it?

MAN (*brushes off hands of* NURSE *and* ASSISTANT): It's got nothing to do with you.

(MAN *gets up, takes a few steps, then his legs buckle under him.* DOCTOR *and* ASSISTANT *prop him up and put him back on the bed.*)

NURSE: He's no slouch when it comes to having his own way.

DOCTOR: I wish you'd try to have more confidence in us.

MAN: I'm absolutely incapable of paying you. You're wasting your time.

ASSISTANT: Your best bet is to mark time here until you feel like getting in touch with your family again. We're not setting any time limits. That's right, isn't it, Doctor? (*Looks to* DOCTOR *for confirmation.*) Nothing is more precious than life.

MAN (*in self-mocking tones*): All it amounts to is marking time until I die anyway.

(DOCTOR *exchanges meaningful glances with the others.*)

ASSISTANT (*pronounces each word slowly and distinctly as if trying to establish something*): What were you running away from, Mister? The police? Creditors? Have you been juggling your accounts? Embezzling company funds? Or have you had a fight with your pals?

DOCTOR: Or perhaps an incurable ailment?

NURSE: An emotional entanglement? A love triangle, maybe?

MAN (*cutting short their speculations*): It was all because of myself.

ASSISTANT: Then you're sick of life, is that it?

MAN (*losing his temper*): For pity's sake, throw me out, right away!

ASSISTANT: But every human being, no matter who he is, has the right to live.

MAN: And the right to die, for that matter.

DOCTOR: But you couldn't have tried to kill yourself without some cause . . . How about it—why don't you leave everything to me?

MAN: What do you mean?

ASSISTANT: Five hundred thousand yen every month!

MAN: I told you, didn't I, that I'm flat broke.

ASSISTANT: No—we'll be paying *you*. Five hundred thousand yen a month, six million yen a year. And on top of that, we'll foot the bill for your living expenses and the rest.

(MAN *remains silent.*)

DOCTOR: Please don't misunderstand me. This will probably be of mutual benefit. You won't lose anything by it. We'll restore your confidence in living, and you'll provide us with confirmation for our hypothesis.

MAN (*sarcastically*): Do you know why I tried to kill myself?

DOCTOR (*glibly*): Suicide is an escape from life. What is life? An escape from death. This means that each of us must die twice. There is the death waiting for us ahead, and the death that comes pursuing from behind. Your trouble is that you're confused. Once you are free at least from the death that

85

comes pursuing you, you can relax and enjoy life as you go along.

ASSISTANT: Let me explain in simple language. Just supposing you knew that in the future you would have absolutely no worries about having enough to eat. Would you still want to kill yourself? What a terrific thing it is—to be free of worries about food! You won't have to slave away or to toady to your boss. And you won't have to adjust your stomach to the size of your savings account.

NURSE (*looking around over the painting of the grassy landscape*): A life of freedom, travelling wherever you please . . .

ASSISTANT (*warms to the theme*): Nothing more than a rucksack on your back, anywhere you feel like going . . .

NURSE: Communing with nature, symbiosis . . .

DOCTOR (*as if to wrap up the argument*): At the very least, it's better than suicide, isn't it?

ASSISTANT (*urging the* DOCTOR): Why not tell him plainly?

DOCTOR: Yes, there's no special reason for hiding. You see . . . if you wish . . . you'll be able to eat grass.

MAN: Grass?

DOCTOR: You'll be able to digest grass, like a herbivorous animal. Grass, straw, pulp—you'll be able to eat them all.

ASSISTANT (*follows up immediately*): Herbivorous doesn't sound too good. How about vegetarian? Lately, there's been something of a craze for vegetarian food. Wild plants from the mountains and the fields—I'm crazy about them myself. The taste is fine, and what's more, they're good for you.

DOCTOR: That's right. They're excellent for one's health. As a general rule, herbivorous animals live much longer than carnivorous ones. And it's not only a matter of longevity. They're full of life. It's nothing more than prejudice to suppose that herbivorous animals are weak or delicate.

NURSE: Yes, just think of the bulls at bullfights or racehorses or elephants or hippopotamuses or gorillas or buffaloes or mandril baboons.

ASSISTANT: It seems that even the penis is longer on herbivorous animals.

DOCTOR: Best of all, you're free. You won't have to depend any longer on the foodstuffs they sell in the stores, their prices

86

swollen by the complicated process of distribution. But it's not only an economic advantage. You can win back your spiritual freedom.

ASSISTANT (*carried away*): You'll never have to carry a box lunch. You can go anywhere, empty-handed, on an eternal picnic . . .

NURSE: Across the seas, to unknown destinations . . .

ASSISTANT: From one field to another, a hiking course over an endless dinner table.

MAN: If it's all that wonderful, why don't you try it on yourselves before you perform this service for other people?

DOCTOR: Of course we will, in time.

ASSISTANT: But it would be rather awkward now, considering our position.

MAN: What do you mean "our position"?

DOCTOR: If a ship was sinking, wouldn't it be utterly irresponsible for the captain and the crew to be the first to make their escape?

(*Pause.*)

ASSISTANT: Five hundred thousand yen a month.

MAN: Mmm.

ASSISTANT: Six million yen a year.

NURSE: And you'll be famous!

DOCTOR: That's right. The first herbivorous man.

ASSISTANT: The star of hope for all humankind.

NURSE: You'll be in demand everywhere—radio, television, lectures . . .

MAN: Well, I suppose I can always kill myself if I decide I want to die.

DOCTOR (*interrupts with a laugh*): Then it's agreed! It's time to begin our preparations . . . !

(ASSISTANT *immediately circles behind* MAN *and presses a pad soaked in ether over* MAN'S *nose and mouth.* MAN *groans and puts up a struggle, but loses consciousness almost at once.* DOCTOR, *aided by* ASSISTANT *and* NURSE, *changes to surgical garb for the operation. He puts on a surgeon's hat, mask, and rubber gloves. He stands by* MAN'S *feet with a large surgical knife in his hand.* ASSISTANT *switches on a light, and a powerful beam throws the bed into high relief.* NURSE *spreads open the lower*

87

The Green Stockings ●

abdomen of MAN'S *pajamas, and uses tweezers to disinfect the area with absorbent cotton.* ASSISTANT *throws a green sheet over* MAN. DOCTOR *thrusts in the scalpel. The gauze pads* NURSE *applies to the incision are quickly stained with blood.*)

DOCTOR: The technique is essentially that of an appendectomy. If the surgeon is sufficiently adept, an incision of three to three and a half centimeters will suffice . . . First, I sever a section of the small intestine . . . (*He lifts up a section of the small intestine.*) The greatest possible care must be given not to damage the peritoneum . . . (NURSE *takes the severed section from him.*) Next, I stitch this to the other end, further on down . . . (*As* DOCTOR *leans over* MAN, ASSISTANT *continues to spray with an atomizer a sort of liquid on the exposed part of the small intestine.*) Next . . . (*Holds out his hand to take the severed section from* NURSE.) I stitch this to the tip of the appendix . . . This reverse bypass creates a short circuit that sends food back from the appendix to the small intestine . . . (*Raises his head.*) And, finally, this is a little invention of my own . . .

ASSISTANT (*holds out to* DOCTOR *a small horseshoe-shaped object*): It was a sudden inspiration. You know the toy frogs that hop around when you inflate them? That's what gave him the idea.

DOCTOR: It opens wide when a fixed pressure has been reached . . . I set this valve a few centimeters from the appendix toward the rectum . . . Here we are . . . While this valve is in operation, the contents of the intestines continue to circulate round and round within the short circuit. (*Concludes the operation.*) To put it concisely, the effect is to make the intestines perform the ruminating process that a cow performs in its stomach. For the time being he'll be on a liquid diet, but this includes bacteria and protozoa with the capacity of resolving dozens of different varieties of cellulose taken from the appendices of herbivorous animals and the internal organs of termites. It's just a matter of time before they begin active digestive functions. (*Removes his rubber gloves. He looks pleased with himself.*) Yes, this may well be termed a reform of the topological structure of the intestines.

88   (*Stage suddenly grows dark.*)

●   *The Green Stockings*

SCENE 7

(*Light from two flashlights probes the interior of the room, the two beams now and then crisscrossing.* SON *and* FIANCÉE *have slipped into the room from the emergency exit at stage left.*)

FIANCÉE: This room gives me the creeps . . .

SON (*light from his flashlight falls on* MAN *in a hospital bed*): He's here!

FIANCÉE: What? Him?

SON: Yes, my old man. No doubt about it. Dad! It's me!

FIANCÉE: How about turning on the lights?

(SON'S *flashlight skims over the grassy fields painted on the wall and comes to a stop at the light switch.*)

SON: That it?

(SON *and* FIANCÉE *go to switch and turn on lights. At the same time, there is a mechanical click as the cube sinks into the floor.* FIANCÉE'S *foot has tripped against the mechanism that kept the cube in place. They jump back in alarm and exchanges glances.*)

FIANCÉE: What was that?

SON: Your guess is as good as mine. (*He gingerly approaches the section of the floor into which the cube has sunk. He peers down, shaking his head in perplexity. He then goes to the bed and shakes* MAN *gently.*) Dad! (*Puts his ear to* MAN'S *chest.*) He's breathing.

FIANCÉE (*peeps over* SON'S *shoulder*): He looks as if he's been drugged.

SON (*shakes* MAN *again, this time vigorously*): Wake up, I say!

FIANCÉE (*looks around her*): There's something suspicious about the atmosphere. Maybe he was being used for a live experiment.

SON: You mean a vivisection?

FIANCÉE (*looks intently at* MAN'S *face*): He doesn't look all that exhausted.

(MAN *mumbles something and turns over in his sleep. His bowels begin to rumble. The sound is indistinct, but more complicated and richer in expression than a normal person's.*)

FIANCÉE: What was that noise?

SON: It must be his stomach.

FIANCÉE (*listens attentively*): You're right.

89

The Green Stockings •

SON: Don't you think it's peculiar? If he's being unlawfully detained, why wasn't the door more securely fastened?

FIANCÉE: Isn't it even more peculiar that a man who's run away from home should suddenly remit four hundred thousand yen?

SON (*puts hand on* MAN'S *shoulder and forces him up into a sitting posture. Then he takes* MAN'S *nose between his fingers and shakes him violently*): Please—open your eyes! (MAN *groans and opens one eye.*) Dad! It's me! Don't you recognize me?

MAN (*in a hoarse voice*): What time is it now?

SON: Three in the morning.

MAN: Give me some water.

(FIANCÉE *pours some water into a glass from a pitcher on the sideboard and hands the glass to* MAN.)

SON: Is something wrong with you?

MAN: How did you find out where I was?

SON: They ought to be more careful about keeping that door locked . . . What happened to your other eye?

MAN (*uses two fingers to open his other eye*): It was just gummed up.

SON: Do you need help?

MAN: Help?

SON: If you want to break out of here, I'll help you.

MAN (*rubs his eyes with his fingers*): It still beats me how you found out about this place.

SON (*in a changed voice*): It was you, wasn't it, Dad, who deposited the money into our account?

(MAN *remains silent.*)

FIANCÉE: So we made the rounds of all the emergency hospitals. (*Looks to* SON *for support.*) This was the twenty-third, wasn't it?

MAN (*looks at her searchingly*): And who are you?

SON (*with feigned cheerfulness*): All the same, I was surprised, I can tell you. It never occurred to me . . .

MAN: That I'd have the nerve to go on living—right?

SON (*apologetically*): That's not what I meant.

FIANCÉE: The present . . .

SON: That's right, the present.

● *The Green Stockings*

(SON *takes from his pocket a small parcel wrapped in paper and hands it to* MAN. MAN *unwraps it. It contains a pair of green nylon stockings.* MAN *takes them halfway out of the bag, then his expression hardens. He steals a glance at* FIANCÉE.)

MAN (*suppressing his emotions*): Does it give you so much pleasure to make fun of me?

SON (*hastily*): You misunderstand me! It couldn't possibly do me any good to make you angry now, Dad. Fetishism has been prevalent, especially among artists, from ancient times. I read it in a book. Go ahead, take it. There's nothing to be ashamed of.

(MAN *lets stockings slip from his fingers, but his eyes seem to be appraising them.*)

MAN: It'd be best not to stay too long.

SON: Ma's also worried. She wonders what the money means, whether she should leave it in the savings account. It's quite a lot of money, and she says she doesn't feel like using it without knowing the meaning.

MAN: It's for living expenses. She should use it any way she likes.

SON (*relieved*): I'm glad to hear it. It's a big help. Some of the money will be turned over to me, with your consent, that is. (*With a gesture of presenting* FIANCÉE.) She's starting a class in handicrafts, but what with one thing and another, it runs into a lot of money.

FIANCÉE: Pleased to meet you. It's a kind of handicraft, but not weaving or anything like that. I do metal carving. I plan to have a show one of these days featuring my own creations.

(MAN *shuts his eyes and puts his hand to his forehead.*)

SON: Do you feel bad?

MAN (*weakly*): Would you mind leaving?

FIANCÉE: That's right. We'll come back at a more reasonable hour, now that we've tracked you down.

MAN: There's nothing to come for. Just leave me alone for the time being, won't you?

SON (*looks at his wristwatch*): All the same, the nurse here is too damned rude. She's so snappish it makes you suspect there's something fishy going on.

FIANCÉE: There must be something going on she doesn't want people to know about.

91

The Green Stockings •

SON: Would you like us to negotiate? We might be able to get more out of her.

MAN: Every month, from now on, I'll be depositing the same amount in the account. That way, I trust I'll have done my duty to you.

SON (*strongly*): Of course! You make me feel as if I've done something wrong. But I still don't get it. I don't know what's wrong with you, but it's certainly peculiar to get paid for being in the hospital.

MAN: I'm not just lying in a hospital bed. I'm doing all that is necessary to earn my pay.

SON: What exactly do you do?

FIANCÉE: Don't be too embarrassed to tell us. You only succeed in upsetting us when you keep your troubles to yourself.

SON: Or if you'd like to get the hell out of here, come along with us. I've got a car waiting outside.

FIANCÉE: This place is like a cell in a looney bin.

MAN: But it suits me just fine . . . I've had an operation. I can eat grass now. I can even eat straw or paper, like a cow or a sheep. I'm a herbivorous man. Unusual, isn't it? (*Picks up the green stockings.*) Where did you steal these? What kind of woman wore them, I wonder. (*Rolls stockings into a ball and sniffs at them.*) They've never been washed! (*Holds them up to the light and inspects them from all angles.*) It looks as if you've tried to pass off a new article on me.

FIANCÉE: They've never been washed, but they're not new. I tried wearing them myself, just a little.

(MAN *looks with surprise at* FIANCÉE. *He lets his glance wander slowly down her legs, all but licking her in the process. The expressions on the faces of* SON *and* FIANCÉE *become constrained.*)

FIANCÉE: . . . I like it . . . green, I mean. It fascinates me. I wonder why . . . Maybe it's because green is connected with happiness. (*Looks around.*) But a place like this that's positively crawling with green is oppressive. Is this the interior decoration? Of course, it must be. I wonder whose design it was?

MAN: I gather it's for educational purposes.

SON: What do you mean, "educational"?

92

MAN: I can't very well let you go away empty-handed. Just a
     second . . .

(MAN *takes a small suitcase from under the bed. He opens it and
arranges the contents—various items of women's underwear, a
dozen or more. He handles each item as if he were caring for some
delicate little animal. He looks around, a pleased expression on
his face.*) Take any one you like. (*His attention returns to the
green stockings. He picks them up gently and brushes them against
his cheek. He sits on the edge of the bed, rolls up one pajama leg,
and pulls on a stocking. He holds up his leg and examines it with
minute attention. Suddenly, to* SON.)

What's the matter? You needn't be shy about accepting.

SON (*mutters something inaudible. Then, to* FIANCÉE): Shall we
     be going?

FIANCÉE (*her voice is dry*): Yes, let's.

SON (*with a forced smile*): Well, I'll be seeing you, Dad.

(SON *and* FIANCÉE *exit awkwardly from door at stage left.*)

SCENE 8

(MAN *slowly rises to his feet. As soon as* SON *and* FIANCÉE *leave,
he fastens the latch on the door. He goes back to the bed, throws
the articles of underwear into the suitcase, and pushes the suitcase
back under the bed. For a moment he remains immersed in
thought. Suddenly he stands erect and begins to dance something
reminiscent of "The Dying Swan" with the other stocking wrapped
around his neck. He expires in swanlike fashion, only to stand the
next moment and deal the coup de grace to his invisible corpse by
stamping on its neck. Breathing a sigh of relief, he puts the
stocking under his pillow. He takes a urine glass from under the
bed. He slowly moves across the room, the urine glass in his hand,
then disappears behind a screen.*)

MAN: All I ask is to be left alone . . . to have nothing to do with
     anybody . . .

(*Sound of his urinating.*)

     I want to slip through the dark spaces separating one human
     being from the next, not interfering with anybody, not being
     interfered with by anybody else . . . The wind at daybreak, a
     half-moon in the sky like a segment of a canned tangerine,

93

The Green Stockings •

and the feel of sand and gravel under my shoes . . . I'll become a shadow, hard as a knife, and mingle with the silent ghosts . . . Grassy meadows waving in the wind will be my dinner table . . . Look! A dinner table fit for a king, and you can eat as much as you like . . . A dinner all by myself, with nobody else around . . . A rabbit on a dark night . . . A black rabbit.

(*The sound of his urinating behind the screen finally stops.*)

Are you happy? Of course you are!

(MAN *appears from behind the screen holding a full urine glass. On one leg, which still has the trouser rolled up, the green stocking all but glows. He places the urine glass on the table, whistling all the while, and measures the amount of liquid with a gauge.*)

Exactly as predicted. My urine has increased by two and a half gradations. The smell has gradually come to resemble a horse's. (*Looks around.*) It won't be long before that picture on the wall becomes reality, and this side of the wall becomes a fake. (*He smiles and, staring at a spot on the wall, continues his soliloquy.*) I'll run away and never turn back. If they think they can catch me, let them try. There's a big difference between me and a horse or a rabbit. My head's still a human being's, just as it's always been . . .

SCENE 9

(*Man suddenly clutches his lower abdomen and stands motionless in his tracks.*)

MAN (*uneasily*): What's happening? . . . I don't like this wriggling. It feels like a snake's running wild inside my guts.

(*His stomach begins to emit a rumbling sound, much more intense than anything previous. The sound is so powerful and so unremitting that it does not seem like a mere physiological phenomenon. The complexity of the sound, composed of many elements, suggests a monkey playing on a wheezing pipe organ. MAN, not surprisingly, is panic-stricken. He rushes to the call bell by the head of his bed. His expression is tense. He keeps his finger*)

● *The Green Stockings*

pressed on the bell. ASSISTANT *rushes in, rubbing his sleepy eyes. He listens in astonishment to the intensity of the roar emitted by* MAN.)

MAN: Do something! Quick!

ASSISTANT (*in dumb amazement*): It's certainly something!

MAN: Is it all right, do you think?

ASSISTANT: I'll call the doctor. (*Picks up interphone on work table.*)

MAN (*nervously*): Maybe something went wrong with the operation?

ASSISTANT: It sounds like the roaring of some kind of animal. A sea lion, maybe . . . (*Into the telephone.*) Doctor, is that you? Please come here in a hurry. His stomach's acting up.

MAN (*impatiently*): The noise! Tell him about the noise!

ASSISTANT: It's making a terrific racket. Like a pig bitten by a duck. Can you hear it? What's that? Just a second . . . (*To* MAN.) Are you in pain?

MAN: In pain? . . . No, there doesn't seem to be any pain.

ASSISTANT (*into telephone*): He says he's not in pain. Oh, really? . . . I see . . . I understand. Well, please do. (*Hangs up.*) He says he'll be here right away. There doesn't seem to be anything to worry about, providing there's no pain. It may be a good sign, instead.

MAN: A good sign?

ASSISTANT: I don't mean to change the subject . . . (*Casually approaches the bed.*) but that's a rather unusual stocking you're wearing.

(MAN *hurriedly rolls down the leg of his pajamas.* ASSISTANT *continues to stare maliciously at* MAN'S *feet.*)

MAN (*pressing his abdomen*): How long is this racket going to last?

ASSISTANT (*nods*): Do you feel more yourself when you make that noise?

MAN: What do you mean?

ASSISTANT: People generally suppose that sexual desire is strongest among meat-eating animals, but that's a mistake. As a matter of fact, grass-eating animals are far more lusty.

(MAN *remains silent.*)

95

The Green Stockings •

ASSISTANT: Am I right in thinking that the underwear in your collection doesn't have to have belonged to any special woman? Or does it make some difference who exactly wore the panties?

(*The rumbling noises suddenly change character.*)

MAN: What is the doctor dawdling over, I wonder?

ASSISTANT: Have you ever tried thinking seriously about your mission in life, what the future holds in store for you?

MAN: What else have I got to do?

ASSISTANT: And it doesn't bother you?

(MAN *remains silent.*)

ASSISTANT: Not afraid?

MAN: Are you trying to tell me something?

ASSISTANT: It doesn't bother me, as long as it's all right with you. Your future's for you to decide.

(*The rumbling noises stop with a final pop, like a champagne cork.* MAN *seems to have broken wind. His expression is one of embarrassment.*)

MAN: Would you put the ventilator on high? The gas is something terrible.

ASSISTANT (*turns the dial of the regulator on the wall*): Congratulations! The bypass seems to have been opened.

MAN: Bypass?

ASSISTANT (*keeping his eyes on* MAN): The experiment's a success! You've just been reborn this second as a herbivorous human being!

MAN (*touches his hand to his abdomen and looks down, as if trying to see inside*): Now?

ASSISTANT: That's right. That noise just now. You can now freely eat even untreated straw or grass. How do you feel? Happy?

MAN: What's keeping the doctor?

ASSISTANT: All the same, it makes a terrible stink. This is awful. (*Covers his nose with his sleeve.* MAN, *turning his back to* ASSISTANT, *starts to pull off the stocking.*)

MAN: I'd like some medicine.

ASSISTANT: Don't be silly. If you stop the gas, it'll ruin the whole point of the experiment. The gas is a symbol, a testimony, the clinching evidence that you, a grass-eating man,

• *The Green Stockings*

are alive and well. It proves that your faculty for resolving cellulose is functioning normally.

MAN: You mean, it'll be like this all the time?

ASSISTANT: We calculate that the bouts will be a couple of hours apart, but there's bound to be some variation, depending on what you eat.

MAN: This wasn't in the agreement! Telephone the doctor and tell him to hurry.

ASSISTANT: But, it's just plain common sense. When you resolve cellulose, it produces gas. It makes a noise even when you blow through a gas pipe.

MAN: It's a question of degree! I never expected that every two hours my stomach would sound off like a military band.

ASSISTANT: I'm sure the doctor'll be upset too.

MAN: If he knew all along, and was keeping it to himself, it's fraud. And if he didn't know, he bungled.

ASSISTANT (*in tones of pity*): I admit that there are little problems like the smell and the noise . . . but when you compare them to this epoch-making event, the fact that you can eat straw and grass . . .

MAN: I thought I asked you to send for the doctor right away!

ASSISTANT (*notices the stocking in* MAN'S *hand*): Wouldn't it be a good idea to put that away?

MAN (*shoves stocking under his pillow*): There's such a thing as dignity. And pride. Man does not live solely to eat. Isn't that what the doctor said? He said he hoped I would become the kind of human being he himself wanted to be.

ASSISTANT: He's not the only one. Every member of the human race would like to turn into what he felt was an ideal human being.

MAN: How about you? How would you like to fart every two hours to the accompaniment of a brass band?

ASSISTANT: If you'd really like to hear my opinion . . .

MAN: I don't give a damn for your opinion. There simply *has* to be something that can be done. This is just too awful.

ASSISTANT: My opinion, whatever you may think, is not entirely beside the point.

MAN: I'll give it my full attention once I've seen the doctor.

ASSISTANT: The doctor's not coming.

97

MAN: Then what was that telephone call?

ASSISTANT: I was only pretending to phone. If we actually had been connected, he would never have been so long.

MAN (*pushes* ASSISTANT *back*): Get the hell out of here!

ASSISTANT (*pulling a stocking from under the pillow*): I'm sure everybody will be interested in this.

(MAN *shrinks back.*)

ASSISTANT (*not giving* MAN *a chance to reply*): I'm sure the doctor will start, the first thing tomorrow, laying the groundwork for the public announcement of the success of his experiment. But to tell the truth, I have a premonition that all is not going to go well. People are unbelievably conservative when it comes to their eating habits. I suppose it will create something of a sensation anyway. You'll make a fine circus attraction, about on a level with a midget. When you've finished reading the morning newspaper, you'll munch your way through it along with your coffee, and you'll say, "Well, that was today's menu." (*Sneeringly.*) I'm sure you'll be quite a hit. And if you can let fly with a good one, the effect will be perfect. But I wonder if anybody will be seriously interested in following in your footsteps. I have a feeling that's a little too much to ask.

MAN: What are you getting at, anyway?

ASSISTANT: In my opinion, there's no need to rush publicizing this.

MAN: That's right.

ASSISTANT: The change that affects you as a human being will be a lot more important than the change as a living organism, and ample time should be allowed for measuring the extent of this change.

MAN: I wish you'd try persuading the doctor to give up the whole thing.

ASSISTANT (*leans forward to emphasize the point*): It's quite unlikely I can persuade him to give it up. He's poured every cent he has into the project.

MAN (*in a display of determination*): Then, supposing I decide to run away?

ASSISTANT (*taken aback*): Run away? Where to?

• *The Green Stockings*

MAN: I won't cause anybody any trouble. I can live now on straw and grass, right? . . . Yes, that's the only way . . . Just as you were saying, the most I can hope for is to disgrace myself by brazenly appearing before people. And I wonder if, in the long run, it wouldn't be better even for the doctor if I ran away. He may feel disappointed for a time, but it's still better than having his pride wounded, isn't it?

ASSISTANT: You don't have to talk in such forlorn tones. Why don't you adopt delay tactics for the time being, and let things take care of themselves?

MAN: I hate the whole business. Even supposing I manage to delay, it'll be just as hateful to me then as it is now. The one thing I absolutely refuse to do is to become a sideshow attraction. The doctor can talk himself blue in the face, but that's the one thing I absolutely refuse.

ASSISTANT: That's why I think your best plan is to keep on delaying, as long as you can. In the end you can have a second operation that will restore your condition to what it was before.

MAN (*shocked*): A second operation? What a terrible thing to suggest. Even you must have had some sort of ideal when this started. Or was it all so much talk, in order to bamboozle me? I'm shocked. The experiment hasn't finished yet, but so far it's been a success. A second operation would be a violation of good faith.

ASSISTANT: How would you like a steak?

(MAN *remains silent.*)

ASSISTANT: A thick, juicy steak sizzling in the frying pan on a bed of thinly sliced onion rings . . . a steak that cuts like butter when you stick a knife in, and spreads open translucent red meat like lips . . .

MAN: Don't try to provoke me.

ASSISTANT: Or maybe you'd prefer turtle soup . . . lobster with drawn butter . . . grilled salmon . . . duck with orange sauce . . . caviar on toast . . .

MAN: Cut it out! You're bothering me!

ASSISTANT: I wonder why people have such conservative appetites? I've become a complete pessimist, ever since our project

99

The Green Stockings ●

for a termite farm was ignored by absolutely everybody. It was obvious even at that stage. Who do you think'll take notice of a herbivorous human being?

MAN: In that case, why didn't you back out of the experiment when you realized what was likely to happen?

ASSISTANT: Even I've got a right to earn a living.

MAN: A right to earn a living?

ASSISTANT: I've worked out a little plan for my future, and if I can manage somehow to stick it out until I've accumulated enough capital . . .

MAN: So that's why you subjected me to this ordeal!

ASSISTANT: Don't forget, my friend, you tried to commit suicide. And you have your ordeal to thank for the five hundred thousand yen you earn each month. How can you have the nerve to gripe?

MAN (*overcome by* ASSISTANT'S *arguments*): But how am I going to stall for time?

ASSISTANT: That's where my special know-how comes in. The doctor is going to ask you to do something, and I want you to agree, right away, without any hesitation. It'll probably be an interview with the director of a publicity agency or something of the sort.

MAN (*suspiciously*): That's not what you promised.

ASSISTANT (*snaps his fingers with an air of self-confidence*): Please leave everything to me. I know a rather unusual company that specializes in dealing with stupid clients who have nothing on their minds but becoming famous.

MAN: You're sure it'll work?

ASSISTANT: In return, I want you to keep pitching. You're to munch on those straw crackers as if you really enjoyed the taste, full of confidence, a cheerful expression on your face . . . (*Pushes the stocking back under the pillow.*) I'm returning this for the time being.

(MAN *is silent.*)

ASSISTANT: This time I'm really going to send for the doctor. Today's likely to be one hell of a day.

(ASSISTANT *exits quickly with a conspiratorial smile on his face.*)

• *The Green Stockings*

SCENE 10

(MAN *takes his suit, which has been hanging behind the screen, and changes as quickly as possible—trousers, shirt, necktie, jacket, socks, shoes . . . Next, he takes a bottle of medicine from a drawer in the work table, and puts it in his pocket. He drinks some water from the pitcher on the sideboard. He turns back and opens a cupboard from which he removes an instrument that looks like a meat grinder, then returns to the bed. He picks up the suitcase containing his collection of underwear and, with some difficulty, squeezes the instrument in. He takes another drink from the pitcher, then starts on tiptoes for the door leading to the emergency exit. He stops, as if recalling he has forgotten something. He goes back to the bed, pulls the green stockings from under the pillow, and stuffs them into his pocket. He puts his hand on the pitcher, but decides this time not to drink. He hurries to the door at stage left.*)

SON'S VOICE (*low*): Dad!

(*Pause.*)

Dad, it's me!

(*Pause. Sound of knocking.*)

I know you're in there. Open up, please. I heard everything. So, open up, I'm asking you.

(MAN *shrinks back toward door at stage right, only to stop in his tracks once again. He has sensed the approach of* DOCTOR *and* ASSISTANT. *A sound of knocking.* MAN, *with the expression of a trapped animal, looks from one door to the other. Finally making up his mind, he climbs up a ladder behind the screen and disappears into the ceiling.*)

SCENE 11

(DOCTOR *and* ASSISTANT *enter briskly.* DOCTOR *seems to be greatly agitated, and he has not quite finished buttoning his white coat.* NURSE *enters next, pushing a serving wagon.*)

DOCTOR (*goes directly to bed*): Congratulations! I hear you've at last had a breakthrough.

ASSISTANT (*noticing that the bed is empty*): Where's he gone, I wonder?

The Green Stockings   •

DOCTOR: He's not here!

ASSISTANT (*looks behind screen*): That's strange.

(*A knocking on the door that leads to the emergency exit.* DOCTOR *and* ASSISTANT *exchange glances of surprise.*)

NURSE: I forgot my contact lenses.

DOCTOR: Shhh.

(ASSISTANT, *leaning forward, touches a finger to his lips as a sign to* NURSE.)

SON'S VOICE: Dad—open up, I'm asking you. I've been thinking over what I said and I'm sorry.

DOCTOR: His son?

ASSISTANT: So it would seem.

NURSE: You're sure he's not here?

ASSISTANT (*looking around*): I still can't believe it.

DOCTOR: The door's locked, isn't it?

ASSISTANT: That's why he's knocking.

SON'S VOICE: If you'll only let me explain . . .

DOCTOR: Then, there was no possible way for him to make his escape.

ASSISTANT: In the first place, he had no reason to run away.

NURSE (*searches under the bed*): It *is* peculiar.

SON'S VOICE: I won't budge until you open this door.

ASSISTANT (*with a click of his tongue*): What're you going to do now?

DOCTOR: Damned nuisance!

ASSISTANT: How did he manage to sniff out this place?

SON'S VOICE: Dad!

DOCTOR: Do you suppose the remittances gave us away?

ASSISTANT: The money was paid directly into his account. How could he possibly have figured it out?

DOCTOR: It can't be helped, then. Let him in.

ASSISTANT: But why?

DOCTOR: It'll make things all the worse if he starts making trouble. This is a crisis.

ASSISTANT: Wouldn't it be better to search for him first?

DOCTOR: The exits are blocked. It's obvious he must still be here.

ASSISTANT: I suppose so.

SON'S VOICE: Dad, I'm begging you.

The Green Stockings

(ASSISTANT *unlocks door that leads to the emergency exit. Door opens.* SON, *unprepared to have it yield so easily, tumbles into the room. He looks around him in bewilderment.*)

DOCTOR: Please come right in.

SON (*looks around him*): Where's my father?

DOCTOR: You're his son, are you? What a big son he has! Would you mind coming in and shutting the door behind you?

SON (*quickly sizing up the situation, he turns back to the door and calls*): Come on in!

ASSISTANT: Is there somebody else?

(MAN'S WIFE *and* SON'S FIANCÉE *enter. Their expressions are tense.*)

WIFE: Please excuse us.

SON: This is my mother and my girlfriend.

ASSISTANT (*sarcastically*): Forced entry by a whole family—and at this hour of the night!

SON: My mother insisted on coming.

FIANCÉE: I'm not yet one of the family.

ASSISTANT (*circles behind the others and shuts the door*): I see.

SON: It was you, wasn't it, who was talking with my father a while ago?

ASSISTANT: Eavesdropping?

DOCTOR: Would you mind explaining your business?

WIFE: Where is my husband?

DOCTOR: That's what's so strange. We've only just come in ourselves.

ASSISTANT (*in a loud voice. Joins his hands in mock supplication*): Please stop playing hide-and-seek with us, and show yourself!

NURSE (*after first taking a look behind the screen, walks around the chairs and sofa*): If he's not here, I give up.

SON: Couldn't he have slipped out the door as you came in?

ASSISTANT: That door can only be opened from the outside, and this one only from the inside. He simply *has* to be here.

(*They all begin an unsystematic search of the room. It does not occur to anyone that to look up inside the ceiling.*)

NURSE (*investigating on the other side of the screen, she finds the pajamas he took off, and comes forward with them in her*

103

The Green Stockings •

hands): What's this? His pajamas—right? And his clothes've disappeared. Look! There's no sign of his shirt or necktie, or even his shoes!

DOCTOR: What does this mean?

ASSISTANT (*angrily*): What do you suppose got into him? I can't figure it out . . . (*Opens cupboard door.*) The hand-cutter's also disappeared!

SON (*to* NURSE): What's a hand-cutter?

NURSE: It's an instrument for cutting straw and grass to make them easier to eat. It was meant for when he traveled. An electric model wouldn't have been of any use in a place without electricity. (*Examines* SON'S *face attentively.*) I've seen you before somewhere. Or it is just my imagination?

DOCTOR (*knocking on his forehead with his clenched fist*): But why should he have run away? What possible advantage could there be in doing such a thing?

WIFE (*to* SON): Are you sure it was Dad?

SON: You don't think I'm lying!

WIFE (*to* DOCTOR): I want to talk with my husband. This is a serious matter, and it may involve all of you, depending on what I find out. You must let me see him.

DOCTOR (*losing his temper*): You want to see him. So do I. But he's not here. There's nothing we can do about it.

SON: It seems pretty definite he's not here.

ASSISTANT: It's about equally definite that he can't be anywhere else.

WIFE: But he couldn't simply have melted into thin air. He's not exactly a snowman.

FIANCÉE: There's no sign of him. There are indications that he tried to run away, but we don't know his escape route. Then, it can be surmised . . .

ASSISTANT: You wouldn't be writing a detective novel, would you?

FIANCÉE: *You* don't seem to be writing one.

ASSISTANT (*barks out a laugh*): Well, since we're all characters in the same novel, let's not be too critical of one another. The fact is, he's *got* to be here. It may seem like he's not here, but there's absolutely no doubt of it.

104

FIANCÉE: It's pretty clear what the motive was. What isn't clear is who did it and how.

SON: What kind of motive do you mean?

FIANCÉE: It's obvious, isn't it? Destruction of the evidence. He was preparing to escape, they tell us. That's an old trick—a false clue, deliberately concocted so as to divert our attention from the case.

DOCTOR: That's one way of looking at it. But I can't imagine why he should have wanted to escape. There really isn't any motive for it.

FIANCÉE (*nods*): He didn't just vanish. Somebody *made* him vanish. This means that the guilty party is whoever most feared that the crime committed here would be exposed.

DOCTOR (*suspiciously*): What do you mean? Against whom are you directing these insinuations? (*He darts a glance at* ASSISTANT.)

ASSISTANT (*annoyed*): Against me, of course. I was so afraid that the experiment would be exposed that, before I went to wake up the doctor, I killed him and stuffed his body down the disposer . . .

NURSE: That's impossible! Not with our disposer.

DOCTOR: Why should you fear disclosure?

ASSISTANT: How should I know?

DOCTOR (*rather emotionally*): Excuse me, madame, but what business brought you here?

WIFE: Nothing that should be referred to in the past tense.

DOCTOR: Use any tense you like!

WIFE: Naturally, I came to bring my husband back.

DOCTOR: Don't be absurd! Your husband's no longer the insignificant creature he once was, a man who can be swayed by petty private emotions.

WIFE: Is it true you've made a cripple out of my husband?

DOCTOR: A cripple? (*Laughs.*) Heaven forbid!

WIFE: But they say he can now eat grass. (*Looks at* FIANCÉE *as if asking her confirmation.*)

FIANCÉE (*to* SON): We heard it from his own mouth, didn't we?

SON: Yes, it seems he can manage straw, paper, or what have you.

105

The Green Stockings •

DOCTOR (*losing his temper*): Why does that make him a cripple? Foolish and ignorant prejudices like yours have always stood in the way of progress. Does being superior to other people make a man a cripple? Does being a champion chess player, getting a gold medal in the Olympics, winning the Nobel Prize, being first in a popular song contest prove that one has become a cripple? I've had enough of these senseless accusations.

FIANCÉE: But surely you're aware that it's illegal to perform an experiment on a living person without his family's consent.

DOCTOR: Then, I'll get him to disown his family. Now, listen to this. (*To* WIFE.) When your husband was carried in here after his attempted suicide—I'd have preferred not to mention this, but you asked for it—the first thing he requested, believe it or not, was that we not get in touch with his family.

WIFE: All the same, I won't feel satisfied until I hear what he thinks from my husband himself directly.

DOCTOR: Go right ahead.

WIFE: With your permission, I'll wait.

DOCTOR (*nonplussed*): But it doesn't make sense to wait for someone who's not here.

(*Pause.*)

FIANCÉE: Is *that* his meal?

NURSE (*picks up something from the serving wagon that looks like a thick slice of pumpernickel bread*): It's the first time, so I made it rather fancy. I used five stalks of sugar cane, three of straw, threw in some cedar shavings and soybean stems, ground them all up to make for easier ingestion, and then steamed them for about twenty minutes.

SON (*takes some in his fingers*): It's like a rotting doormat. And is this his whole meal?

NURSE: It amounts to a fairly big quantity when it's been broken down.

ASSISTANT: Besides, his diet calls for more than three meals a day. It takes time to digest grass and straw. He'll have to eat eight meals a day.

SON: Eight meals? Then, if he eats at two-hour intervals he'll have to keep eating all day.

ASSISTANT: Americans chew gum all day.

• *The Green Stockings*

(*Pause.*)

WIFE (*crosses room and sits in one of the chairs in the living room set*): I intend to go on waiting here, no matter how long it takes.

DOCTOR: I think you're wasting your time. Your husband's not the same husband he was.

WIFE: No, he's just the way he was. He hasn't changed in the least. I'm a tiny bit disappointed, but I'm relieved all the same. His sickness is exactly the same as before . . .

DOCTOR: What sickness?

SON (*holding out the breakfast tray prepared for* MAN): But Ma, he can eat this. You've got to admit there's been some change . . .

FIANCÉE: That certainly is a change.

WIFE: Not any more serious than if his hair became thin or he developed a paunch.

DOCTOR: You're wrong. Your way of looking at things—how shall I put it . . . ?

WIFE: Shall I tell you what his sickness is?

SON: Stop, Ma.

WIFE: My husband has a special interest in women's underwear. I wonder if that's what is called a perversion?

NURSE: Ah-hah.

DOCTOR (*unruffled*): In other words, a fetishism.

SON: Wasn't it you, Ma, who said we weren't to criticize him? You're contradicting yourself. I gave Dad a present of her stockings. It was part of a carefully conceived plan to break down the barriers between us and make it possible for our conversation to move ahead smoothly. There's nothing for you to get so worked up over. It's a complete contradiction.

WIFE: I'm *not* criticizing him. As far as I was concerned, he was just a human being.

DOCTOR: He still is a human being. That's obvious, isn't it? A fine human being.

(*Short pause.*)

WIFE: Just because he can eat grass doesn't mean that everything's been settled.

(*Short pause.*)

NURSE: They say herbivorous animals are the most active.

(*Short pause.*)

ASSISTANT: You know, I think that women in the future are likely to wear underwear made of cotton that's as edible as possible.

NURSE (*raising her voice*): Ugh! Disgusting!

DOCTOR: You mustn't ridicule the idea.

ASSISTANT: Still, sex isn't as serious a problem as his appetite.

DOCTOR: Of course, we also bear a share of the responsibility.

NURSE: Do you suppose that was what was depressing him?

ASSISTANT: He was certainly a nervous guy.

SON: Dad must understand how we're all worrying about him this way.

FIANCÉE: The fact is, human beings are just plain lonely . . .

DOCTOR: Yes, when he comes back, this time we'll have to give him a heartfelt welcome.

(*Suddenly,* MAN'S *rumbling noises resound from the ceiling.*)

SCENE 1 2

(*They all look up at the ceiling in astonishment.*)

ASSISTANT: That's where he is!

DOCTOR: Damn!

NURSE (*to* SON): I forgot to put on my contacts.

SON: Dad, come down, right away!

(*A green stocking flutters down.*)

MAN'S VOICE: That was what you wanted, wasn't it? Pick it up and get the hell out of here.

WIFE (*with feeling*): Please, I beg you, come down.

MAN'S VOICE: Go away, I tell you.

WIFE: I won't leave without you.

MAN'S VOICE: It's too late now.

WIFE (*more urgently than before*): I've heard everything. Is it true, as they say, you can eat grass now? But what difference does that make? No matter what you eat, you're still the same you.

DOCTOR: No, you're wrong!

WIFE (*picks up the green stocking from the floor and pushes it into* DOCTOR'S *face*): He's just the same! Look! Isn't this proof he's exactly the same as before?

108

- *The Green Stockings*

DOCTOR: He's been unfaithful. The only difference is that it's been with underwear rather than with a woman. Infidelity in men is not so much a sickness as a physiological necessity.

(NURSE *claps her hands and bursts out laughing.*)

WIFE (*again calls to her husband inside the ceiling*): Let's go home. I've had a good talk with the principal at your school and I've completed all the formalities for an official leave. Your desk, your bookcase, your slippers, your dressing gown— they're all just the way you left them.

SON (*hesitantly*): But aren't you taking too one-sided a view of the situation? As long as he's here, he earns close to three times his salary at school . . .

DOCTOR: That's right. And it's possible he may earn even more, depending on circumstances.

WIFE (*to* SON): How can you calmly . . . You're like some sort of parasite or tick!

SON: But if Dad himself doesn't want to go home, there's nothing we can do about it, is there?

WIFE (*to* MAN): Why were you dissatisfied? What didn't you like?

ASSISTANT: You're on the wrong track. It's simply that he likes this place too much to leave. (*To* MAN.) That's right, isn't it? (*Looks round each of the people present.*) A new life! A new existence as a human being!

WIFE: Is that noise he makes what you call a new life?

FIANCÉE (*to* SON): Don't you think it'd be a good idea if we went away for a while?

MAN'S VOICE: That's right. The best thing you can do is leave.

DOCTOR (*to* WIFE): You see, that's what your husband has to say.

ASSISTANT: At this rate, he won't be able to eat his meal in peace.

NURSE (*looks into the dishes on the serving wagon*): Everything's turned stone cold.

ASSISTANT: Poor guy—his stomach must be complaining.

WIFE (*suddenly uneasy*): I wonder if he's all right. He's been rumbling on for quite some time . . .

DOCTOR: There's nothing to worry about. He's just hungry. (*Calling to* MAN.) How about coming down and having some breakfast? It sounds as if you've got rid of the gas. You must be pretty well starved by now.

ASSISTANT (*standing beside the wagon, picks up a card*): Well, what do you know . . . "Information for Herbivorous Human Beings." (*Reads.*) "One. Eating of the first meal should commence within five hours after the expulsion of gas, and special care must be taken to ensure that no less than twelve percent of the matter remaining in the appendix consists of unresolved cellulose."

WIFE (*imploringly, to* MAN): Let's go home. I've been thinking over things since you left. I intend to help you, until you've completely recovered.

MAN'S VOICE: Help me do what?

WIFE: I can look over the lay of the land in advance. Or I can distract people's attention after you've staked out a clothesline.

NURSE: You needn't go to such trouble. Right? (*She turns to* ASSISTANT *for confirmation.*) . . . Here he doesn't have to feel the least bit constrained.

WIFE: And what do you mean by that?

NURSE: It doesn't bother me. I can always get the doctor to pay for whatever's been stolen. And as long as he keeps stealing my things, it saves me the trouble of having them laundered.

(WIFE *springs at* NURSE. NURSE *dodges, then counterattacks with a slap to* WIFE'S *face.* DOCTOR *and* ASSISTANT *separate* NURSE *and* WIFE. *Ad lib exchange of dialogue during fight.*)

MAN'S VOICE: Stop it, you damn fools!

(*Even as he speaks* NURSE'S *underwear cascades down from the ceiling like a shower of multicolored blossoms. They are all taken aback.*)

MAN'S VOICE (*as if holding back the tears*): Get out, get out, all of you! Right away!

(*Short pause.*)

DOCTOR (*politely pushes the members of* MAN'S *family toward the door*): Now that you've seen the situation, I trust you'll understand for the time being . . .

MAN'S VOICE: You too, doctor. All of you, get out! I don't want one of you left here. Vamoose!

(*Short pause.*)

The Green Stockings

WIFE (*resolutely*): I intend to stay.

NURSE: You're jealous, that's what!

WIFE: Whore!

ASSISTANT: Cut it out!

DOCTOR (*to* MAN, *in explanatory tones*): This will be your first meal, your first meal consisting exclusively of grass and straw . . . Surely you wouldn't be so irresponsible as to insist on eating it with absolutely nobody to witness this important event. I hope you'll understand . . .

MAN'S VOICE: I don't want to understand.

DOCTOR: But it's your duty, isn't it?

WIFE: He has his duties to me, too.

(*Rumbling noises abruptly stop.*)

FIANCÉE: It's stopped!

MAN'S VOICE (*his voice suddenly rises to something close to a scream*): Damn it! I want to take a crap!

DOCTOR: That's to be expected, now that the gas has escaped.

MAN'S VOICE: And to piss, too!

DOCTOR: Hydrolytic resolution has been accelerated.

MAN'S VOICE (*defiantly*): If you absolutely refuse to leave, give them back! (*A small suitcase drops from the ceiling.*) I want every last one back!

(ASSISTANT, *catching the suitcase, looks up in confusion, not knowing what to do.*)

The underwear! The underwear! All of it, right away!

(ASSISTANT *hurriedly scoops together the underwear lying on the floor and stuffs it into the suitcase.*)

The stocking, too!

(WIFE *picks up the green stocking that has been left lying on the edge of the bed.*)

FIANCÉE (*at once makes a grab for the stocking*): Stop! I'm leaving.

WIFE (*vigorously brushes her hand away*): You keep out of this!

(ASSISTANT *takes the stocking and pushes it into the suitcase.*)

ASSISTANT: Satisfied now?

MAN'S VOICE: What happened to the padlock?

ASSISTANT: The padlock? (*Thinks a minute, then goes to the sideboard and opens a drawer.*) I was sure it was here . . . Yes, here it is.

The Green Stockings •

MAN'S VOICE: Attach it to the emergency exit door.

(ASSISTANT *goes toward the door to do what he has been told.*)

FIANCÉE (*clutches* SON'S *arm and urges him forward*): Wait!
We're leaving!

MAN'S VOICE: Hurry!

(ASSISTANT *quickly fastens the lock, then removes the key.* MAN'S
hand stretches down from the ceiling.)

MAN'S VOICE: Give me the key.

(ASSISTANT *puts the key in* MAN'S *hand. The hand is with-
drawn.* FIANCÉE, *still clutching* SON'S *arm, darts glances around
the room, instinctively searching for another way out.*)

While you're at it, how about the key for the hall door, too?

(ASSISTANT *hurriedly removes a key from the keyholder on his
belt and holds it up. The hand stretches out and snatches it. This
time it is* SON *who urges* FIANCÉE *toward the hall door. He grabs
the knob and tries twisting and shaking it.*)

NURSE (*in explanatory tones*): It's no use. The inside and outside
of the auto-lock are reversed.

SON: Of all the crazy tricks!

FIANCÉE: It's illegal confinement!

(MAN'S *feet appear from the hole in the ceiling. He jumps down
to the floor, brushes the dust from his clothes, and with a somewhat affected gesture, stretches out his arms, his fingers interlaced
and bent away from him. He slowly looks from one person to
another. They all burst out at once.*)

WIFE: I didn't expect to see you looking so well.

SON: What are you trying to do, anyway?

DOCTOR: Congratulations!

NURSE: Are you ready for your breakfast?

ASSISTANT: Would you like me to put on some music?

MAN: Stop bothering me! (*Points to wall at stage left.*) Line up
there, and don't move til I tell you.

(*They hastily line up alongside the wall.*)

First I'm going to piss and then I'll have a crap.

SCENE 13

(MAN *picks up suitcase and disappears behind the screen. They
all stare at the screen. Nobody so much as budges. The sound of*

● *The Green Stockings*

MAN'S *urinating begins.* STAGEHANDS *appear and cover with sheets, one after another, the people lined up against the wall. They rearrange the furniture and make a few other changes.*)

DOCTOR (*sticking out his head from under the sheet*): Did you put out the "No Consultations Today" sign?

STAGEHAND A: Of course.

DOCTOR: It looks as if seeing patients will be the least of my concerns for the time being. (*Draws his head back under the sheet.*)

STAGEHAND A: Just leave everything to us.

(WIFE, SON, *and* FIANCÉE *poke out their heads from under the sheet like snails and exchange glances. They turn toward the screen. Then, their eyes following what the* STAGEHANDS *are doing, they begin to confer secretly in rapid whispers.*)

SON: His whole personality seems suddenly to have changed.

FIANCÉE (*to* SON): I'm fed up. I've had all I can take of keeping you company.

STAGEHAND E: But he's a sick man, isn't he?

SON: If we could only figure out his motives . . .

STAGEHAND F: It's just a whim. He's crazy.

WIFE: Did you say he was crazy?

FIANCÉE: Forget about his motives. We've got to find a way out somehow.

SON: But we need the key in order to get out. And in order to get the key, we need to know his motives. Right?

WIFE (*her voice is suddenly animated*): You know, I wonder if Dad might not be planning a fast?

SON: A fast?

WIFE: Yes. His food looks like a rotten doormat, and after all, he's not a rabbit.

STAGEHAND F: Isn't that a bit far-fetched?

FIANCÉE: If he really dislikes the food, all he has to do is refuse it point-blank.

SON: That's right. He doesn't have to ask our opinions.

WIFE: When you can't hold back your urine, you can't.

STAGEHAND F: Women are certainly frightening!

(ASSISTANT *moves closer to* NURSE *under the sheet, making a rustling sound.* WIFE, SON, *and* FIANCÉE *hastily hide under their sheets. The sound of* MAN *urinating becomes fainter.*)

113

The Green Stockings •

NURSE (*with a coquettish laugh*): You mustn't! Not in a place like this!

ASSISTANT: Just a little bit.

(MAN *appears from behind the screen, a urine glass in his hand. He addresses* STAGEHAND C.)

MAN: Excuse me, but would you mind . . .

STAGEHAND C (*takes glass with a show of reluctance*): It's certainly full.

MAN: I've omitted the larger item. (*Reaches for pitcher on sideboard.*)

STAGEHAND D (*snatches away the pitcher*): Sorry, I didn't realize it was empty.

(STAGEHANDS C AND D *exit, carrying respectively the urine glass and the pitcher.* STAGEHAND A *pulls the serving wagon with the meal on it to stage center.* STAGEHAND B *places an adjustable chair on the other side, spinning it around until it reaches the right height for the wagon.* MAN *removes his jacket and hands it to* STAGEHAND B. *He sits on the chair.* STAGEHAND A *drapes a napkin, bib fashion, around* MAN'S *neck.* STAGEHAND B *hangs* MAN'S *coat behind the screen.* MAN *officiously inspects the meal on the wagon.* STAGEHAND D *returns with the pitcher and* STAGEHAND C *with the parts of a machine—aluminum case, cord, tripod, etc.* STAGEHANDS A AND B *set to work assembling the parts of what prove to be a 16–mm movie camera and a small recording apparatus.*)

MAN: Which of you play the people from the special news service?

STAGEHAND A: I do, and she does, too. (*He points at* STAGEHAND B.)

STAGEHAND B: I'm the interviewer, and he's the cameraman.

MAN: What about the rest of you?

STAGEHAND C: I'm a patient in this hospital.

STAGEHAND D: And I look after him.

STAGEHAND C: I realize there's a shortage of help but this place lacks even the basic amenities. It's bad enough we have to cook for ourselves, but they even make my wife take my temperature.

STAGEHAND D: And, when it comes to impudence, I've never met anyone like that nurse.

114

STAGEHAND B (*to* C): What're you suffering from?

STAGEHAND C (*masochistically*): Everything!

STAGEHAND D: I'm told his blood is mildewed.

STAGEHAND B: I've never heard of that sickness before.

STAGEHAND C: It seems to be the result of environmental pollution.

(*During this conversation,* STAGEHANDS A AND B *change costumes in order to assume the roles of employees of a Special News Service company.* STAGEHAND A *becomes* CAMERAMAN, *and* STAGEHAND B *an* INTERVIEWER.)

MAN: Have you been thoroughly briefed on the purpose of this assignment?

CAMERAMAN: Yeah, we got the general idea from the phone call.

MAN: How many feet of film have you brought with you?

CAMERAMAN: We figured on a finished product of five minutes.

MAN: Only five minutes?

INTERVIEWER: The budget's only 500,000 yen. You can barely squeeze five minutes out of that. And, from the point of view of sales, it's an easy length to sell.

MAN: You think you can sell it?

INTERVIEWER (*to* CAMERAMAN): Do you remember that man—the one who ate glass? What ever became of him?

CAMERAMAN (*as if reluctant to answer*): It was only glass, and glass's become a little old.

STAGEHAND C (*gesturing at* MAN *with his chin*): What about him? Does he do something unusual?

INTERVIEWER: They say he eats grass and straw.

CAMERAMAN (*encouragingly*): He can even eat paper and mattress stuffing.

MAN: That's still no match for glass.

STAGEHAND B: You mean his teeth are particularly strong?

CAMERAMAN: That's a good point. A toothbrush manufacturer might buy it.

INTERVIEWER: Don't you think someone in the dairy products line would be more likely?

MAN: Why dairy products?

INTERVIEWER (*throws herself into the act*): Look—we've already got the background provided. (*Her eyes travel over the wall,*

115

The Green Stockings ●

only to stop somewhere, as if her attention had been caught by one particular spot.) Lush green meadows, stretching out as far as the eye can see, and one lonesome human figure in the midst . . . Zoom up. Now we can see the happy expression on his face. He's having a picnic! Zoom up even closer. He's eating grass! (*Carried away, she hums the first couple of bars of the theme music from* Plein Soleil. *Her voice rises with excitement.*) "Let's drink the sunshine! Something or Other Milk!"

(*Short pause.*)

MAN: You're really on the ball, aren't you?

INTERVIEWER (*with a shy smile*): We try never to lose our enthusiasm for our work.

MAN (*suddenly stands and, with a self-confident air, puts a question to the world*): Am I the star of hope for this world? A hero who will radiate light on tomorrow? (*The strength goes from his voice.*) No, I'm just a laughingstock, a cripple rejected by society. (*Directs a self-mocking glance at* CAMERAMAN *and* INTERVIEWER.) Do you know what I'd really like to eat now? A fried pork chop. Or maybe rice and eels would be good . . . A human rabbit who dreams of pork chops and eels even while he's eating grass . . . (*Begins to sing with desperate intensity.*) "Bunny, bunny, what makes you so funny? When you see the moon on top, all you do is hop, hop, hop."

(CAMERAMAN *and* STAGEHANDS, *embarrassed, shift uneasily on their feet.*)

STAGEHAND C: You think we might be starting?

INTERVIEWER (*with a little nod*): Yes, let's.

(STAGEHANDS C AND D, *as if trying to escape from* MAN'S *gaze, hurriedly remove the sheets from the figures along the wall.*)

STAGEHAND D: It's been five hours and eighteen minutes since this started.

STAGEHAND C: The fourteenth scene is about to begin.

STAGEHAND D (*bunching the sheets together*): We'll be seeing you!

(STAGEHANDS C AND D *exit hurriedly after making their final salutations to the others. In performance, several of the latter, as they watch* C AND D *go, may call out, "Thanks for all your*

● *The Green Stockings*

trouble" and similar things. The people who have been under the
sheets on emerging stretch and turn their heads from side to side.
Once they are back into the swing of things, they resume their
roles as if nothing had happened.)

SCENE 14

DOCTOR (*reassuringly pats the shoulders of the cowering*
CAMERAMAN *and* INTERVIEWER. *In resolutely cheerful tones*):
There's nothing for you to get so frightened about. It's true,
he's not very sociable, but you've got to take into account
that a little unsociability is to be expected in his case. You
won't have any trouble with him as long as you recognize his
worth and listen to him with due deference. (*Gazes at* MAN
from the angle of the camera.) Just look at him now . . .
brimful of individuality . . . a uniquely human appeal . . .
Arrogance? Don't be absurd! That's not arrogance but a self-
awareness that comes from complete confidence in his own
existence. Can you grasp the immensity of the question
presented to modern society by the appearance of a herbivorous human being? Even you must read at least the newspapers. According to the statistics compiled by the United Nations, the present population of the world, some three billion
eight hundred million people, will reach seven billion eight
hundred million by the end of the century, and fifty years
from now it will be one trillion seven billion. Do you understand what this means? Mankind, which has always been a
part of nature, has reached a point where it is too much for
nature to accommodate. Let us reject the arrogance of our
civilization and make peace with nature! And that is how I
happened to ask him if he would become the first herbivorous human being . . . (*To* MAN, *in gentle tones.*) Would
you mind standing?
MAN: I *am* standing.
DOCTOR: Sorry. (*To* CAMERAMAN.) Are you shooting this?
CAMERAMAN (*rather confused*): Start! (*He begins to turn the*
camera.)
MAN (*unconsciously striking a pose*): Will anyone really want to
buy this film?

117

The Green Stockings •

DOCTOR (*opens a notebook and intones the following in a romantic manner*):

Were it not for you

The globe would grow old and decrepit,

The earth would cease to be our mother;

Only tears would water the soil.

Children weeping with hunger,

Multitudes of starving people,

A silent star that had breathed its last.

MAN: When?

DOCTOR: Eh?

MAN: When's the earth going to become silent? If it's not right away, I won't have any part of this. I absolutely refuse to become a public spectacle for the sake of the future unless there's a definite time schedule. (*Sits down on chair.*)

DOCTOR: A public spectacle? Still harping on that theme, are you? You are our last ray of hope, the lifeline of humankind, the pioneer, the prophet, the explorer, the vanguard, the morning star, the first to clear the barrier . . .

ASSISTANT: How would it be if I put on some music?

INTERVIEWER: Yes, it's easier to get into the mood when there's background music.

(ASSISTANT *manipulates the tape deck on the work table. An explosive blast of rock music blares forth.*)

FIANCÉE (*covering her ears, she shrieks*): Stop it! Stop it! (*The music stops.*)

ASSISTANT: Well, how about this? (*He puts on another tape, a Chopin nocturne.*)

FIANCÉE (*in tones of distress*): I'm not feeling well.

ASSISTANT (*goes up to* FIANCÉE): Then, what kind of music would you like? (*He begins to massage her back.*)

INTERVIEWER (*stopping the tape*): I wonder if you haven't some sort of music with grassy fields as its theme?

ASSISTANT: You mean Western?

INTERVIEWER: Wouldn't Latin be better?

DOCTOR: Are you all right? Would you like me to examine you?

FIANCÉE (*she gives* ASSISTANT *a coquettish look, then gets up*): Thank you. I'm feeling much better . . .

118

• *The Green Stockings*

DOCTOR: Don't be afraid of imposing on me.

SON (*irritatedly*): She's just hungry, that's all. Dad, it's a question of human rights. It'll soon be eight hours since you shut us up in here. What do you want us to do? If you've got some request to make, why not come out with it plainly?

MAN (*vaguely*): I suppose it boils down to the fact that I was afraid to be alone . . . Or maybe what I really wanted was to be completely alone . . .

SON: I can't make the least sense of what you're talking about. When I get hungry, I lose my patience. Go easy on the funny business.

DOCTOR: No, I understand him.

SON (*defiantly*): What do you understand?

DOCTOR: His feelings . . . his mind . . . his first meals as a herbivorous human being . . . the moment of his birth, which is also the moment of his leave-taking from his former flesh that nurtured itself on meat and cereals . . . Can't you understand? Amidst the joy of the first flush of dawn, a note of sadness has crept in . . . When you set out on a journey, you want somebody to see you off.

WIFE: There's no need for that.

DOCTOR: Why not?

WIFE: What sense does it make to see off somebody who's not leaving? I assure you, my husband's not going anywhere.

DOCTOR (*sarcastically*): Sooner or later the facts will show which of us is right. (*To* NURSE.) How about serving the meal?

NURSE (*steps forward to the side of the serving wagon. She spreads the "straw bread" with a paste and sprinkles some kind of powder over it*): The paste is made from sheep's appendix, and the powder is dried termites . . . And this teapot contains termite juice . . .

CAMERAMAN (*giving a sign to show dissatisfaction*): Sorry, but your hands are in the shadow. Would you move just a little?

DOCTOR: The menu has been specially selected to strengthen the digestive processes of a herbivorous man.

NURSE: Should he drink the juice first? (*She pours a milky white liquid from the pot into a glass.*)

WIFE: You don't have to do what they tell you. We're with you.

DOCTOR (*to* MAN): Please begin.

119

The Green Stockings   •

MAN (*he looks around at the others, then lowers his glance to the serving wagon*): I feel kind of embarrassed, eating all by myself . . .

DOCTOR: Don't be foolish! It's a feast for us just to be able to be present on this historical occasion. Please go ahead. No need to stand on ceremony.

WIFE: Is that meant to be eaten?

MAN (*to* WIFE): What makes you say that?

WIFE: Surely you don't want to eat anything like that.

MAN: Why not?

WIFE: Are you asking me why?

MAN: What's wrong with eating grass? Is eating grass such a terrible thing?

WIFE: It's too miserable, no matter how you explain it.

MAN (*to* DOCTOR): You're going to have your hands full, Doctor, just dealing with obstinate people like that . . .

DOCTOR: It's a question of image. Prejudices arise because of a poverty of the imagination with respect to images.

ASSISTANT (*rapidly*): It's all because people are so conservative in their eating habits. Some degree of coercion will probably be necessary. For example, a special appendix tax law could be enacted under which punitive taxes were collected from people who had not been herbivorized. Or, it could be done the other way, by expanding the amount of national forest and meadow land for the exclusive use of grass-eaters. Or special legislative measures could be considered for the propagation of herbivorization . . .

DOCTOR (*chiming in*): It's all a matter of image . . . Tell me, what image have you of grass-eating?

INTERVIEWER (*with a feeling of having at last been given a cue for her to appear. She readies the microphone*): Let me start off by asking a few questions. Doctor, what associations does the word herbivore have for you? (*Holds out the microphone.*) Please.

DOCTOR (*looking around at the picture on the walls*): Green . . . freedom . . . peace . . . nature . . .fertility . . . harmony . . . travel . . . clouds . . . the sun . . . picnics . . . full stomachs . . .

INTERVIEWER: What was that last?

• *The Green Stockings*

DOCTOR (*annoyed*): Full stomachs—because these fields, stretching as far as the eye can see, are all edible. The world is full of edibles.

WIFE (*with a mocking laugh*): That's a hackneyed image for you!

INTERVIEWER: What did you say, please?

WIFE: I said he was being hackneyed.

INTERVIEWER: Then, next I'll ask our subject's wife for her associations. (*Turns the microphone toward* WIFE.) Please.

WIFE: First of all, cowardice . . . Next, vacillation . . .

ASSISTANT (*bursts out laughing*): She's got a point!

WIFE: What's so funny?

ASSISTANT: I beg your pardon.

WIFE: Grass-eating animals wind up as food for meat-eating animals, don't they? There's not much chance of finding a decent image for them.

NURSE: How about the Green Mountain Boys?

INTERVIEWER: What was that? Would you mind repeating?

NURSE: Green Mountain Boys. Green Belt.

INTERVIEWER (*before she realizes what she is saying*): We've heard that before. Sorry, but a cliché's a cliché. Anybody else?

FIANCÉE: I don't know how to put it . . .

INTERVIEWER: Go right ahead.

FIANCÉE: Green makes me think of silence, or maybe it's loneliness. I get the feeling of a terribly distant star . . .

WIFE: Don't be so pretentious!

FIANCÉE: But there aren't any green animals, are there? Only plants and minerals . . .

WIFE: There're lots of green animals. How about praying mantises and grasshoppers?

NURSE: And there are green snakes and frogs.

ASSISTANT: Some birds are also green, at least in part.

MAN (*suddenly*): Tropical fish, too.

FIANCÉE: But all the same . . .

MAN: Why don't we let it go at that? What month were you born in?

FIANCÉE (*without thinking*): May.

MAN: I thought as much. Your birthstone is the emerald. I'm crazy about emeralds, too.

121

The Green Stockings •

WIFE: You only think of yourself! The woods and fields used to look beautiful to me, too . . . a long time ago. I can't believe in such things any more. Green is finished as far as I'm concerned.

CAMERAMAN: In Europe they say about something unripe or inexperienced that it's green.

ASSISTANT: They also use it for jealousy and envy.

WIFE: Are you being nasty?

INTERVIEWER: If green's no good, how about Tarzan? Tarzan!

CAMERAMAN: Tarzan?

INTERVIEWER: That's right, Tarzan.

DOCTOR (*claps his hands*): An excellent suggestion!

INTERVIEWER: I'm sure Tarzan lived on grass.

CAMERAMAN: Hmm. He's not exactly my picture of Tarzan.

NURSE: Are you sure Tarzan ate only grass?

ASSISTANT: The other animals wouldn't have trusted him if Tarzan ate meat, would they?

DOCTOR (*to* INTERVIEWER): It's a wonderful image. Exactly what I had in mind.

NURSE (*slaps* MAN *on shoulder*): They say you're Tarzan!

(MAN *tumbles awkwardly from the chair.* ASSISTANT *and* NURSE *hurriedly help him to his feet.*)

ASSISTANT: Are you all right?

NURSE: I'm sorry.

WIFE: Some Tarzan!

(MAN *smiles weakly and reseats himself on chair. Pause.*)

MAN: . . . You know, I feel somehow forlorn.

DOCTOR: Why should you?

MAN: I'd feel a lot surer of myself if somebody even indicated a willingness to follow me.

(*Short pause. Each darts glances at the expression on the faces of the others.*)

WIFE: There, you see! There's nobody. Did you suppose anyone would be willing? If you do exactly what these people ask of you, in the end you'll be left all alone.

DOCTOR: But there *are* people who'll follow him. Of course there are.

WIFE: What did you do with the key? We're leaving. No point in wasting any more time . . .

● *The Green Stockings*

DOCTOR: Drawing lots might be the best way to decide. If it were simply a matter of volunteering, of course we'd all volunteer.

SON: Drawing lots is a funny way to reach a decision. Wouldn't it be better to proceed on the basis of mutual discussion?

ASSISTANT: Yes, but as an expedient, the obvious companion would be a woman . . .

FIANCÉE: But his taste is for underwear. After all that's happened, a woman might be too much.

MAN: Yes. Sometimes they dazzle me. Women, I mean.

NURSE: Then maybe a man—a pal—would be better.

SON: But presenting the problem in terms of whether it's to be a man or a woman is in itself . . .

MAN: It's all right. I feel a lot happier just realizing that you're willing to discuss it. (*He takes the glass of termite juice and drinks some.*) Well, I guess I'll begin my meal.

WIFE (*muttering*): He's hopeless . . .

(MAN *tries taking in his fingers a piece of the "straw bread" on the plate.*)

NURSE: There's a knife and fork, if you'd like them.

(MAN *spears the "straw bread" with the fork and starts to cut it with the knife.*)

MAN: It's tough.

NURSE: Try from this side, cutting along with the fibers, as much as you can.

MAN: It's faster with my hands. (*Tears "bread" apart in his hands.*)

DOCTOR (*striking a pose*): Behold! This is a truly historic moment!

(*As they all watch with bated breaths,* MAN *puts a piece of "straw bread" in his mouth and chews on it.* NURSE *presses a stopwatch.* MAN'S *expression suggests he is chewing on rubber. For all his chewing, he does not seem to be able to get any down.*)

DOCTOR (*to* ASSISTANT): You probably didn't cut it fine enough.

ASSISTANT (*to* NURSE): That's not true, is it?

DOCTOR (*to* MAN): There's no fear of indigestion even if you swallow it whole.

MAN (*rests from chewing. Sighs*): At this rate, I'll never get it down.

123

The Green Stockings •

ASSISTANT (*with gestures*): The trouble is you're chewing verti-
cally. You should try chewing more the way a horse or a cow
does, with a horizontal movement, like this . . .

DOCTOR: Yes, laterally, like a stone mortar.

ASSISTANT: It's not so much biting as grinding.

DOCTOR: That's it. Now you're on the right track!

SON: Use your back teeth more.

FIANCÉE: That's why there're called molars.

SON: Grrr . . . grrr!

FIANCÉE: As if you were grinding your teeth.

DOCTOR: How's it coming?

ASSISTANT: He seems to have got the knack.

(MAN, *with great effort, manages to swallow the first mouthful.
He heaves a sigh.*)

WIFE: It's too painful to watch.

DOCTOR: That kind of emotional judgment is most upsetting. I
feel positively envious of him, so envious that I'm quite
incapable of speech.

MAN: Then keep quiet.

(MAN *begins to massage his temples with the inner surfaces of his
fingers.*)

NURSE (*looking at the stopwatch*): Eight meals a day—right?
He'll have to do slightly better than that.

(ASSISTANT *quickly calculates with the aid of a small scale the
amount of "straw bread" remaining. He jots down figures on a
slip of paper.*)

INTERVIEWER (*at the prompting of* CAMERAMAN): What I have
just witnessed is not a mere curiosity—a man who craves
unnatural food or someone who enjoys eating odd things—
but a sight that gives me the impression of what I might call
a religious austerity, something spiritual like yoga. I wonder
if I am correct. (*She points the microphone at* MAN, *but he is
totally unresponsive.*)

ASSISTANT (*to* NURSE): How many seconds did it take him to
eat the first mouthful?

NURSE (*looks at the stopwatch*): One minute and thirty-three
seconds.

ASSISTANT (*continues his calculations*): In that case, it has taken
him one and a half minutes to eat one seventy-second of his

The Green Stockings

meal . . . At the present rate, it will take him 108 minutes, in other words, one hour and forty-eight minutes to consume the whole meal. (*To* DOCTOR.) If he doesn't do better than that, it's quite possible that it'll be time for his next meal before he's finished eating the previous one.

WIFE: I really envy him.

DOCTOR (*to* ASSISTANT): Isn't there some way of setting the blades of the cutter a little closer together, or else of speeding up the revolutions of the pounder?

ASSISTANT: There's a limit to what you can do. You can put mattress stuffing through a meat grinder, but that still won't make it a marshmallow.

MAN: That's OK. I'll try again. (*He begins to chew the second mouthful.*)

INTERVIEWER: At any moment the expression on his face is sure to change and become strong and powerful . . .

(*Pause.*)

DOCTOR: It all depends on how one looks at things. They say that the length of time it takes to eat a meal stands in direct ratio to the level a civilization has attained. Moreover, the vigorous movements of the jaws stimulate the salivary glands and we can hope that this will have a rejuvenating effect.

WIFE: Would you say that dumb silence, being incapable of uttering a word, is a mark of civilization?

DOCTOR: Silence is golden, they say.

(*Pause.*)

SON (*urgently*): I'm hungry!

DOCTOR: If you like, I'll perform an operation on you.

(SON *remains silent.*)

CAMERAMAN: Damn! That's the end of the film.

(*Nobody responds.* CAMERAMAN, *a perplexed expression on his face, exchanges glances with* INTERVIEWER, *then folds his arms.*)

MAN (*making various inarticulate sounds*): Oo yoo reeree en ee ee? (*Making a mighty effort, he swallows. He touches his hand to his throat, and washes down the food with the rest of the juice.*) How many minutes this time?

NURSE (*consulting her stopwatch*): One minute and twenty-four seconds.

The Green Stockings   •

(MAN *leans his elbows on the serving wagon and massages the area around his jaws.*)

ASSISTANT: You've cut it down nine seconds!

DOCTOR: He's gradually getting the hang of it.

SON: Dad, what were you trying to say?

MAN (*continuing the massage*): When?

SON: Before you swallowed.

MAN: I just thought I'd ask if you really envied me. Well, now for the next bout! (*He begins to chew the third mouthful.*)

(*Short pause.*)

FIANCÉE (*to* SON): Find the key, right away!

SON: I'll find it if there's any way to find it.

FIANCÉE (*her eyes fixed on* SON): I'm about to have an attack of hysteria.

DOCTOR (*automatically*): Please come here. I'll examine you.

SON (*rushes up to* MAN. *Speaks over his shoulder*): Dad, I'm asking you. Won't you let just the two of us leave? We're only in the way.

INTERVIEWER (*timidly*): Mightn't we be excused, too? We've used up all the film.

CAMERAMAN: There's nothing more we can do here.

ASSISTANT: Not much chance of your leaving! You're leading candidates for an operation.

INTERVIEWER (*her attitude suddenly stiffens*): It's a criminal offense, you know, if you keep us here against our will. It's illegal detention.

CAMERAMAN: That's right. You'll answer for this!

FIANCÉE (*screams*): Give me the key!

(MAN *moans.*)

SON: What's that? What did you say?

INTERVIEWER (*her tone is again beseeching*): We make a solemn vow. We'll never breathe a word of this, no matter what happens.

(ASSISTANT *begins to stroke her back.* CAMERAMAN *tries to rescue her.* MAN *plants his elbows on the serving wagon and braces his chin with his palms. He continues to chew painfully, shaking his head all the while. No one can say a word in face of this heartrending spectacle.*)

126

• *The Green Stockings*

NURSE (*consulting the stopwatch*): It's taking longer than the first time! Thirty-four . . . thirty-five . . . thirty-six.

(MAN, *with a final effort, manages to swallow the food. He strokes his esophagus with his fist and hiccups.*)

WIFE: Are you all right?

MAN: Would you bring me a cold towel? The muscles of my jaws are getting hot.

(NURSE, *in response to a signal from* ASSISTANT, *goes behind the screen.*)

DOCTOR: That's because those are muscles you don't normally use.

WIFE: And that's why I've been telling you to stop!

SON: What were you saying?

MAN: When?

SON: Just now.

MAN (*shakes his head*): I've forgotten.

(NURSE *returns with a wet towel.* WIFE *takes the towel, passes it under* MAN'S *jaw, then presses it to his temples.*)

NURSE: It's not very cold.

DOCTOR: You should've had some ice ready.

WIFE: That's right. You should suspend an ice bag over his head and put his head inside the loop.

DOCTOR: You seem to have had a change of heart.

WIFE: I haven't changed in the least. But what else can I do? I can't bear just watching.

DOCTOR (*to* MAN): Did you hear her?

WIFE: I would like to make it perfectly clear, lest I be misunderstood, that I am not concerned with what my husband eats. As long as it frees him from his sense of guilt over the underwear . . .

DOCTOR: Does that worry you so much?

NURSE: A sex maniac—and at her age!

WIFE: How dare you!

DOCTOR: Come, come . . . (*Puts his arm around* WIFE'S *shoulders.*)

WIFE (*collapses limply against* DOCTOR): It's so hard for me . . .

(*Suddenly there is a short but loud rumbling noise. They all start.*)

The Green Stockings   ●

MAN: Well, shall I try once more? (*He crams in the fourth piece and chews it. The serving wagon begins to zig-zag across the room, following the shaking of his head.*)

FIANCÉE (*her body rigid*): I'm growing impatient!

DOCTOR (*removing his arm from* WIFE'S *shoulders*): Wouldn't you like to lie down for a while?

(ASSISTANT, *having lost interest in* INTERVIEWER, *hurries over to* FIANCÉE.)

WIFE: Doctor, I have a favor to ask. While you're at it, I wonder if you'd mind sterilizing my husband?

DOCTOR: What did you say?

(MAN *stops chewing.*)

WIFE: Sterilize him.

DOCTOR: That's rather extreme . . .

WIFE: After all, he can't transmit to children his ability to eat grass, can he? It's an acquired ability that lasts for only one generation, and it can't be inherited. Wouldn't you agree that his reproductive powers are of no use whatsoever?

DOCTOR: Well, yes . . .

WIFE (*to* MAN): You yourself have no use for them. Why don't you take advantage of the opportunity and ask for an operation?

SON (*exasperated*): No, it'd be better for him to have a companion, a woman . . . How about it, Dad? If it's a woman, who would you like? I'm in favor of discussions, but in the end it has to be someone Dad likes.

WIFE: It won't work. Your father has always had too many ideals concerning women. Do you think he would be satisfied now with some woman who just happens to be here?

SON: But there's no harm in asking. Dad, who shall it be?

INTERVIEWER: What does he say?

(MAN *mumbles something incomprehensible. With great difficulty he forces down the fourth mouthful.*)

SON: What do you say, Dad? Which one's your choice? Who?

MAN (*looks around with a pained expression, his eyes upturned*): The stockings are enough for me. The green ones . . . Always trembling like a leaf on a tree, but never resisting, shy as a blade of grass, but never attempting to run away. (*To* FIANCÉE.) If you can get another pair like that . . . (*Sud-*

denly MAN'S *rumbling noises resound.* MAN *runs behind the screen, his hands pressed against his abdomen.*)

WIFE: I've had all I can take! (*She knocks the dishes from the serving wagon, scattering the contents on the floor. The rumbling stops.*)

ASSISTANT: Well, who will it be? If you like, you can have the whole lot.

DOCTOR (*grabs the microphone. He sounds intoxicated*): Snip! Snip! I connect the section of the small intestine I have cut off to the end of the appendix, creating a bypass. That's all there is to it.

ASSISTANT: It's perfectly simple. How about it? Who will it be?

MAN (*indistinctly*): Ye I atsaaa . . . in aaa . . .

DOCTOR: Let us try to imagine how glorious it will be when human beings are at last freed from the fear of hunger. (*He gestures toward the painting on the walls.*) Those fields, stretching as far as you can see, are all edible!

(PATIENT [STAGEHAND C] *and* PATIENT'S WIFE [STAGEHAND D] *enter.*)

PATIENT: We're getting desperate. Do something, please.

PATIENT'S WIFE: The kitchen's full of straw!

PATIENT: How can we possibly prepare a meal?

PATIENT'S WIFE: If you light the stove in a place like that, there's sure to be a fire.

PATIENT: I'm going to die here, not of sickness but of starvation.

DOCTOR: I can't believe you're going to die because of a little straw.

ASSISTANT (*leaps on* PATIENT): There's nothing wrong with straw.

(*The others join forces to overpower* PATIENT *and* PATIENT'S WIFE *and force them to breathe ether.*)

DOCTOR: Body and mind steeped in green. Freedom, nature, calm, peace.

ASSISTANT: The world's crammed with things to eat.

SON (*peers behind screen. In a frightened voice*): Dad! Where's he gone?

(*The others, who have been crouching over their victims, search the place.*)

DOCTOR: What . . . has he disappeared again?

129

The Green Stockings •

SON: He was there just a minute ago . . .

ASSISTANT (*looks up at ceiling*): Does it make you so light on your feet when you take to eating grass?

WIFE: He didn't go up there. I've been here all along. (*She looks under the bed.*)

CAMERAMAN: It's absolutely unbelievable.

INTERVIEWER (*to* CAMERAMAN): I've given up all hope for you.

FIANCÉE (*stares at a spot on the wall*): Look, there, in the middle of the fields . . .

(*They concentrate their attention on the spot she has indicated.*)

SON: That's my old man, isn't it?

ASSISTANT: Hardly!

NURSE: I forgot my contact lenses.

FIANCÉE: He's running. It looks as if he's escaping . . . Look!

SON: Yes, it's my old man, all right. He's running away.

WIFE: How can he think only of himself?

(*Pause.*)

(DOCTOR *slowly walks up to the wall and peers at it. The next instant he whips off his slipper and slams it against the wall.*)

DOCTOR (*in jovial tones*): It was a bug! Just a stupid little bug!

(*They continue to stare at the stain on the wall.*)

Curtain.

● *The Green Stockings*

The Ghost is Here
A Play in Three Acts

Kunie Tanaka
(right) as MARUTAKE
and Hisashi Igawa
as ŌBA SANKICHI in a
production of *The
Ghost is Here*.

▲

CAST

OF

CHARACTERS

Fukagawa Keisuke

Ōba Sankichi

Ōba Toshie (Sankichi's wife)

Ōba Misako (Sankichi's daughter)

Hakoyama Yoshikazu, a newspaper reporter

Mayor

Torii, a newspaper publisher

Marutake, a building contractor

the real Fukagawa Keisuke

Fashion Models

Citizens

Laborers

Old Woman

Ghost (cannot be seen)

ACT I, SCENE 1

(*It is raining. A steady stream of* CITIZENS *go by under umbrellas, pausing briefly, only to go off quietly. The scene is under a bridge. A tramp* [ŌBA SANKICHI] *is warming himself by a fire.*

Translator's Note: This play was first performed and published in 1971. The present translation, however, was made from the text prepared by Mr. Abe for the 1975 production of the play. It differs only slightly from the earlier text (which is printed in his collected works), but one character—the older brother of Torii, a financier—has been omitted, and his lines assigned to other characters. I myself prefer the somewhat smaller number of characters, and have therefore used the later text.

He wears corduroy breeches. He is about fifty, judging by his thinning hair. He holds a small mirror in his left hand and in his right a pair of scissors with which he is trimming a mustache whose Ronald Colman-like elegance does not go with the rest of his appearance. An unprepossessing man in his early thirties [FUKAGAWA KEISUKE] *comes shuffling over the bridge. The road is muddy. He stops directly above the man underneath the bridge, looks up at the sky, and clicks his tongue. He unsteadily removes one of his rubber boots and, turning it upside down, shakes out the water inside.*)

ŌBA: (*looking up*): God damn you!

FUKAGAWA (*confused*): I'm sorry. (*Looks under the bridge and holds out his rubber boot.*) It's got a hole in it. There's nothing more unpleasant, is there, than a rubber boot with a hole in it . . . It's like walking with a suction pump on your foot.

ŌBA: While you're at it, why don't you cut open another hole to let the water out?

FUKAGAWA (*seriously*): I hadn't thought of that . . . That's an interesting suggestion.

ŌBA: What the hell are you talking about, anyway?

FUKAGAWA (*leans further forward to get a better look*): Hey, it looks like you've got a good set-up there . . . You don't mind if I warm myself a bit? (*Pulls on the boot and, without waiting for an answer, comes down the flight of steps at the side of the bridge.*)

ŌBA: Some guys have their nerve . . . What've you got?

FUKAGAWA: What do you mean?

ŌBA: I'm asking if you've got something to eat.

FUKAGAWA: I've got aspirin.

ŌBA: You've got what?

FUKAGAWA: Aspirin.

ŌBA: Of all the stupid . . . Who's said he had a headache? (*Abruptly changes his mind.*) But let's have a look at it anyway.

FUKAGAWA (*takes box from his pocket*): Even if you haven't got a headache, it's good for the jitters. There's still a lot left.

ŌBA (*takes the box of aspirin, examines it, then stuffs it in his pocket*): Go ahead, warm yourself.

▲   *The Ghost is Here*

FUKAGAWA: Are you taking all that aspirin?

ŌBA (*in tones that suggest he won't take no for an answer*): I'm letting you warm yourself as long as you like.

FUKAGAWA (*timidly chooses a place for himself by the fire when suddenly he notices what ŌBA has in his hand*): Oh . . . that's a mirror, isn't it?

(ŌBA *looks puzzled.*)

FUKAGAWA (*pronouncing the words with difficulty*): Excuse me, but would you mind putting it away? I hate to bother you . . .

ŌBA: What a peculiar guy! (*For a moment he seems uncertain what to do, but he finally puts the scissors and the mirror in his pocket, and pulls out a huge green handkerchief. Blows his nose.*)

FUKAGAWA: I'm sorry, but whenever I see a mirror, it gives me a headache. (*Sits himself opposite ŌBA, then, shifting over a little, addresses an invisible person next to him.*) You sit here . . . (*He acts as if he is making room for his invisible companion.*)

ŌBA (*looks up in astonishment*): What the hell are you doing, anyway?

FUKAGAWA (*uneasily*): Can you see him?

ŌBA: No . . . (*Swallows hard.*) Is somebody there?

FUKAGAWA (*calmly*): Yes, a ghost . . .

ŌBA (*startled*): A ghost? Whose ghost?

FUKAGAWA: A friend of mind. But there's nothing to worry about. (*To* GHOST.) Try warming your feet. (*Removes his boots and stands them upside down. While drying the soles of his feet.*) It's already April, but isn't the weather awful?

(*Pause.*)

ŌBA: Where've you come from?

FUKAGAWA (*smiles*): Sorry, but I can't tell you.

ŌBA (*puzzled*): Then, when did you and this ghost become acquainted?

FUKAGAWA: Mmm . . . I see . . . You think we've escaped from a lunatic asylum, don't you?

ŌBA: No, why should I . . .

FUKAGAWA: You don't have to worry about hurting our feelings . . .

135

The Ghost is Here ▲

ŌBA: It's not that . . .

FUKAGAWA: Still, you can't really believe he's here, can you? (ŌBA *remains silent.*)

FUKAGAWA: It's quite all right. Why, even he doesn't get upset over anything like that. (*To* GHOST.) How about it?

GHOST: . . .

FUKAGAWA (*interprets*): He says it's only natural you can't believe it. Anybody who's so silly he can admit the existence of ghosts right off the bat is bound to be pretty feeble-minded.

ŌBA (*cautiously*): But I suppose *you* can see him.

FUKAGAWA: Naturally. (*To* GHOST.) Right?

GHOST: . . .

FUKAGAWA: He says you can touch him if you like.

ŌBA (*in confusion*): No, that won't be necessary.

FUKAGAWA: Go right ahead. You won't be able to feel anything, anyway. Here . . . (*Forcibly takes* ŌBA'S *hand.*) This is his head . . .

ŌBA (*nervously gropes with his fingertips*): I see . . .

FUKAGAWA: That's his nose.

ŌBA (*with movements of his hands that suggest he is testing the temperature of bath water*): Then, this must be his stomach, around here.

FUKAGAWA: You don't feel anything at all, do you?

ŌBA: Hmmm. (*Pause.*) And what are your plans now?

FUKAGAWA: I've got all kinds of plans . . . I must pay back my debt to him.

ŌBA: What do you mean, debt?

FUKAGAWA (*brusquely*): Every human being, no matter who he is, owes a debt to the dead. (*With a sigh.*) But it makes me sick . . . Whatever you try to do, you need money. Without money, you can't do a thing.

ŌBA: What would you do if you had the money?

FUKAGAWA (*his face suddenly brightening*): Do you have any? . . . The first thing we'd like to do is buy up pictures of dead people, all kinds.

ŌBA: What did you say?

FUKAGAWA (*enthusiastically*): Photographs of dead people. That's to help identify the ghosts. The best thing would be to take

136

pictures of the ghosts themselves, but there's not much chance of that.

ŌBA: Hopeless, is it?

FUKAGAWA: Hopeless is the word . . . (*Returning to his main concern.*) But will you lend me the money?

ŌBA: Don't be ridiculous. What makes you think I've got money?

FUKAGAWA (*disappointed*): So that's the way it is . . . (*Answering* GHOST.) What's that? . . . (*Bows his head apologetically in all directions.*) I'm really sorry.

ŌBA: What are you doing?

FUKAGAWA: The others also seem to have been counting on it.

ŌBA: What others?

FUKAGAWA: They're all over the place. He's the only one I can see . . . (*Follows the movements of* GHOST.) There, and over there, and here too . . . There are two right behind you . . . He says they've been listening to our conversation . . .

ŌBA (*somewhat flurried, he nods with excessive emphasis*): Of course . . . Of course . . . But if that's the situation, there's a chance we may be able to team up together.

FUKAGAWA: Team up together?

ŌBA (*with an air of importance*): For business reasons, I try insofar as possible not to give out my real name but, very well, just this once I'll come out with it. The fact is, I'm . . . Ōba Sankichi from Kitahama.

FUKAGAWA (*unaffectedly*): Pleased to meet you. I'm Fukagawa Keisuke.

ŌBA: You've never heard my name?

FUKAGAWA: Well . . .

ŌBA: No, even if you haven't, that's all right too. I may not look like much now, but I've had a fair amount of experience in this line. I mean, if I felt like it, I could show you how to turn even a stone like this into 100 or 200 yen, easy as can be. But, you know. I detest petty trickery. I won't touch anything unless it's big, first class. I may seem a trifle down on my luck right now, but it's—what shall I call it?—a period of recuperation.

FUKAGAWA: You mean you're an inventor?

ŌBA (*laughs*): That's a good one! You really said a mouthful!

. . . But you're quite an inventor yourself, and young, too. Ghosts . . . and on top of that, photographs of dead people . . . Yes, you've got talent, no doubt about it. We definitely should be able to make some money out of this . . .

FUKAGAWA (*suspiciously*): Make money?

ŌBA: That's right. Make money.

FUKAGAWA: That's funny. I wonder if you haven't misunderstood something.

ŌBA: Don't worry. I tell you, don't worry. I understand everything . . . But, if you'll permit me to express an opinion, it's a shame you don't give your ghost one final twist. Something essential is missing.

FUKAGAWA: A final twist?

ŌBA: Let me ask you a question, if I may. Is your ghost a man or a woman?

FUKAGAWA: A man, of course. (*Turns to* GHOST.) How about that?

ŌBA: That's no good. The trouble with your story is that the ghost *has* to be a woman.

FUKAGAWA (*looks at* GHOST *and bursts out laughing*): A woman? He thinks you're a woman!

ŌBA (*annoyed*): What's so wrong with it being a woman? You still don't understand, do you?

FUKAGAWA (*to* GHOST): Shall we be on our way? It seems to have stopped raining. (*Starts to get up.*)

ŌBA (*hurriedly*): Wait a minute. It wouldn't be impossible for me, depending on the case and the circumstances, to raise a little money.

FUKAGAWA (*his faces brightens*): Do you mean it?

ŌBA: In traveling a companion, in life sympathy, as they say.

FUKAGAWA (*with emotion*): I'm really grateful . . . (*To* GHOST.) Isn't it wonderful to have met up with such a kind man? (*To* ŌBA.) You can't tell just by looking at somebody what kind of man he is, can you?

(*They leave the stage together.*)

138

▲ *The Ghost is Here*

SCENE 2

(*In center, a table and five chairs. On the rear wall, a filing cabinet and a large map of the city of Kitahama.*

TORII, *the publisher of the* Kitahama News, *presents an utterly slovenly appearance. He is leaning back in a chair, busily cleaning his ear with an earpick.* MARUTAKE *bursts in precipitously. He is the leading building contractor of the city, a local man of means, as is apparent at a glance.*)

TORII: Oh, Mr. Marutake . . .

MARUTAKE: I have news for you, big news.

TORII: I was just looking into this book, *Investment Economy*, it's called . . . (*He holds up the book that he has been using for a pillow, and shows it ostentatiously.*)

MARUTAKE: Mr. Torii, today I went to the station to meet the Mayor. He was coming back from Tokyo on the train that gets in at 5:50 . . .

TORII: That was a clever thing to do . . . But what makes this book interesting is the explanation it gives of how, as a city develops, the value of land goes up in the surrounding area . . . Yes, it's really interesting.

MARUTAKE: I'll be glad to hear about it one of these days.

TORII: You shouldn't make fun of scholarship, Mr. Marutake.

MARUTAKE: That's the last thing I had in mind. Mr. Torii, just now at the station . . .

TORII (*ignoring him*): Do you follow me? The basic question is the price of land. The owner of the land and the political authorities together . . .

MARUTAKE (*with a sour look, determined to squelch him*): I saw Ōba Sankichi! With my own eyes!

TORII (*startled*): Ōba?!

MARUTAKE (*nods, hammering it in*): I was waiting at the place they punch the tickets, when from the platform there came an old man and a young one, both of them looking like they needed a square meal . . . I thought, I've seen them before, the old one anyway . . . Who could it be? After they'd gone by, I looked back at them, and then it occurred to me, it must be . . .

TORII: Ōba Sankichi?

MARUTAKE: Right.

(*Pause.*)

TORII: Did he notice you?

MARUTAKE: No, it was too crowded for that.

TORII: But there are such things as accidental resemblances.

MARUTAKE: No, there's no mistaking him. He had a mustache like this. (*Gestures.*) At first I was a bit unsure, but nobody else has a behind that sticks out this way or a mushroom-shaped head like his.

TORII: Hmmm . . . So he's come back at last, has he? Well, how did he look? Did he seem to be doing well?

MARUTAKE: Anything but. (*He nods emphatically, then, as if he had first realized it was there, he sits down on a chair.*) In the first place, his clothes looked like a stock farm for lice.

TORII: Damned nuisance!

MARUTAKE: Nuisance is the word for it. Especially this year, when there's the election for mayor. The mayor has been terribly worried as it is . . .

(*Scene shifts to a street.* CITIZENS B AND C *enter, carrying umbrellas.*)

CITIZEN B: Have you heard? They say Ōba Sankichi's back.

CITIZEN C: Is that guy still alive?

CITIZEN B: It's just a rumor.

CITIZEN C: Any rumor about him is likely to be true. He's always been tricky enough to make money even out of a fire by scraping up the ashes.

CITIZEN B: Yes, there was that scheme of his for building a breeding ground for edible mice. It seems funny when you think about it now, but at the time . . .

CITIZEN C: To hear him tell it, it was perfectly feasible . . . (*He snickers.*)

CITIZEN B: Then there was that city councilman who ran off one night. That was the same incident, wasn't it?

CITIZEN C: There're plenty of people even now who'll be embarrassed if he's really come back. (CITIZENS *disappear, laughing in unison.*)

MARUTAKE: . . .And there you have it.

TORII: But there wasn't any evidence that definitely proved he was guilty . . .

▲ *The Ghost is Here*

MARUTAKE: No evidence, but people will talk all the same.

CHORUS OF CITIZENS:

A plausible rumor
Seems a lot more believable
Than the truth itself
When it doesn't seem likely.
The reason why people don't have four fingers
Is because fingers have to fit gloves.
The reason why there's no crack in the wall
Is to give mice something to gnaw their way through.

MARUTAKE: Anyway, the best we can do is to stay on the alert.

TORII: Incidentally, who do you suppose the man with him was?

MARUTAKE: I haven't the faintest idea.

TORII (*thinks*): Should I have one of my reporters track his movements?

MARUTAKE: That was just what I was going to ask you.

TORII (*opens the door and calls*): Is Hakoyama around? If he is, tell him to come here for a minute. (*To* MARUTAKE.) He's from another part of the country, and he doesn't know much about what happened here in the past. But he's quite sharp . . . (*Suddenly recalling something, he begins rummaging through the filing cabinet.*)

MARUTAKE (*lighting a cigarette*): But, you know, I think it's a good idea for him not to get too involved. Rather than provoke Ōba unnecessarily, the best thing is to let sleeping dogs lie.

(HAKOYAMA *enters.*)

HAKOYAMA (*extremely businesslike*): What can I do for you?

TORII (*still searching in the cabinet*): There's something I'd like you to do . . . You know Mr. Marutake, don't you?

HAKOYAMA: Yes . . . (*He bows.* MARUTAKE *responds with a condescending nod.*)

TORII: Here we are . . . (*Returns to his chair, a photograph in his hand.*) This is the man . . . (*Takes out a pencil.*) Mr. Marutake, would you mind drawing in his mustache?

MARUTAKE: Let me see . . . (*Draws in the mustache with exaggerated seriousness.*) Ummm. It's like this.

TORII (*stares at the photograph, then hands it to* HAKOYAMA): This is Ōba Sankichi. Know him?

HAKOYAMA: I can't say for sure.

MARUTAKE: It's all right, even if you don't.

TORII (*silencing* MARUTAKE *with his eyes*): He's suddenly come back to town, after eight years away. He bears watching, and I'd like you to keep track of his movements . . . (*Points at the map.*) There's that electric appliance store—what's its name?—just above the cliff on Hill Street. What was the name again?

MARUTAKE: I suppose you mean Sunbeam Electronics.

TORII: That's it. Sunbeam Electronics. I'm positive his wife and daughter are still running the shop.

SCENE 3

(*Hill Street. A shabby-looking building on the edge of the bluff fronting the sea. A sign reads "Sunbeam Electronics." It is still not quite dark outside, but lights have already been turned on inside the building. Front door, a door leading to the kitchen, stairs leading up to the second floor. A partition in the form of a counter near the entrance. A desk, several chairs, and a display case with various electrical appliances. On the desk, papers, repair tools, and a telephone. ŌBA MISAKO emerges from the kitchen.*)

MISAKO (*lifts the receiver with a bright smile*): Sunbeam Electronics.

(*Kitchen door opens and her mother, TOSHIE, peeps in, wiping her hands on her apron. She looks worried.*)

MISAKO (*her voice sounds rather discouraged*): Yes. Thank you for your patronage. It was a C tuning transformer, wasn't it? I'm really sorry. We expect to get it in by tomorrow afternoon at the latest . . . Yes. No. This time, I promise you . . . I'm really sorry . . . Yes. Definitely. Yes . . . (*Puts down the receiver. Sighs.*)

TOSHIE: What are they complaining about?

MISAKO (*recovering her spirits*): Nothing special . . . Oh, I think something's burning.

TOSHIE: You're right. (*She hastily retreats to the kitchen.*)

MISAKO (*in dejected tones*): I simply must do something . . .

(*ŌBA and FUKAGAWA appear at the base of the cliff. They climb the stone steps with ŌBA in the lead.*)

▲ *The Ghost is Here*

FUKAGAWA (*on the way up, to* GHOST): Look—there's the ocean! (*To* ŌBA.) Terrific, isn't it? Pitch black, and it looks swollen.

(ŌBA, *paying no attention, climbs to the top of the stairs and stands before the building. His expression is rather tense.*)

FUKAGAWA (*catching up*): Well, what do you know? An electric appliance store. Isn't that something?

ŌBA (*turns to him*): Shhh . . .

(FUKAGAWA *looks puzzled. Inside the house,* MISAKO, *startled to hear voices, strains to hear more. A sound of waves.* MISAKO, *deciding she must have been mistaken, sighs. She happens to notice a book beside her.* ŌBA, *creeping up on tiptoes, peeks into the house through a crack in the shutter.*)

FUKAGAWA (*whispers*): What's up?

ŌBA (*whispers*): It's my first visit home in quite some time. I'd better reconnoiter the situation a little.

(FUKAGAWA, *finding another crack, also peeks in.* MISAKO, *opening the book, starts to read.*)

FUKAGAWA (*whispers*): Is that your daughter?

ŌBA (*whispers*): Mmm. So it seems. She was fifteen then, so she must be twenty-three now.

FUKAGAWA: Quite a pretty face. (*He urges* GHOST *to take a look, too.*)

MISAKO (*suddenly looks up from the book*): A standard rectifier circuit results when a 5–volt coil of an electric power transformer and a block condenser are connected as shown in the diagram below . . . Because the current is allowed to flow in only one direction, between a and b . . . the voltage with a as the positive and b as the negative . . . there is also, as in the diagram below, a pulsation . . . a pulsation . . . a smooth circuit . . . the first half-cycle at the poles a and b. (*Her voice trails off. She looks abstracted.*)

ŌBA (*in a low voice*): What was all that?

FUKAGAWA (*in a low voice*): She's studying. I'm impressed.

MISAKO: Yes! There are no two ways about it—this is the age of electricity! . . . (*Crooning.*) Electricity is a magic-working servant who never complains, never spares himself, a servant you need never fear to impose on . . . Improvements in your lifestyle begin with electrification! (*Tilts her head to one side and flashes a smile.*)

143

The Ghost is Here ▲

FUKAGAWA (*whispers*): I'm amazed!

MISAKO: Yes, this product represents an absolute savings. Now on special sale, with all kinds of extras thrown in.

(TOSHIE *pokes in her head from the kitchen. She looks surprised.*)

TOSHIE: For goodness sake! I thought it was a customer.

MISAKO (*with a show of determination*): I've made up my mind. Starting tomorrow, I'm going outside the town to try and find some customers there.

TOSHIE: You're wasting your time. It's too late. Wherever you go, you'll find the customers are monopolized by the farmers' cooperative . . . Let's have dinner. (*She goes back into the kitchen.*)

MISAKO (*putting away the things on top of the desk*): But we've *got* to do something.

TOSHIE'S VOICE: If worse comes to worst, we'll withdraw our savings.

MISAKO: That won't do much good. (*Turns toward the door.*) In six months' time we'll be back where we started.

(MISAKO *exits.*)

ŌBA: Good! In general, the situation is under control. There's no sign of another man having moved in.

FUKAGAWA: So it would seem . . .

ŌBA (*slides open the door and steps in*): Good evening!

FUKAGAWA: You're sure its all right?

ŌBA: Leave everything to me, I tell you. It's my house, isn't it?

(MISAKO *enters.*)

MISAKO: Yes, what can I do for you?

ŌBA: Mmm. Good evening . . .

(*Pause.*)

MISAKO: Err . . . we're rather short of stock, what with inventory clearance and the like, but if you wouldn't mind ordering from a catalog . . .

FUKAGAWA (*steps forward*): It's your father!

MISAKO (*catching her breath*): Ohh!

ŌBA: I don't suppose you recognized me with a mustache.

MISAKO (*unconsciously shrinking back. She calls to kitchen*): Mother . . . come here a minute. It's Father!

ŌBA (*a little embarrassed. Snickers.*)

▲   *The Ghost is Here*

(TOSHIE *rushes in. She stands transfixed, an expression of disgust on her face.*)

ŌBA (*with a nervous laugh*): I've brought a rather unusual guest with me. This is Mr. Fukagawa.

(FUKAGAWA *bows, with a broad grin.*)

ŌBA (*to* FUKAGAWA): Please come right in. (*He removes his shoes and starts to go inside.*)

FUKAGAWA (*removes his rubber boots and dumps out the water*): Excuse me. There's a hole in them.

TOSHIE (*not entirely recovered from the shock*): So you're still alive!

ŌBA: What's that? You want to bring me bad luck? (*Laughs.*) Ghosts are *his* speciality. (*Points to* FUKAGAWA.) Right?

(FUKAGAWA *nods with a smile.*)

ŌBA (*steps inside and looks around*): Hmmm. It hasn't changed a bit, has it?

TOSHIE (*her voice is stifled*): This is going too far!

ŌBA (*not at all fazed*): What do you mean?

TOSHIE: What do I mean? Not one letter in eight years . . . eight whole years.

ŌBA: What's so bad about that? . . . Yes, old lady, we're both a lot older . . .

TOSHIE: What are you planning to do?

ŌBA: What I plan to do. (*To* FUKAGAWA.) First of all, let's have something to eat. Or would you rather go to the public bath?

FUKAGAWA: My stomach comes first, I guess . . . But is it all right?

ŌBA (*cuts* FUKAGAWA *short with a gesture. To* TOSHIE): If you go on standing there like a stick, don't you realize it'll make our guest feel he isn't welcome? (*To* FUKAGAWA.) Please, come right in. (*Lays his bag on the desk.*) How's business these days?

MISAKO: You'll make it dirty. (*Takes bag and puts it on the floor.*)

ŌBA (*to* MISAKO, *removing his jacket*): Well, well. You're fully grown now, I see . . . Has some lucky fellow chosen you for his bride?

TOSHIE (*interrupting*): Misako, make some tea.

(MISAKO *exits to kitchen.*)

ŌBA (*following after her, removes his socks at the kitchen door*): I thought I really must buy you a present, and I gave quite a bit of thought to it, but somehow I couldn't think of anything suitable . . . On second thought, it's just as well I didn't buy anything. I never expected you'd become such a raving beauty . . . (*Starts to remove his trousers.*)

TOSHIE: What are you undressing for? You've got nothing to change into.

ŌBA: That's a pretty harsh way to talk. (*With an expression of annoyance he pulls on his trousers again.*) What have I ever done to be treated in this unfriendly way?

TOSHIE: You wouldn't talk that way if you knew all that she's been through.

ŌBA: Hmm. Is that so? (*Flustered, but quickly recovers his composure.*) But what's done is done. It's time to turn over a new leaf, and for the whole family to join forces together.

TOSHIE (*goes up to him and speaks rapidly in a low voice*): How about telling me plainly, exactly what prompted you to come back here, all of a sudden?

ŌBA: But this is my house, isn't it?

TOSHIE: Then, why did you stay away at your own sweet pleasure for eight whole years? You left town, didn't you, because you promised Mr. Torii you'd stay away for a year, until all the excitement over that business had died down.

ŌBA (*in a whisper*): Can't you understand anything? I couldn't write you letters because there was also a little misunderstanding at the place where I went, and I was using a phoney name at the time. It's a good thing everything turned out all right in the end, but if the truth ever came out, it'd mean perjury and a second offense. And, on top of everything else, they might've started stirring up that old business again, and there would've been hell to pay. I waited patiently until the statute of limitations ran out so I could come back home and walk around without feeling ashamed before anyone.

TOSHIE: The statute of limitations? For that incident?

ŌBA: That incident! Don't keep talking about it that way! It was just a rumor, right? (*He moves away from* TOSHIE.)

TOSHIE (*sharply*): Was that *all* it was?

146

▲ The Ghost is Here

ŌBA: There was no evidence of any kind . . . But I'm tired of talking about it. Let's change the subject.

(MISAKO *brings in a tray with two cups of tea. It has become completely dark outside.*)

ŌBA: Sorry to put you to the trouble. (*To* WOMEN.) Wouldn't you like a cup with us?

MISAKO: I've had all I want.

ŌBA: Oh? . . . (*Beckons to* FUKAGAWA.) Mr. Fukagawa, here's tea for you . . . (*As he lifts the cup to his mouth, he addresses* MISAKO.) No matter where your daddy was, it always gave him pleasure to boast about his girl . . .

(FUKAGAWA, *inviting* GHOST *to accompany him, unassertively walks toward the desk, but when he notices the window, he quickly turns his back to it.*)

FUKAGAWA: Ohh . . . that window . . . can't you draw the curtain? I told you, didn't I, that whenever I see a mirror, it makes my head hurt.

(MISAKO *and* TOSHIE *are taken aback.*)

ŌBA: Of course. (*Stands hurriedly and pulls the curtain over the window. To the women.*) Mr. Fukagawa is quite a character. Even on the train coming here, as soon as the train went into a tunnel, he couldn't stand looking at the window anymore. It's strange . . . (*To* FUKAGAWA.) It's all right now.

FUKAGAWA (*nonchalantly sits on a chair by the desk. He takes a teacup*): Well, if you'll excuse me . . . (*He nods slightly to* GHOST *by his side.*)

(*The others are mystified by the gesture, and* ŌBA, *who had supposed* FUKAGAWA'S *last words were addressed to himself, is particularly annoyed, as if somebody has pulled a fast one on him.*)

FUKAGAWA (*explaining*): Of course, he himself can't drink any-thing. (*Takes a sip.*) He tells me not to worry about him, but, all the same, I can't help feeling embarrassed . . . (*He and* GHOST *exchange glances.*) Maybe it's just my self-compla-cency. (*He takes another sip.*)

ŌBA (*his hand holding the teacup remains motionless before his mouth. He thinks, hesitates. Finally making up his mind, he imitates* FUKAGAWA *in offering the teacup to* GHOST): By your leave . . .

147

The Ghost is Here   ▲

FUKAGAWA: He's over here now. (*Points to a different place.*) But he says he doesn't want you to worry so much about him.

ŌBA: Don't mention it. (*He offers the cup again, this time in a different direction, then, with an uncertain expression, begins to drink.*)

(MISAKO *and* TOSHIE *exchange glances that combine alarm, surprise, and suspicion. They look first at one man and then at the other.*)

FUKAGAWA (*turns toward the women with a smile*): He's a ghost. (*Makes gestures of introducing them to him.*)

ŌBA (*after a brief fit of coughing*): That's right, a friend of Mr. Fukagawa.

(*A short but charged pause. A figure appears at the foot of the stone steps. It is* HAKOYAMA.)

TOSHIE: I can't stand any more! Get out, I beg you! Right away!

ŌBA (*alarmed*): What's that?

TOSHIE: I thought all along it would be something like this. But a ghost! I won't hear another word. I've had enough! After all I've put up with over the years, just when I thought I could at last settle down to a peaceful life like other people, without anybody pointing a finger at me, you come back. Then, the next thing I know, it's this!

ŌBA (*soothing her*): Calm down, and listen to me, please. I'm going to make money out of this.

MISAKO: If you intend to make money, go somewhere else and make it there!

TOSHIE: That's right. This is a respectable house. Get out!

(FUKAGAWA *stands in alarm.* HAKOYAMA, *after first looking around him, slowly climbs the stairs.*)

ŌBA (*taken aback*): No interest in money, eh? Just when I had a good plan worked out, you have the nerve . . .

TOSHIE: That's why we've been telling you to go somewhere else to make your money.

ŌBA: That's all very well, but without some capital . . .

TOSHIE: Capital?

FUKAGAWA: It's my fault. I've coaxed him into it. It's so I can collect photographs of dead people.

148

▲ *The Ghost is Here*

TOSHIE (*stammering, out of an excess of rage*): The gall of you! You know perfectly well we haven't got money for that sort of thing.

ŌBA: But I'm sure you must have put aside quite a bit of rent money.

TOSHIE: Rent money?

ŌBA (*his voice is uncertain*): This house is registered in my name. In other words, in my opinion, the two of you have been renting the house from me.

(TOSHIE *looks at* MISAKO *in dismay.* HAKOYAMA *peeps in.*)

MISAKO: He seems to be completely out of his mind.

ŌBA: Don't misunderstand me. I'm not insisting on the rent money. I'm ready to forget it . . . But there are other things. For example, we were raising chickens here, weren't we?

MISAKO: The weasels got every last one.

(HAKOYAMA *looking up, strikes a match, and compares* ŌBA *with the photograph in his hand. He nods. Next, he goes around the building to the back door.*)

ŌBA: You don't say! Weasels, here? That's interesting. Weasels make good money. They multiply quickly . . . Who would have thought there'd be weasels . . . The first thing to do is to hire some middle-school kids as part-time employees, and have them hunt for weasels. They'll be glad to do it for fifty yen a day. Once we have a male and five females, they'll increase in geometrical progression.

TOSHIE (*to* FUKAGAWA): Now you can see what sort of man he is. Please leave without any further discussion. Please, I'm asking you.

FUKAGAWA: I'm going . . . (*He hastily starts to leave.*)

ŌBA (*grabs* FUKAGAWA'S *arm and pulls him back. To* TOSHIE): Such rudeness to a guest! . . . It's disgraceful. And at your age!

TOSHIE: How about you? At your age isn't it about time you washed your hands of your swindling?

ŌBA: Swindling! Don't give me a bad reputation! (*Takes out his big handkerchief and brandishes it.*) I'll ask you one question. Where can you get a handkerchief like this for nothing? Nowhere, right? If you buy it, it'll cost you 35 yen. At any

149

rate, that's what it's worth. But why? Why is it worth that much?

MISAKO: That's obvious. The material and the labor.

ŌBA: Don't be silly! Supposing somebody whittled down a log as big as a telegraph pole to make one toothpick—who do you suppose would pay the cost of the materials and the labor? Nobody. Do you follow me? The only reason why this is worth 35 yen is because somebody is willing to pay that much. The value of a thing or a person is determined by what somebody else is willing to pay. If there's somebody willing to pay, that's what it's worth. There's no such thing in this world as a swindle.

FUKAGAWA: That's an interesting idea . . . He also agrees with you.

ŌBA (*flustered, despite himself*): I'm sure he does.

TOSHIE: But never once has one of your schemes worked out.

MISAKO: And, on top of everything else, you hocked the family furniture every time, saying it was for campaign expenses, or whatever it was.

ŌBA: That was because I didn't have enough capital.

TOSHIE: This time it's the same thing, isn't it?

ŌBA: It's not! . . . Anyway, you've got savings, haven't you?

(TOSHIE *and* MISAKO *shrink back, in shock.* HAKOYAMA, *having made a complete circle of the house, returns to his original position. This time, he presses his ear against the wall.*)

FUKAGAWA (*smiling*): We overheard you talking a while ago.

(HAKOYAMA, *startled by the word "overheard" jumps back from the wall.* TOSHIE *remains silent.*)

ŌBA: There's nothing to worry about. This time, I tell you, it's in the bag . . . But how about something to eat?

TOSHIE (*firmly*): Please leave.

(HAKOYAMA, *hearing this, hurries down the steps.*)

ŌBA (*heaving a sigh*): Are those the words you address your husband when he returns after eight years?

(*He looks at* MISAKO, *as if imploring her help, but she lowers her eyes.*)

FUKAGAWA (*conferring with* GHOST *about something*): It would seem the best thing we can do is leave.

▲ *The Ghost is Here*

MISAKO (*beseechingly*): Yes, I beg you.

ŌBA (*fiercely*): No, I won't let you. Not unless you first hand over the ghost.

FUKAGAWA: Hand him over to you? (*Bursts out laughing.*) I can't very well do that.

ŌBA: Of course not . . . (*To* TOSHIE, *with an expression of "I told you so."*) I tell you plainly now, no matter what you say, we are absolutely not going to budge from here. The more you talk, the less effect it'll have. Anyway, this is my house, and if you've got any complaints, I can sell the house any time I like. Come, Mr. Fukagawa. (*Points to kitchen.*) Let's get something to eat . . . You can never make headway with a woman, can you?

(ŌBA *exits to kitchen, pushing* FUKAGAWA *before him.*)

MISAKO: What're we going to do?

ŌBA (*sticks his head out*): Would you mind getting me some cigarettes?

TOSHIE: Why don't you try buying them yourself?

ŌBA: I see. That's the way things are, is it? . . . Very well . . . One of these days you're going to discover my true worth. The solidity of a family line is based on the thickness of the wad of banknotes at its foundation. (*Exits.*)

TOSHIE: More of the usual style.

MISAKO: All the same, he doesn't seem to have enough money to buy cigarettes . . . I wonder if we couldn't at least get rid of that Fukagawa or whatever he's called.

TOSHIE: It's no use. He seems even cleverer at it than your father.

MISAKO (*sighs*): I suppose this means we'll have to close the shop.

TOSHIE: I won't let that happen! (*With an air of having firmly made up her mind.*) If that's what he's after, I have a way of dealing with him. Yes, any time he takes it into his head . . .

MISAKO: Takes it into his head?

(*Pause.*)

TOSHIE (*nods toward the kitchen*): Daddy, would you mind coming here a minute?

ŌBA'S VOICE: What is it?

TOSHIE: I have something to discuss with you.

(ŌBA *emerges, mumbling something.* HAKOYAMA *slowly climbs back up the stairs.*)

TOSHIE (*to* MISAKO): You go back to the kitchen. Why don't you offer them some pickles?

ŌBA: Pickles? That would be fine.

(MISAKO *gives her mother a dissatisfied look, then exits.*)

TOSHIE: Now that things have come this far, I might as well speak my mind . . . It'll make things difficult for me if you're going to insist on having your own way as you have, so I'm giving you fair warning. I know *everything* about you.

ŌBA: What are you talking about, anyway?

(*Grinning, he grabs* TOSHIE'S *hand, and tries to put his hand up her skirt.* TOSHIE *jumps aside with a sharp cry.* ŌBA, *taking out his handkerchief, wipes around his mouth. He frowns.*)

I'll have to have this laundered.

(MISAKO *quietly enters. The others do not notice her.*)

TOSHIE (*still somewhat flustered*): I'm talking about that little incident . . . You claim there's no evidence, but I know of some . . . There was somebody who saw everything.

ŌBA (*excitedly*): Are you telling the truth?

MISAKO: Then, it wasn't just a rumor! (ŌBA *and* TOSHIE *turn in surprise.*) You really killed a man!

ŌBA: No, I didn't . . . I mean, that old guy Yoshino had terrible heart trouble . . . All I did was shoot off a toy pistol near him. Bang! You know, the kind they use at track meets . . . That's not what's meant by killing a man. It was an accident. The worst you could call it would be accidental homicide.

TOSHIE: Wasn't that the way you planned it from the start?

ŌBA: Don't talk to me like a policeman! Who was the witness, anyway?

TOSHIE: You don't think I'm going to give that away so easily!

ŌBA: Don't give yourself airs of importance.

TOSHIE: If you continue to do whatever you like, disregarding us, I can go straight to the police and tell them the name of the witness.

ŌBA: Oh? Is that what you have in mind? (*His tone gradually becomes more menacing.*) If that's the situation, why don't

▲   *The Ghost is Here*

you do it? Yes, go right ahead . . . It'll earn you quite a reputation . . . That's the woman who sold her husband . . . That's the wife of the murderer . . . (*Abruptly changes his tone.*) That's why I keep telling you that nothing good'll come of it if you lose your head . . . You may intend to drive me away, but in the end you won't be able either to stay in this town . . . How about trusting me? (*Suddenly sentimental.*) I'm fifty-five, an old man. When I was young, I could bounce back from things like a brand-new rubber ball, but now that I've reached this age, I need a home, a place where I can relax . . . the warmth of my own home . . .

MISAKO (*she attempts to rally her mother, who shows signs of weakening*): But it's better than letting him get his hands on our savings . . .

TOSHIE: That's right. It'd be better, even if we had to leave town.

ŌBA (*backing down*): I see. It's come to this. I leave my eyes off you for a little while, and the next thing I know you've turned stingy. Well, if that's the way things are, I won't bother you for another penny. It makes me feel lonely . . . Well, I'll finish off what I started eating. (*Exits.*)

(HAKOYAMA *slowly makes his way around to the back of the building.*)

SCENE 4

CHORUS:
When the clever man says something
Believe his lies implicitly:
Then golden flowers will bear fruit
On the lips of dead men.

(*A road at night.* ŌBA *and* FUKAGAWA *enter from stage left.* ŌBA *carries posters and* FUKAGAWA *a can of paste.*)

ŌBA: At last, only three sheets left . . . How about pasting one somewhere around here? (*He shines his flashlight on a telegraph pole.*)

FUKAGAWA (*smearing paste with a brush on the telegraph pole*): But you know, I can't help worrying somehow.

The Ghost is Here ▲

ŌBA: What about?

FUKAGAWA: Your wife's in a terrible mood. That bothers him, too. (*To* GHOST.) That's right, isn't it?

ŌBA: There's nothing to worry about. An old woman like that!

FUKAGAWA: But even your daughter . . .

ŌBA: It's all right, I tell you.

FUKAGAWA: I bet this'll create quite a sensation tomorrow.

ŌBA: What could be better?

FUKAGAWA: It's already raised quite a stir among the ghosts, too. Right now there are more than fifty of them following behind us.

ŌBA: You don't say . . . (*He looks back uneasily over his shoulder.*)

FUKAGAWA (*finishes applying the paste*): I guess this is all right . . . I hope we're not overdoing things.

ŌBA (*sticking on a poster*): What's the point in worrying at this late stage? . . . But, changing the subject, what's your impression of my daughter?

FUKAGAWA: She's really nice. Why, even he's fallen head over heels.

ŌBA: You don't say so. (*Finishes sticking on the poster.*)

(*Text of poster*)

> Wanted: Photographs of the Dead
> High Prices Paid
> Sunbeam Electronics, Hill Street

ŌBA: You know, her mother when she was young was quite something . . . She was nice and plump around the middle if you know what I mean . . .

FUKAGAWA: You don't say . . . ? (*Picks up can.*)

ŌBA: She was about average in looks.

FUKAGAWA: I see.

ŌBA: Very sensitive. She was from Niigata.

FUKAGAWA: Is that so?

ŌBA: And when you pinched her bottom, it sprang back with a snap.

FUKAGAWA: Not really?

ŌBA: Incidentally, you're a bachelor, aren't you, Fukagawa?

FUKAGAWA (*embarrassed*): That's right.

154

▲   *The Ghost is Here*

ŌBA (*lowering his voice*): Has Misako made eyes at you?

FUKAGAWA: Don't be silly.

ŌBA: That's no way for her to behave! It's shocking! She's just too damned indifferent when it comes to men. Right?

FUKAGAWA: There's something more to the point. *He's* fallen completely for Misako.

ŌBA: We mustn't rush things . . . (*Darts a glance at* FUKAGAWA *from the corner of his eye.*) There's plenty of time for him to court her, patiently . . . But, you know, the more I look at it, the better this poster seems . . . In the first place, it stands out, hits you in the eye.

FUKAGAWA: It stands out almost too much.

ŌBA: Still two left, aren't there? (*Starts walking.*) If we make some money, what's the first thing you'll buy, Fukagawa?

FUKAGAWA (*catching up*): Let me see. The first thing I'd like is a new pair of rubber boots.

(*The two men exit.* HAKOYAMA *emerges from the shadows and stealthily watches them leave. He rips from the telegraph pole the poster that was just pasted there, stares at it, reads it aloud, then folds it and puts it in his pocket.*)

SCENE 5

(*The scene, the same as in Scene 3, is the building of Sunbeam Electronics. A signboard proclaims: "Wanted: Photographs of the Dead. High Prices Paid." It is about ten in the morning. The curtain rises on* ŌBA SANKICHI. *He is alone, sitting on a chair. As usual, he is trimming his mustache, a mirror in his left hand.*)

FUKAGAWA'S VOICE: Mr. Ōba, somebody's come! Somebody's here!

(ŌBA *hurriedly puts away the mirror and the scissors.* FUKAGAWA *rushes back in from outside. The kitchen door opens.* TOSHIE *peers in to see what is happening.*)

FUKAGAWA: This time there's no mistaking it . . . She's paced back and forth before the building no less than three times. (*To* GHOST.) Right?

(CITIZEN D *enters. She carries an umbrella and a shopping*

basket. *After darting glances to left and right, she hurries up the stone stairs. ōba stands, rubbing his hands in anticipation. He stands up and awaits her before a long table.*)

CITIZEN D (*she hesitates a moment at the entrance, then, making up her mind, goes in*): Excuse me, please . . .

ŌBA (*with an expression of having been waiting for her a long time*): Do come in.

CITIZEN D (*she nervously fumbles in her shopping basket*): Err . . . I saw your sign downtown and . . . (*She takes out a photograph the size of a calling card that is wrapped in a piece of newsprint.*) How much is a picture like this worth?

ŌBA: May I examine it, please? (*He takes the packet and opens it.* FUKAGAWA *peeps at it from behind.*)

TOSHIE (*fiercely*): Can I see you a minute?

ŌBA (*with a click of his tongue, turns to her*): Stop bothering me! Can't you see I'm busy? (*He tries to push* TOSHIE *back into the kitchen.*)

TOSHIE (*as she is pushed*): Don't forget, I know a witness!

ŌBA: If you're looking for hush money, first present your bill! (*After pushing her into the kitchen, he shuts the door.*) Damnation! (*Returns to* CITIZEN D.) Sorry to have kept you waiting . . . Are you quite sure that the person in the photograph is really dead?

CITIZEN D: Yes, we had a proper burial service for him two weeks ago. (*Suddenly begins to sob. She wipes her nose with the sleeve of her kimono.*) He was my husband's younger brother. Such a good-natured, kind man . . . This is the only picture we have of him, and it means a lot to my husband.

ŌBA: I see. If it's so valuable, I can have a copy made for you, but in that case the price is somewhat lower. I'll be able to give you only 50 yen for the photograph.

CITIZEN D (*hastily*): No, what's so precious about it, anyway? Having it won't help to fill any stomachs . . . But he's a handsome man, isn't he? Just like an actor.

FUKAGAWA: Hasn't the picture been retouched a bit too much?

ŌBA (*to* CITIZEN D): Does it look like him?

CITIZEN D: Exactly like him.

▲   *The Ghost is Here*

FUKAGAWA: Isn't there any distinguishing feature that doesn't show in the photograph? A birthmark or a mole, for instance?

ŌBA: That's right . . . a birthmark or a mole.

CITIZEN D (*warily*): Let me see . . .

ŌBA: We pay somewhat more when there are distinguishing features.

CITIZEN D (*flushed*): Now that you mention it, the skin was always peeling on his upper lip.

FUKAGAWA: I see. (*Notes this on the back of the picture.*)

CITIZEN D: What about the payment?

ŌBA (*holds out toward her a piece of paper and a pen. He points at another piece of paper on the counter*): Before we get around to that, I'd like you to fill in this form, just as in the model here . . . It's a personal survey . . . Date and place of birth, domicile, occupation during his lifetime, cause of death and surrounding circumstances, family connections and, if possible, something on the deceased person's hobbies and personality . . . This is how we establish the amount of money to be paid . . .

FUKAGAWA: Also, the clothes he was wearing when the picture was taken and at the time of his death.

(CITIZEN D *hesitantly begins to write.*)

ŌBA: It looks as if our posters are beginning to show some results. What a relief!

FUKAGAWA (*listening to* GHOST, *turns to* ŌBA): The ghosts all seem to be terrifically excited.

ŌBA: Shhh. Didn't you promise not to say a word about the ghosts until we'd collected ten pictures?

FUKAGAWA: I'm sorry.

ŌBA: Once we've accumulated ten pictures, we'll spread the rumors far and wide. Until then, mum's the word. We've got to keep it between us.

(HAKOYAMA *enters. He slowly and cautiously climbs up the stairs.*)

CITIZEN D: Excuse me, but what should I write here, where it asks for the surrounding circumstances?

FUKAGAWA (*goes up to her*): Did he die of something special?

CITIZEN D: No . . . he just had lung trouble for a long time.

ŌBA: That's all you have to write.

(CITIZEN D *continues to write.* FUKAGAWA *notices* HAKOY-AMA, *who has approached the entrance.*)

FUKAGAWA: Another customer . . .

(*The two men exchange glances.* HAKOYAMA *hastily beats a retreat.* FUKAGAWA *looks puzzled.*)

ŌBA: What happened?

FUKAGAWA: Search me . . . (*He walks back toward* ŌBA.) I wonder if he'll come back? But what made him so furtive?

ŌBA: Don't let it worry you. It's because he's still unacquainted with our lofty ideals. (*Takes out his handkerchief and blows his nose.*)

CITIZEN D: Is this all right?

ŌBA: Let me see . . . (*Takes paper, examines it gravely, then makes calculations on an abacus.*) Hmm. This'll fetch you quite a good price. It comes to 250 yen.

CITIZEN D (*happily*): Really?

FUKAGAWA: Two hundred fifty yen, right? (*Writes something on a piece of paper, stamps it with his seal, then hands it to* ŌBA.)

ŌBA (*gives the paper to the woman*): Here's your claim check. Exactly two hundred fifty yen . . . We will pay in cash one week from today.

CITIZEN D: Are you sure it's all right, a scrap of paper like this?

ŌBA: Absolutely. Nothing to worry about. There's a guarantee attached.

(CITIZEN D *looks dubiously at the claim check and at* ŌBA'S *face, seeming to compare the two. She finally resigns herself, and tucks the claim check into her sash.*)

CITIZEN D: But what possible use have you for photographs of dead people?

ŌBA: We're making a survey. All kinds of things.

(CITIZEN D *bows and starts to leave.*)

FUKAGAWA: Please come again.

CITIZEN D (*looks up in surprise, but quickly collects herself*): I wonder . . . the old man at our place has been sick such a long time . . . do you suppose a photograph of him would be worth anything?

FUKAGAWA: But he's still alive, isn't he?

▲   *The Ghost is Here*

CITIZEN D: It's not much different from being dead. I could sell it cheaper, if you'd like . . .

FUKAGAWA: Out of the question, even stretching a point. (*Laughs.*)

CITIZEN D: Excuse me for having asked . . . (*Exits, all but running.*)

ŌBA (*extremely pleased*): How about that? What a woman!

(HAKOYAMA *emerges from the shadows, watches as* CITIZEN D *leaves, then exits, following her.*)

FUKAGAWA: You know, the room is full of ghosts now. They're all hoping to get a look at the picture.

ŌBA (*returning to himself*): Oh? . . .

GHOST: . . .

FUKAGAWA (*interpreting*): They're making quite a fuss. They say we should start operations as soon as possible.

ŌBA (*suddenly uneasy, as he looks around him*): We still have some way to go . . . We've only got one photograph, and that's the essential thing.

GHOST: . . .

FUKAGAWA (*interpreting*): They say, couldn't you at least set a time for beginning? . . . It seems to be terrifically popular. How about telling them, say, that we'll begin at seven tonight? We can set a deadline of six o'clock for people who want to sell photographs.

ŌBA (*vaguely*): That's an idea . . .

FUKAGAWA (*to* GHOSTS): We can't possibly take care of you and the customers at the same time.

ŌBA: Wouldn't it be better to put it off a while longer? For the time being, we'll just collect photographs.

GHOST: . . .

FUKAGAWA: He says they can't wait any more.

ŌBA (*at a loss what to say*): They do? . . . Well, then . . .

FUKAGAWA (*nods. To* GHOST): Tell everybody we're beginning at seven.

(*He sees the other ghosts as far as the door and nods at his ghost, who seems to be talking to the others.*)

ŌBA (*watching this, cocks his head dubiously*): I don't get it. It's a bit too elaborate for anyone just putting on a performance . . . (*Stands and goes toward kitchen. When he opens the*

159

The Ghost is Here   ▲

door, TOSHIE *is standing there.*) . . . What are you doing there? Trying to startle me?

TOSHIE (*slowly*): I was just wondering how you would react if, while you were performing these antics, the ghost of the man you killed were suddenly to appear.

ŌBA: This is no time for jokes.

(TOSHIE *crosses the room and exits quickly.*)

ŌBA (*to* FUKAGAWA, *who has turned around and come back*): I'm sure, Mr. Fukagawa, you don't still question my sincerity.

FUKAGAWA: Don't be foolish. Why, even the ghosts are extremely grateful to you.

ŌBA: I'm touched. (*He nods in different directions.*) . . . Leaving that aside, you know there's something I'd like you to reveal, only to me, quite frankly.

FUKAGAWA: What is it?

ŌBA: Tell me, do the ghosts really exist?

FUKAGAWA: You mean, you still doubt it?

ŌBA (*presses him*): Do they really exist?

FUKAGAWA (*to* GHOSTS): You really exist, don't you?

ŌBA: Then, would you prove it?

FUKAGAWA: You're asking too much . . . If that was possible, living people would certainly be a lot nicer to the dead than they are.

ŌBA: Hmm.

GHOST: . . .

FUKAGAWA (*nods*): That's right . . . If it's all that difficult for you to believe in ghosts, we won't impose on you any further. We're willing to give up the project and leave . . . It's unfortunate, but it can't be helped.

ŌBA (*in confusion*): No, there's no need to do that . . . Yes, I do believe in ghosts . . . I will believe in them . . . Believing won't hurt me any . . . Right! I am now a believer!

FUKAGAWA: You mean, Mr. Ōba, that all this time, even though you didn't believe in ghosts, you've been helping them in so many different ways . . . You really are kind.

ŌBA: It's not worth mentioning . . . By the way, just to satisfy my curiosity, would you mind asking Mr. Ghost if there is in his vicinity a ghost with this description: it's the ghost of a big

▲ *The Ghost is Here*

fat man, about 65 years old, height around up to my chin, bald head with a dent in the middle like a loaf of bread, glasses with gold rims, and a big mole a little to the right of center of his forehead . . .

GHOST: . . .

FUKAGAWA (*interpreting*): He says there's nobody of that description around here now . . .

ŌBA (*directly to* GHOST): Well, if he does show up, I suggest you be careful. He doesn't make a very desirable companion. You must watch your step all the time.

SCENE 6

(*Same as Scene 2. Office of the President of the Kitahama News. Sitting around the table are* TORII, MARUTAKE, *and the* MAYOR. HAKOYAMA, *standing to one side, is making his report.*)

HAKOYAMA (*spreading open the poster for the others to see*): . . . This is the handbill I mentioned . . .

MARUTAKE (*reading*): "Wanted: Photographs of the Dead. High Prices Paid." Well, who'd have thought . . .

HAKOYAMA: They went around pasting fifteen or so of these handbills at various places. It hasn't taken long to get results. This morning a woman came to sell a picture. I sounded her out afterward, and she said they asked her all kinds of questions about the dead person and finally paid her 250 yen.

(*They all show signs of agitation.*)

TORII: Have you found out anything about his accomplice?

HAKOYAMA: He's not particularly impressive . . . To sum up the situation in the style of a newspaper headline, "Business is tough. New tactic for catching customers: pictures of the dead."

TORII: I thought I told you that you didn't have to think about an article.

HAKOYAMA (*sullenly*): Force of habit, I suppose. It's my business, after all. Well, what do you want me to do now? Should I still keep a watch on them?

TORII: Just a second . . . (*Takes in the expression on the faces of the others.*) We're about to have a discussion on the matter, so please wait outside for a while.

161

The Ghost is Here ▲

(HAKOYAMA *exits.*)

MARUTAKE: I wonder what he's up to now.

TORII: The court has already handed down a verdict of innocent on the case, so there's no need to . . .

MAYOR: I know, but . . .

MARUTAKE: That's right. Elections are won by chance. It only takes some crazy rumor to bring about an upset.

TORII: Mmm. Right now I'm studying a book called *Investment Economy.* According to this book, political power without financial power is no political power, and financial power without political power doesn't rate as financial power. Each election marks a fresh start in the connections between the two.

MARUTAKE: That's right. A man whose whereabouts were unknown for eight whole years suddenly reappears, and that just before an election.

TORII: Anyway, until things become a little clearer, what do you say to keeping him under surveillance?

(*All nod in agreement.*)

SCENE 7

(*Sunbeam Electronics.* HAKOYAMA *appears under the stone steps, then gradually comes closer. After a while the kitchen door opens and* ŌBA *enters, wiping his mouth with his handkerchief.* HAKOYAMA *assumes an attitude of readiness.* FUKAGAWA *follows* ŌBA *onstage.*)

ŌBA (*tapping his belly*): Soup with noodles is not much. That kind of food doesn't last an hour. Taking all things into consideration, it's not worth the trouble of eating.

FUKAGAWA (*looks around, considers various places*): Mr. Ōba, would you lend me a hand in moving this desk?

(*They carry the desk to the middle of the room.* HAKOYAMA *peeps in through a crack in the door.*)

ŌBA: Wouldn't it be better to have it face this way?

FUKAGAWA (*decisively*): No, this is the way he wants it.

(MISAKO *enters.*)

MISAKO: Do you mind if I have a look?

FUKAGAWA: Go right ahead . . .

▲   *The Ghost is Here*

MISAKO (*over her shoulder to the other room*): Mama, wouldn't you like to see, too?

ŌBA: This is nothing to joke about.

FUKAGAWA: It's all right. He also wants them to see. It makes things livelier . . .

ŌBA: You can use the ghost to justify anything, can't you?

FUKAGAWA (*cuts him short, with vehemence*): You mustn't say such things. There's nothing he hates so much as being talked about in that way.

(TOSHIE *enters.*)

GHOST: . . .

FUKAGAWA (*nods*): Well, let's begin! Sorry to bother you, Mr. ōba, but would you mind opening the front door?

TOSHIE (*to* MISAKO): What can they be up to?

FUKAGAWA: We're letting the ghosts in.

TOSHIE (*to* MISAKO): There's no need to open the door for ghosts.

ŌBA: That's right. They can pass even through the walls . . .

FUKAGAWA: Can't you understand? . . . It's a matter of self-esteem. Of course they can pass through walls. They can't bump against a wall even if they want to . . . Or would you rather not open the door?

ŌBA: Nobody's said he won't. (*Goes to the door and opens it.*)

(HAKOYAMA, *alarmed, tries to make his escape.*)

ŌBA: And who are *you*?

(HAKOYAMA *trips over a worn place in the steps and falls.* ŌBA *jumps out with a snarl, grabs* HAKOYAMA, *and pins him down.*)

HAKOYAMA: I'm not a crook.

ŌBA: Then get to your feet without making any fuss and come in.

HAKOYAMA: I will.

(ŌBA *leads* HAKOYAMA *in.* HAKOYAMA *rubs his shoulder as if in pain. Everyone is tense.*)

ŌBA: What were you doing there? Just loitering? Eh?

HAKOYAMA (*brushing the dirt from his suit*): This is violence, pure and simple . . .

ŌBA: A sneak thief?

HAKOYAMA: No.

ŌBA: A burglar, maybe?

HAKOYAMA: Don't make me laugh.

FUKAGAWA: You know, I've seen him before.

HAKOYAMA: That's not likely.

GHOST: . . .

FUKAGAWA (*nods*): Yes, that's right. He's the man who came here this morning but didn't come into the shop.

TOSHIE: Yes, I remember him, too. He's the man I ran into a while ago at the bottom of the hill.

(HAKOYAMA *remains silent.*)

ŌBA: If you won't talk, I'll investigate on my own. (*Thrusts his hand into* HAKOYAMA'S *pocket.*)

HAKOYAMA (*pulling himself free*): All right, I'll talk. I'll tell you everything. I'm a newspaper reporter.

ŌBA: Ah-hah. You work for Torii, right? (*To* FUKAGAWA.) What'll we do with him?

MISAKO (*forcefully*): Nothing! Just get him to leave as soon as possible.

FUKAGAWA: But if he wants to see, why not let him?

HAKOYAMA: If I might impose . . .

ŌBA: Of all the nerve! After having come to spy on us!

FUKAGAWA: But if we can get it published in the newspaper, it'll save us the trouble of writing handbills again.

ŌBA: I see . . . You're right . . . OK, I forgive you. But in return you're to write an article exactly as I dictate it.

FUKAGAWA (*pointing to* GHOST): You mean, exactly as *he* says, don't you?

ŌBA: Yes, yes . . .

HAKOYAMA (*baffled*): As who says?

FUKAGAWA: The ghost.

HAKOYAMA (*surprised*): Is he . . . there?

ŌBA: Will you write the article?

HAKOYAMA (*not completely recovered from his surprise*): But, you know, promotion articles come high. A minimum of 50,000 yen for half a column.

ŌBA: Don't talk nonsense! If we could afford to pay for it, nobody would ask *you*. If you're not willing, make yourself scarce!

HAKOYAMA: Lay off the violence . . . I can't do what you want unless the newspaper publisher agrees, can I?

ŌBA: The publisher? To hell with him!

TOSHIE (*seizing the opportunity*): Yes, why don't you leave now, before things get more complicated?

ŌBA: Shut up and keep out of it, woman.

MISAKO: Mother, wouldn't it be better to come out with it and plainly say who the witness was?

FUKAGAWA: Witness? What do you mean by that?

ŌBA (*a smile lighting up his face*): Wait . . . I have a good idea! (*To* HAKOYAMA.) Will you write the article if your boss says it's all right?

HAKOYAMA: If he says so, I will.

ŌBA: Then, it's perfectly simple . . . You just go back and tell Mr. Torii that Mr. Ōba Sankichi has his hands on an eyewitness to a certain event.

TOSHIE: How can you?

FUKAGAWA: What is this all about? An eyewitness? A witness? . . .

ŌBA: It doesn't concern you.

MISAKO: What'll you do, Mother?

TOSHIE: What do you mean, what'll I do?

HAKOYAMA: There's something going on that I don't understand.

FUKAGAWA (*at the insistence of* GHOST): When you've reached an agreement, will everybody please quiet down? It's time to begin. (*Steps forward.*) . . . I'm sorry to have kept you all waiting. We're opening the reception desk now. Please come in one by one . . . The ghost here is my friend, my old wartime buddy, but, as you can see, he's dead and one of you. The present experiment was entirely his idea. I'm sure you're all satisfied.

HAKOYAMA (*to* ŌBA): What kind of make-believe show is this, anyway?

ŌBA: Shhh.

(FUKAGAWA *sits on chair.*)

HAKOYAMA (*to* MISAKO): Can you see them, too?

MISAKO: Not much likelihood of that, is there?

FUKAGAWA: Mr. Ōba, the pictures, please.

(ŌBA *hastily pulls a string, revealing a drop curtain with photographs pasted in a row.*)

HAKOYAMA: Damn it! If only I had brought my camera!

165

The Ghost is Here ▲

FUKAGAWA: These are the photographs we've collected to date. They are all of deceased persons. We owe Mr. Ōba a great debt for his help. (ŌBA *bows his head in all directions.*) Please examine them carefully. Isn't there one of a friend, or someone you know of? I believe it might be easier if you formed teams of two each and investigated the photographs by turns. You'll find all the basic information—name, original domicile, residence at time of death, cause of death, brief personal history. Please do not hesitate to inform us if you recognize anyone. We will do everything in our power to lend assistance in uniting you to your family and doing anything else that will bring you closer to the past. I myself, of course, am unable to see you or even to sense your presence, but since *he* has taken on himself the task of serving as an interpreter, I urge you, please, to speak up without hesitation and let me know whatever is on your mind. One further remark. From now on, we will be open every day for three hours, beginning at seven in the evening. Please pass on the word to any of your friends who may not already have heard about it. (*Pause.*) Thank you very much. I feel as if I can hear your applause.

(TOSHIE *leans forward, pressing her hands to her stomach.* MISAKO, *alarmed, supports her.*)

MISAKO: Are you all right?

TOSHIE: I can manage by myself . . . But this is too awful to watch . . . (*She goes off toward the kitchen.*)

HAKOYAMA: Anemia, no doubt . . .

FUKAGAWA (*to* ŌBA): Please help me. We are going to begin registration now. (*Opens a notebook.*) In addition to the verification of identity by means of photographs, we will record, with *him* as the interpreter, the distinguishing features of each of you. It's a kind of ghost census. From now on, whenever new photographs come in, we will compare them with entries in this registry, and if they correspond, we will issue a number, and in time inform you. (*To* GHOST.) Is this satisfactory?

GHOST: . . .

FUKAGAWA (*nods*): Very well, let's begin then, from the first on line. (*Getting a signal from* GHOST.) Your number is A-2. I

▲   *The Ghost is Here*

have given number 1 to my friend. But A-2 is also an important number. A stands for the very first register. Well, then, Mr. A-2, please stand before the wall chart. We're going to measure your height. Is anything the matter? Hmm, I see. Well, then, I have no choice but to write just that. (*Writes.*) "Measurement of height not possible because upper half of body has gasified . . . Right half of face missing . . . Scar on left cheek . . . Lower half of body? . . . Black pants, leggings, foot gear resembling soldiers' boots made of pigskin . . . I see. A student during the war or possibly a civilian air-raid warden." (*Stops writing.*) I suppose he must've been killed during an air raid.

HAKOYAMA (*to* MISAKO): He seems absolutely serious, doesn't he?

(MISAKO *swallows hard but does not say anything.*)

FUKAGAWA: Next, evolution of self-awareness as a ghost.

HAKOYAMA: Evolution of self-awareness! The guy is quite an intellectual!

FUKAGAWA (*begins writing, repeating aloud* GHOST'S *words*): "Eight years and six months ago . . . The place was inside a Shinjuku department store in daytime . . . Until quite recently haunted the vicinity of Kabuki-chō. Since then . . . Hobby is riding trains . . . At the time he enjoyed crowds, but at present has a tendency to be attracted instead by solitude . . . Chief worry now? . . . Fear . . ." (*Puts down his pen and nods.*) That's fine. Please remember your number is A-2. And do come again.

ŌBA (*to* HAKOYAMA): How about it? Does it look as if it'll make a story?

HAKOYAMA: It certainly will. The headline will be something like "Extend a Loving Hand to Homeless Ghosts."

ŌBA: Not bad!

FUKAGAWA: Nothing to report concerning verification of photographs? . . . Well, then, next is A-3.

Curtain.

(*Somewhere in the town.*)

CITIZEN A (*reading the newspaper*): What's this—"Extend a Loving Hand to Homeless Ghosts!" . . . "Unhappy Ghosts Wander the Streets" . . . What *is* this? Sounds exactly like the tear-jerking language the reds always use, doesn't it? This beats everything. Who'd have supposed that even Torii's newspaper would be infected with reds?

(*Elsewhere in the town.*)

CITIZEN D (*reading the newspaper*): Good grief! Ghosts! If *his* ghost comes back, it will really be terrible.

(*Elsewhere in the town.*)

CITIZEN B (*reading the newspaper*): Damn! Next we'll have the soldiers' ghosts . . . Reverting to reaction, is it? Makes me sick.

(*Elsewhere in the town.*)

CITIZEN E (*reading the newspaper*): I must tell my sister as soon as possible. She'll be so happy if he comes back, even as a ghost. She's had such a hard time of it.

(*Sunbeam Electronics. It is the morning when the newspaper appeared. ŌBA, FUKAGAWA, and HAKOYAMA are talking together. TOSHIE and MISAKO, standing beside them, are trying to get a look at the newspaper.*)

HAKOYAMA: Your magical formula about a witness certainly seems to have worked. The publisher was stunned . . .

ŌBA (*flattering him*): How can you say that? Surely it's because your article was so well written.

FUKAGAWA: It really was a good article. *He* was absolutely delighted. (*To* GHOST.) At this rate, we'll soon have a fine collection of photographs.

TOSHIE: It's nothing to joke about. If you go on acting in this irresponsible manner, pretty soon the people who sold you photographs will flock here to demand their money, and they're sure to look absolutely woebegone . . . And if this happens, I don't know anything about it.

ŌBA: Stop bothering me! How many times do I have to tell you before you can understand that a woman has place in this business?

TOSHIE: If you really mean it, that's just fine with me. I hope you won't forget what you just said. (*Exits.*)

ŌBA: At last! When a woman loses her sexiness, it's the end.

MISAKO: It's incredible you can say such things. You're just taking advantage of Mother's timidity.

ŌBA: Her timidity?

MISAKO: If it was up to me, I wouldn't waste a minute in sending somebody straight to the police.

(*Exits to kitchen.*)

ŌBA You'll never get a man to marry you if you keep on talking that way.

HAKOYAMA: But, you know, when I mentioned the witness, there was something positively abnormal in the look of surprise the publisher gave me.

(FUKAGAWA *also looks interested and starts to say something when he is interrupted.*)

ŌBA (*suddenly unpleasant*): It's best for you not to get too deeply involved with things you haven't been asked to do.

HAKOYAMA (*miffed*): Oh, is that so? . . . Anyway, I've got a pretty good idea . . .

ŌBA: Isn't that just dandy?

HAKOYAMA (*lighting a cigarette*): I should tell you that I wasn't exactly serious when I wrote that article.

FUKAGAWA: Meaning what?

HAKOYAMA: All I'm saying is when you shoots off your mouth, the aftertaste is likely to be bad.

ŌBA (*intimidatingly*): Are you trying to be funny?

HAKOYAMA (*to* FUKAGAWA): You, too. You're going to enormous trouble to help the ghosts of strangers, but you don't seem to be in the least interested in tracking down the identity of your friend. Right?

FUKAGAWA: That's a misunderstanding.

HAKOYAMA: Then, who is he, anyway? . . . Don't say you don't know. He was a wartime buddy of yours. I definitely heard you say so.

FUKAGAWA (*nods*): But he refuses to believe me, because I can't prove it. (*To* GHOST.) That's right, isn't it?

HAKOYAMA: You can't squirm out of it that way. You have no

169

The Ghost is Here ▲

way of proving even what the ghost just answered. Why can't you be more specific?

FUKAGAWA: Do I have to say something?

HAKOYAMA: It'd be better if you did, assuming you can.

ŌBA: You don't have to say anything.

GHOST: . . .

FUKAGAWA: All right, I'll tell you . . . because he says I should . . . It's a very strange story . . . I was personally responsible for his death during the war. He'd told me about his family, so I went searching for them as soon as I could. I took *him* along. But the people in his family seemed completely perverse. They were so suspicious of us that they didn't even try to believe. Far from it. They went to the trouble of producing a photograph of some total stranger, and said *this* was the son who went into the army. I had nothing to say. Once things'd reached that pass, there was no way I could convince him, no matter how much I tried, that this was in fact his family. I simply didn't have any proof . . . It was a disappointment for him, and I was at the end of my rope . . . But I persisted, and kept trying to persuade them. Then, they must have misunderstood something. They forcibly locked us up in a certain place. Probably they thought I intended to use him to blackmail them.

HAKOYAMA: Locked you up? Where?

FUKAGAWA: I can't tell you. I've only just managed to escape.

HAKOYAMA (*mutters to himself*): It *does* make some sort of sense.

ŌBA: Didn't I tell you?

HAKOYAMA: Your ghost is very solicitous about the others, isn't he? Considering the terrible experience he had.

FUKAGAWA: It's self-respect on his part. Everybody—even a living person—wants to do something which only he can do. That's what they mean by human feelings.

HAKOYAMA: No fooling . . . (*He stares at* FUKAGAWA *as if trying to figure him out.*) . . . Yes, I can see why . . .

(*The telephone rings just as* ŌBA *with an expansive gesture is about to launch into an opinion of his own.*)

ŌBA (*taking the phone*): Yes, that's right. It is . . . (*Excitedly.*) Oh, thank you . . . I understand. Yes . . . Yes. That's fine. Yes . . . yes . . . thank you. (*He bows his head to the other*

▲   *The Ghost is Here*

party and hangs up.) Mr. Ghost! You're a big success. That was the radio. They say they've seen the newspaper and want to interview you.

FUKAGAWA (*to* GHOST): Is it all right?

ŌBA (*worried*): They say they're coming about noon.

GHOST: . . .

FUKAGAWA: He says it's all right.

ŌBA (*pleased*): Of course. I knew he would. Radio's on a totally different scale from Torii's newspaper. This'll make terrific publicity . . . (*Turns to* HAKOYAMA. *Severely.*) You've finished your business, I trust.

HAKOYAMA: No, this is getting interesting.

ŌBA: Damn you! How much do you want?

HAKOYAMA: You can't buy me with a mere pittance.

ŌBA (*makes a lunge at him*): Damn you!

HAKOYAMA (*avoiding him, gives a thin smile*): I'll be coming back to see you again from time to time. (*Dodges* ŌBA *and exits.*)

ŌBA: Damnation! Face like the underside of a caterpillar!

FUKAGAWA: It would have been better to talk more calmly. Newspaper reporters have no manners.

(MISAKO *emerges from the kitchen. She starts to cross the room diagonally, heading for the front door, without saying a word.* FUKAGAWA *stops her.*)

FUKAGAWA: Where are you going?

MISAKO: I have work to do.

(CITIZEN D *enters. She runs into* HAKOYAMA *under the stone steps. They exchange glances of surprise.* CITIZEN D *hurries up the stairs as if anxious not to be seen.* HAKOYAMA *watches her go with great interest, then exits.*)

ŌBA (*his voice is excited*): Look! Here they come! (MISAKO *stops in her tracks.*) If you have business to do, hurry up and do it.

MISAKO: That's for me to decide.

CITIZEN D (*out of breath*): Good morning.

ŌBA: What's up? Has your father died?

CITIZEN D: Heaven forbid! I'd like you to return the photograph I gave you yesterday . . . (*Holds out the receipt.*)

ŌBA: Ah-hah. You've seen the *Kitahama News*, have you?

CITIZEN D (*speaking rapidly*): No, it's just that it weighed on

171

The Ghost is Here ▲

my conscience . . . You see, it was after a long illness, and I was all wrought up, and then, you know what they say, being brothers is the beginning of being strangers . . . Anyway, for a tiny sum of money like that . . .

ŌBA: I understand completely. Yes, I understand your feelings, but for us it's a valuable item of research material . . .

CITIZEN D: But if I had known that ghosts were coming back, I would never, from the very beginning, have . . .

ŌBA: Don't say that. If his ghost appears before you, meet him as you normally would.

FUKAGAWA: Yes, ghosts would like very much for people to see them.

CITIZEN D: Heaven forbid!

ŌBA: But I'm sure you're aware that when somebody's extremely anxious to buy something, no matter what it may be, the price goes up.

(*Pulls a string that lowers the photograph. Compares the number with the number on the receipt.*)

MISAKO (*to herself*): I wonder if everybody gets to be disliked that way once they're dead?

FUKAGAWA (*hastily, out of regard for the* GHOST's *feelings*): That's not the case. It's simply that people are afraid of themselves.

ŌBA: This is it, all right . . . Yes, the look on his face suggests he might come back at any moment.

CITIZEN D (*holding out her hand*): Please, I beg you.

ŌBA: I want it, and you want it, too . . . It's getting more and more valuable.

MISAKO (*to* FUKAGAWA): He's trying to sell it!

FUKAGAWA: Don't worry. He'll sell it for a good price. He certainly won't take a loss.

CITIZEN D: How much do you want?

ŌBA: How much can you give?

MISAKO: Is it all right to do such a thing?

FUKAGAWA: Of course, it's all right. Even if we sacrifice one photograph, it'll come back two or three times. It's a shame to give it up, but at the moment the most urgent need is to increase our capital.

▲ *The Ghost is Here*

CITIZEN D: Three hundred yen . . .

ŌBA: You must be joking. I was about to ask for 3,000 yen, but I'll make you a special price. How about 2,000 yen?

CITIZEN D: Five hundred yen . . .

(ŌBA *tilts his head to one side. He takes out a pair of scissors and starts to trim his mustache.*)

MISAKO: I *thought* it would come to something like this.

FUKAGAWA: But he seems terrifically pleased.

CITIZEN D: Please say something. I only have 1,000 yen on me.

ŌBA (*coolly*): Very well. Shall we settle on 1,000 yen?

CITIZEN D (*resigns herself. Takes a 1,000–yen note folded up small from her obi*): In this world there's no such thing as easy money.

ŌBA: You're absolutely right . . . (*Takes bill, opens it out, holds it up against the light. He then returns the photograph to her.*) Do come again.

CITIZEN D: Heaven forbid! (*Puts away the photograph.*)

ŌBA (*laughs*): Don't say that! Next time, how about bringing the picture of some total stranger you don't have to worry about? A total stranger, so that even if his ghost returns, it won't bother you in the least.

CITIZEN D (*her hopes reviving*): Would that be all right?

ŌBA (*in a kindly manner*): Of course. And in that way you can get back what you lost today.

CITIZEN D: I'll go look for some right away. I'm glad that's over, but thank you for your kindness. (*She exits, all but fleeing.*)

ŌBA (*flourishing the banknote*): It went well. Just as I planned . . .

CHORUS:
The clever man has spoken;
So, in full confidence
Trust in his lies.
Then, on the lips of the dead
Golden blossoms will bear fruit.

ŌBA: Two hundred yen makes a thousand yen, a thousand yen makes five thousand yen, five thousand yen makes twenty-five thousand yen, twenty-five thousand yen makes one hundred twenty-five thousand yen, one hundred twenty-five thousand yen makes—let me see—six hundred twenty-five thousand yen. (*Laughs.*)

FUKAGAWA (*to* MISAKO, *at the prompting of the* GHOST): Excuse me, but he says that if we make any money he would like to buy something for you, Misako.

(MISAKO *leaves without replying. As she goes, she passes* CITIZEN E, *who enters.*)

CITIZEN E: Excuse me, please.

ŌBA (*in a coaxing voice*): Do come in.

CITIZEN E: Is this where Mr. Ghost is?

FUKAGAWA: Yes, he's here. (*Points.*)

CITIZEN E (*bows her head*): The old man at our house has suffered for years from rheumatism . . .

ŌBA: That won't do, madame . . . He's got to be dead.

CITIZEN E (*dismayed*): Good grief!

ŌBA: But we'd like you to bring it once he's dead.

CITIZEN E: Bring what?

ŌBA: What do you mean "bring what"? We're talking about photographs, aren't we?

CITIZEN E: I came here thinking I was going to ask him for a cure.

ŌBA: I beg your pardon . . . A cure, is it? . . . Let me see.

CITIZEN E (*still annoyed*): Can't I ask him?

ŌBA (*turns to* FUKAGAWA): In other words, you'd like the ghost to work a cure?

CITIZEN E: The old man saw it in the newspaper. He won't take no for an answer.

(ŌBA *gazes fixedly at* FUKAGAWA, *and* FUKAGAWA *in turn at* GHOST. ŌBA *itches with anticipation.*)

FUKAGAWA (*to* GHOST, *dubiously*): Can you do it—something like that?

GHOST: . . .

FUKAGAWA: It's always a good thing at least to try, no matter what it is, but still . . . (*He looks at* ŌBA, *perplexed.*)

ŌBA (*to* CITIZEN E): Very well. Bring him whenever you like. The fee will be . . . let's see . . . this'll be the first visit, so we'll give a special reduced rate. Two hundred yen a session.

CITIZEN E: It's only to soothe the old man . . .

174

ŌBA: That's no way to look at it. Why, there's even a theory that ghosts are a kind of electricity.

CITIZEN E: I'll come back in a little while. (*Exits.*)

ŌBA: Yes, please do.

CHORUS:

Soon on the lips of the dead
Golden flowers will bear fruit.
People will hear the voices of the dead
And kneel before their invisible shapes.

ŌBA (*claps his hands happily*): How about it? Isn't it just what I said? The value of a thing is determined by what somebody is willing to pay for it.

FUKAGAWA (*to* GHOST): You see, it's always a good thing at least to try . . .

ŌBA (*to* GHOST): Mr. Ghost, you're terrific . . .

TOSHIE (*comes down from upstairs. Her fingers make a gesture of counting banknotes*): Where's the money you just got?

FUKAGAWA: Excuse me?

ŌBA: Pay no attention to her.

TOSHIE: How much do you think it's cost for the food you've eaten up to now?

ŌBA: All right, all right. Bring me an itemized bill.

TOSHIE: I certainly will. (*She crosses room and disappears into the kitchen.*)

(CITIZEN A *enters.*)

CITIZEN A: I'm sorry to bother you.

ŌBA: Are you from the radio station?

CITIZEN A: No, to tell the truth . . .

ŌBA: Then, you've got photographs?

CITIZEN A (*shakes his head. Looks around him warily. He lowers his voice*): You're Mr. Ōba, aren't you? Do you remember me?

ŌBA (*surprised*): Why, it's . . .

CITIZEN A: I have a big favor to ask of you . . . But before I do, there's something I want to verify . . . (*Earnestly.*) I gather that this ghost you have here has come back from the South Pacific. Is it true? . . . You're sure he's not some ghost who's been brainwashed in the Soviet Union or in Communist China?

175

The Ghost is Here ▲

ŌBA: What are you talking about, anyway?

CITIZEN A: They say he's the ghost of a soldier, but any soldier who refuses to resign himself to being dead and comes back as a ghost is probably not to be trusted. He wouldn't be a deserter, would he?

ŌBA: Have you come here just to complain about with him?

CITIZEN A: No, not at all . . . It's just that the Yasukuni Shrine has been revived of late, and the ghost has no reason to wander around anywhere like this.

ŌBA: But the Yasukuni Shrine's already full.

FUKAGAWA (*leaning forward*): What's all that?

ŌBA (*trying to restrain him*): It's nothing at all.

CITIZEN A: Are you the wartime buddy of the ghost?

FUKAGAWA: Yes.

CITIZEN A: Then, I'd like to ask you what rank the ghost had.

FUKAGAWA: Superior private.

CITIZEN A (*throwing out his chest*): I was a major!

ŌBA (*unable to contain himself*): And I was a lifetime first-class private. What's wrong with that?

CITIZEN A: There's nothing to get excited about. It's simply that I can't figure out why a superior private should be the spokesman for a million heroic dead. Only a general is qualified to be a spokesman.

FUKAGAWA (*guilelessly*): Ah, I see. And did you do anything during the war to make the soldiers hate you?

CITIZEN A: How dare you! (*Wheels about.*) I have no further business in a place like this!

ŌBA: Don't get so upset, mister . . . (*Follows after him, catching up at the stone steps.*) Why did you come here? It couldn't have been just for the fun of it.

CITIZEN A: That ghost of yours is a red!

ŌBA: That's a surprise . . . It couldn't be that you've never heard of me.

CITIZEN A: You're a swindler.

ŌBA: That's right, I am a swindler. But I would like you to think a moment. Do swindlers and reds ever get together?

CITIZEN A (*hesitates*): I see . . . That's true, I suppose . . . All right, then, on that one point you're someone who can be fully trusted.

176

ŌBA: You see?

CITIZEN A: To tell the truth . . . I have something to ask of you that has to be handled with care.

ŌBA: Ah-hah.

CITIZEN A: I'll give you the whole story. You know, there's a factory that makes cardboard boxes behind here. This factory hasn't been doing too well lately. I've thought it over, and it's my hunch that there's a red who's infiltrated the factory workers. Now, if your ghost is not a red . . .

ŌBA: You mean, you'd like him to play the detective?

CITIZEN A: Exactly . . . A ghost is made to order for the job.

ŌBA: I see. (*Nods expansively.*) I understand perfectly. Just leave everything to me . . .

CHORUS:

The clever man has spoken;
So, in full confidence
Trust in his lies.
Then, on the lips of the dead
Golden blossoms will bear fruit.

SCENE 2

(*From loudspeaker on publicity van.*)

ANNOUNCER: Ladies and gentlemen. The Ōba Trading Company, known to you all because of the ghosts, has an important announcement to make. According to statistics, in the last fifty years a total of 48,500,000 people have died in all parts of the country. Even if we pay an average of only 200 yen for each photograph, it comes altogether to the immense sum of approximately 97 million yen.

(*Somewhere in the town.*)

CITIZEN D (*as if relating a secret*): I'm told you've opened a photographer's studio.

CITIZEN B: Yes, and I'm doing quite well, thank you.

CITIZEN D: But recently just to hear the word "photograph" has been enough to make people shrink, hasn't it?

CITIZEN B: That's true of people who've done something to make the dead hate them. But, to tell the truth, I (*Lowers voice.*) . . . I really don't believe in ghosts.

CITIZEN D (*contradicting him*): How can you say such a thing?

CITIZEN B: Anyway, there's a fad now for husbands and wives especially to have their picture taken side by side . . . The meaning is, "I certainly won't be afraid, even if you die and become a ghost." It's a testimony of love, I suppose . . . Regardless of whether people believe in ghosts or they don't, the morality of people of this town has definitely improved.

CITIZEN D: If you keep the photographic plates, in the future they'll be a tremendous asset.

CITIZEN B (*happily*): Yes, I think so, too. And that's why I'm working my darndest right now.

(*Loudspeaker on publicity van.*)

ANNOUNCER: Even if we pay an average of only 200 yen for each photograph, it comes altogether to the immense sum of approximately 97 million yen. This is a truly extraordinary asset for our impoverished Japan, which has lost land and possessions because of the war. The ghosts are offering themselves to their country for a second time in order to bring about a recovery of the Japanese economy.

(*Somewhere in the town.* CITIZEN D *is sneaking off with a parcel under her arm.*)

CITIZEN A'S VOICE: Hey! Wait!

(CITIZEN D *hastily hides the parcel under her umbrella. Then, with an unconcerned expression, she turns around and begins to walk in the direction from which she has just come.*)

CITIZEN A (*running up*): Excuse me, have you seen anyone running away from here?

CITIZEN D: What's that?

CITIZEN A: It's peculiar . . . (*Looks around distractedly.*)

CITIZEN D (*looks around with him*): It couldn't have been a sneak thief, could it?

CITIZEN A: That's exactly what it was, a sneak thief.

CITIZEN D: How frightening! What did he look like?

CITIZEN A: He? . . . Yes, I suppose it was a man.

CITIZEN D: Surely it was a man, considering it's a sneak thief.

CITIZEN A: What makes you so sure it was a man?

CITIZEN D: Oh, no special reason . . . But what was it that got stolen?

CITIZEN A: That's what's so annoying. A photograph album!

178

CITIZEN D: An album!

CITIZEN A: Yes, a memento of my days in the military.

CITIZEN D: I suppose it contains pictures of soldiers who got killed in the fighting.

CITIZEN A: That's exactly it. It's this disgusting craze. Just supposing it falls into the hands of that guy Ōba. It'll take a fortune to buy it back . . .

CITIZEN D: I'm sure it will.

CITIZEN A: Photograph thieves have been positively rampant— here, there, everywhere. Just the other day, a gang of three burglars broke into a photographer's studio on the coast . . . Some people have had every last picture of their family stolen, and some have got into such terrible debt in order to buy back the photos that they've even committed suicide.

CITIZEN D: This Mr. Ghost is certainly popular . . .

CITIZEN A: His popularity is based on a misconception! I am second to no one in the respect I have for Mr. Ghost. In my opinion, Mr. Ghost has come back to this world because he cannot bear to witness the degradation that has taken place in people's hearts since the end of the war. No one who thinks *he* is watching can possibly do anything bad.

CITIZEN D: You're right, I'm sure . . .

CITIZEN A: Anyone who thinks he can run away is making a serious mistake. Mr. Ghost can see through everything . . . Why, just the other day, I asked Mr. Ghost to investigate and see if there were any reds in my factory. He told me then that a man with a squarish jaw who wears black-rimmed glasses looked suspicious. I searched for someone of that description and—what do you think?—I found *two* just like that! I was astonished, I must say. I fired both of them at once.

CITIZEN D: Dear me.

(CITIZEN A *turns on his heel and exits.* CITIZEN D *furtively takes the parcel from under her umbrella.*)

CITIZEN A (*running back*): Wait! I *thought* it was something like that!

(CITIZEN D *runs off, followed by* CITIZEN A. *Both exit.*)
(*Publicity van.*)

ANNOUNCER: The ghosts are offering themselves to their coun-

The Ghost is Here   ▲

try for a second time in order to bring about the economic recovery of Japan. Please bear these sincere feelings in mind and cooperate with our enterprise. This is also a golden opportunity for you all to build a fortune without any capital. Do not let this opportunity slip by. We cordially invite you to visit us.

(*Sunbeam Electronics.* FUKAGAWA *is alone.*)

FUKAGAWA (*uneasily, looking from the corner of his eyes at* GHOST *beside him. He trembles slightly.* GHOST *seems to have turned in his direction, and* FUKAGAWA *forces a smile*): It's nothing. I was just thinking a little. I wonder if Mr. Ōba's way of doing things, especially that story about the witness, isn't a bit excessive . . . What's that? You really seem to have changed . . . (GHOST *hits him all of a sudden.*) Oh! What are you doing? . . . What do you mean by hitting me? . . . What? . . . Ohh. (*Suddenly conciliatory.*) It's all right, perfectly all right . . . I'm sure you tried hitting me just as an experiment. It doesn't bother me. It's not as if it hurt . . . What's that? . . . Oh, that hurt! That really hurt! . . . (GHOST *hits him again.*) Owww . . . (*Staggering.*) You're hurting me. Stop it, please. It hurts, I tell you . . . It really hurts. You're terrifying . . . (*He is hit again.*) Owww. That's violence! Ha-ha-ha. It hurts as if it were real . . . (*Staggers off.*)

(ŌBA *enters. He wears a suit of rather good quality.*)

ŌBA (*cheerfully*): Playing tag?

FUKAGAWA: No . . .

ŌBA: How do I look? (*Shows off his clothes.*) Does it become me?

FUKAGAWA: You seem very prosperous.

ŌBA: It's a big deal, being the mouthpiece for Mr. Ghost. (*He goes toward the front door.*)

(*Enter* CITIZEN C.)

CITIZEN C (*pompously*): Forgive the intrusion. (*He holds out his card.*)

ŌBA: Have you come to buy back a photograph?

CITIZEN C: What's that? . . . No . . .

ŌBA (*officiously*): Then you want to sell one? I'm asking people who wish to sell photographs to do it through an agency. There are a great many of them, you know . . .

180

CITIZEN C: That's not why I've come. (*Thrusts his card at* ŌBA.) I am from the Federation of Japanese Religious Societies . . .

ŌBA: What's that?

CITIZEN C: We would like to ask Mr. Ghost to give a lecture and to take part in a panel discussion . . .

ŌBA: I see . . .

CITIZEN C: I hope you understand that, although I have said there will be a discussion, it will most assuredly not involve any disrespect. We have the most heartfelt feelings of respect and affection for the departed ones.

ŌBA: How about the rental?

CITIZEN C: Rental?

ŌBA: I mean, the lecture fee . . .

CITIZEN C: From our point of view . . .

ŌBA: Our Mr. Ghost comes a little high . . . Two thousand yen an hour . . . Or, you can rent him by the day at the special price of 15,000 yen . . .

CITIZEN C: I see.

ŌBA: It's our fixed price . . . It may seem a bit high, but, after all, our Mr. Ghost . . .

CITIZEN C: I wasn't complaining. That's fine.

ŌBA: I thought you'd understand . . . (*Nods, to* GHOST.) Is it all right with you?

FUKAGAWA: He says it's all right.

ŌBA: In that case, we accept your offer. What about the time and place?

CITIZEN C: We were thinking of some time around Sunday next week.

ŌBA: Sunday next week . . . (*Turns to* FUKAGAWA.)

FUKAGAWA (*turns the pages of a notebook*): He seems to be free that day.

CITIZEN C: If he would like, we will be glad to send a car to take him to the auditorium.

ŌBA: Well, then, we would like one.

CITIZEN C: Then I'll leave the rest to you . . . If anything should come up, please telephone the number on my card.

ŌBA: Thank you for your trouble.

181

The Ghost is Here ▲

(*Exit* CITIZEN C.)

FUKAGAWA (*to* GHOST): It's all right, isn't it? A federation of religious societies, he said.

ŌBA: It's fine . . . It'll give him class . . . and bring us luck. This is a good omen, just before our important conference today . . . Well, I'll be leaving now.

FUKAGAWA (*to* GHOST): How about it? Can you talk on something that difficult? . . . What's that? (GHOST *hits him.*) Owww!

ŌBA (*startled*): What was that?

FUKAGAWA: Nothing, nothing at all.

ŌBA (*controls his laughter*): Well, Mr. Ghost, I'll be seeing you . . . I leave everything in your hands. Don't get involved in too many quarrels! (*Changes the tone of his voice.*) And don't forget to telephone at four.

FUKAGAWA: Is there any aspirin left?

ŌBA: I haven't touched it. Have you caught a cold?

FUKAGAWA: My head feels heavy somehow.

ŌBA: That will never do . . . If you're going to get sick on me . . . (*Searches in his pockets.*) Oh, it's in my other clothes, the old rags . . . I'll go and get it.

FUKAGAWA: That's all right. I'll get it.

ŌBA: Will you? Well, take care of yourself. Swallow the whole lot if you want . . . There's no need to stand on ceremony. Just tell Misako or the old lady to do whatever you want. (*Raises his voice.*) Hey, Toshie! Misako! Damn it. Where could they have gone?

FUKAGAWA: It's all right. If I need them, I'll look for them myself.

ŌBA: Will you? Then I leave things to you. I'm sorry to keep reminding you, but you won't forget the telephone call, will you?

(ŌBA *exits.* FUKAGAWA *looks relieved. In response to urging from* GHOST, *he forces a smile.*)

FUKAGAWA: Don't worry . . . It's nothing important . . . I'll take some aspirin. (*Exits.*)

(*By the time* ŌBA *reaches the bottom of the stone steps,* TOSHIE *appears.*)

TOSHIE (*calling, to make him stop*): There you are!

▲   *The Ghost is Here*

ŌBA: What is it? You gave me a start.

TOSHIE: I've just been to see the person who claims to have witnessed the incident.

ŌBA: What made you do that?

TOSHIE: Don't worry—it's not what you think. I made some arrangements. It was *you* who asked me to find out how much the other party wanted.

ŌBA: Damn it! Who is it? Enough is enough—I want to know his name!

TOSHIE: It's not that easy. I've got to have at least one trump card.

ŌBA: Hmm . . . Well, how much does he say he wants?

TOSHIE: The other party is well aware just how prosperous you are now.

ŌBA: Don't talk nonsense.

TOSHIE: Fifty thousand yen every month.

ŌBA: You're crazy! No more of your bad jokes. Where does he suppose I can find that much money?

TOSHIE: If you don't like it, that's all right with me. It doesn't affect me one way or the other.

ŌBA: Goddamn . . . At least get him to reduce it to something like twenty thousand yen.

TOSHIE: From fifty thousand yen down to twenty thousand? I wonder how that'll go down.

ŌBA: All right, then. Thirty thousand . . . I won't give a red cent more than that.

TOSHIE: I see . . . I can't predict the reaction, but there's no harm in my asking.

ŌBA: Humph . . . (*He starts to leave.*)

TOSHIE: Just a second. What about the money?

ŌBA: What money?

TOSHIE: You don't expect me to go there empty-handed to discuss matters.

(ŌBA, *with an angry click of his tongue, takes out a wad of bills and counts them.*)

ŌBA: Well, take this. What a sordid business, and on a day of celebration!

TOSHIE: I don't want you to tell Misako about this.

ŌBA: Why not?

183

The Ghost is Here ▲

TOSHIE: She's still innocent about such things.

ŌBA: That's one way to put it.

TOSHIE: Why can't you ever talk to me the way that husbands and wives talk? Really, you make me feel terrible.

ŌBA: What, in broad daylight?

TOSHIE: It's raining!

ŌBA: Well, if you insist on talking about such indelicate matters, tonight I'll ask you to warm the futon next to mine.

TOSHIE: The nerve of you!

(*She hurries off stage left.* ŌBA, *after first looking around, furtively starts to follow her.*)

TOSHIE'S VOICE: You're wasting your time trailing me. I'm not going there right away.

ŌBA (*laughs*): Can't be helped. It's an investment of capital . . .
(*Turns around and exits to stage right.*)

(HAKOYAMA *shows himself. He watches the two of them depart, looks at his watch, and writes something in his notebook. It suddenly grows dark and rain beats fiercely down.* HAKOYAMA *runs off, looking for shelter.*)

SCENE 3

(CITIZENS *enter carrying paper lanterns inscribed:* "High Prices Paid for Photographs of the Dead." *They form a single line at the front of the stage.* MISAKO *is alone in a different, enclosed space.*)

MISAKO: Ahh, I'm fed up. Things that really serve some useful purpose don't sell, and things of use to no one sell like wild fire. What's happening to the world?

CHORUS:
Things have value
Because somebody buys them,
Because somebody pays money;
If you can find a buyer,
Even a lie is worth a thousand yen.

MISAKO: That's a lie!

CHORUS:
That's why we say
Even a lie

▲   *The Ghost is Here*

Will fetch a thousand yen.

(TOSHIE *enters.*)

MISAKO: I wish you'd been firmer, Mother.

TOSHIE: But, you know, it's not easy for a woman to run a household.

(*Enter* CITIZEN H.)

CITIZEN H: Sorry to bother you. I've come about permission for an agency. You remember, I asked you last week . . .

TOSHIE: You mean you've come again, after I told you it was useless? We're absolutely full.

CITIZEN H: But I hoped that somehow . . .

TOSHIE: Why, even in this town alone there are more than a hundred people . . .

CITIZEN H: But I was hoping . . .

CHORUS:

If you can find a buyer,
Even a lie is worth thousand yen.

TOSHIE: Well, there *are* some people who say they're willing to sell their rights. If you're willing to pay . . .

CITIZEN H (*very seriously*): About how much would it come to?

TOSHIE: They're talking in terms of 120 or 130 thousand yen . . . It may actually be a bargain at this price. The price keeps going up and up . . . If you'd like, I can discuss it with them . . .

CITIZEN H: Would you? . . . I'll come back after I've had a chance to think it over.

TOSHIE: But if you don't hurry, they may have already sold the rights.

CITIZEN H: Yes, I understand, yes. (*Exits.*)

CHORUS:

That's why we say
Even a lie
Will fetch a thousand yen.

(TOSHIE *watches* CITIZEN H *leave, rubbing her hands.*)

MISAKO: I can't leave things to you any longer, Mother . . . Why don't you tell me who the witness is?

TOSHIE: Life isn't as simple as you suppose.

MISAKO: Is deceiving people with ghosts what you mean by life?

TOSHIE: "Deceiving people"—that doesn't sound respectable!

CHORUS:

> Once the clever man has spoken,
> The intelligent man
> Garners the harvest:
> Flowers open on the mouths of the dead,
> An invisible bouquet of golden flowers.

MISAKO: Then do you believe, Mother, that ghosts really exist?

TOSHIE: It's all the same, whether they do or they don't.

MISAKO: It's not the same.

TOSHIE: My expectations are not as high as yours. (*She disappears.*)

MISAKO (*to herself*): My expectations high? All I want is to lead an ordinary life . . . Ordinary? . . . What does ordinary mean? If ghosts have all that much value, the best thing might be for me to kill myself.

CHORUS:

> If you should kill yourself,
> Be sure to give me your photograph—
> It's worth three hundred yen!

(*Enter* FUKAGAWA, *pursuing the* GHOST.)

FUKAGAWA (*reproaching the* GHOST): What a crazy thing! Forget it!

(MISAKO *turns around in surprise.*)

GHOST: . . .

FUKAGAWA: No, no . . . All right, I'll tell her . . . But whatever happens afterward is none of my concern . . . (*Hesitantly.*) Excuse me, Miss Misako, but he says that if you're going to kill yourself, he'd like you to do it somewhere he can see.

MISAKO: Good heavens!

FUKAGAWA: Don't take it amiss. He's misunderstood something . . . (GHOST *hits him again.*) Owww!

GHOST: . . .

FUKAGAWA: Of course, I'm of the same opinion as yourself. That's obvious, isn't it? . . . (*To* MISAKO.) He means, in other words, that if you do it while he watches, he can become friends with your ghost before he loses sight of it. He doesn't intend you the least harm . . . (*To* GHOST.) Right?

MISAKO: I don't believe in ghosts! (*Starts to leave.*)

FUKAGAWA (*urged on by* GHOST): Just a second, please. He says

186

it doesn't make any difference even if you don't believe in ghosts. If you are really serious about finding out—I mean, if you really intend to kill yourself—you'll find out just as soon as you die and become a ghost yourself.

MISAKO: Who's going to commit suicide, anyway?

FUKAGAWA (*relieved*): Oh, you're not going to kill yourself? That's fine . . . (GHOST *hits him again.*) I mean, it'd be fine even if you killed yourself.

(*Pause. Lightning flashes.* MISAKO *shrinks back in fear.*)

FUKAGAWA: Wow! Terrific! Oh, the rain seems to have stopped . . . (*Follows with his eyes the* GHOST, *who has gone to the window. Quickly, to* MISAKO.) Please don't get upset by what the ghost says . . . (GHOST *seems to have come back.* FUKAGAWA *changes his tone.*) Ah-hah. Even somebody who runs an electric appliance store is afraid of lightning . . .

(MISAKO *slaps* FUKAGAWA *in the face.*)

CHORUS OF CITIZENS: Ha-ha-ha-ha.

(*Thunder.* FUKAGAWA, *pursued by* GHOST, *runs this way and that trying to escape him.*)

SCENE 4

(*Somewhere by the sea, a place that looks completely deserted. However, the sea is invisible because the place is situated on high ground. There is only the roar of the waves.* MISAKO *stands there vacantly.* HAKOYAMA *appears.*)

HAKOYAMA: Hello, there. I've trailed you.

MISAKO (*looking the other way*): As long as you're trailing someone, wouldn't it be a better idea to trail my father?

HAKOYAMA: I know where *he's* gone. But how about you—are you neglecting to make the rounds of your customers today?

(MISAKO *does not answer.*)

HAKOYAMA: Have I made you angry? . . . That was clumsy of me. I consider myself to be your ally.

MISAKO: Then tell me what you think of Mr. Fukagawa.

HAKOYAMA: Well, in my opinion, he's nothing more than a faint-hearted madman—right?

MISAKO: How can you dismiss him in those terms?

HAKOYAMA: What? Do you think there really is a ghost? If there really is, there must be a lot of other ghosts wandering around here, listening to our conversation, and they may report us to him. Heaven preserve us!

MISAKO: They have their self-respect, and they wouldn't do anything like that, he says . . .

HAKOYAMA: What provoked that?

MISAKO: I asked him why the ghost had appeared.

HAKOYAMA: This is getting interesting. What did he say?

MISAKO: It's a really frightening story . . . Mr. Fukagawa and his friend, just the two of them, were running around in the jungle somewhere in the South Pacific, trying to escape . . . They only had one canteen of water, and there was gradually less and less of the water left . . . They couldn't drink the local water because of the parasites. It was hot, and the place they were heading for was still a long ways off . . . Each gradually became suspicious of the other over the canteen. They were like animals, over the canteen . . . In the end, they became afraid of each other, and tossed a coin to see who would get the canteen . . . Mr. Fukagawa lost. He sat down and covered his face with his hands, patiently waiting for his friend to go away . . . But no matter how long he waited, the friend showed no signs of leaving . . . Waiting was frightening. It was waiting for death . . . Finally, when he couldn't stand it any longer, he lifted his head and looked. The friend had gone out of his senses . . . There was nothing to do but to sit the friend there in place of himself, and to take the canteen . . . And then the friend died . . .

HAKOYAMA: I see . . . But that's what war is like. Anyone who's ever been on a battlefield has had an experience like that once, if not more often . . . But they generally manage to forget it.

(*Distant thunder.*)

MISAKO: But don't you think the ghost wants to have his way too often?

HAKOYAMA: The world is full of all kinds of ghosts . . .

MISAKO: Mr. Fukagawa is absolutely serious!

HAKOYAMA: In short, this ghost is made for the sticks.

(MISAKO *does not answer.*)

HAKOYAMA (*stretches*): It's really boring here in the sticks . . . What do you do for amusement?

▲   *The Ghost is Here*

(MISAKO *remains silent.*)

HAKOYAMA: Sorry, sorry. (*Looks up at the sky.*) When the rain stops, the price of fish goes down.

MISAKO (*suddenly points to something in the distance and screams*): Ahh!

HAKOYAMA: What happened?

MISAKO: Somebody's fallen from the edge of that cliff over there . . . No, he must have jumped!

HAKOYAMA: Probably a swimmer, practicing his diving.

MISAKO (*shakes her head*): Not fully clothed!

HAKOYAMA: I'll go take a look. (*Runs off.*)

SCENE 5

(*Office of the publisher of the Kitahama News. Four people—* TORII, *the* MAYOR, MARUTAKE, *and* ŌBA SANKICHI *in a new suit. A bottle of beer and glasses on the table.* ŌBA *is in high spirits; the others are strangely subdued.*)

ŌBA (*drinking the beer*): Public interest has been aroused, and, I'm glad to say, what with one thing and another, business has considerably increased . . . Transactions in photographs alone have amounted to 120 or 130 thousand yen in five days. In addition, we have an average of fifteen or sixteen people a day who want to rub the ghost, and—though we don't ask for it—some of them leave money. It's nothing to sneeze at. We also have requests for consultations on personal problems and for detective work.

MARUTAKE (*suspiciously*): Can the ghost really do detective work?

ŌBA: Yes, indeed. He's acquired quite a reputation. And that's why, at this stage, I'm planning even further developments. I'd like very much, as I've explained to you, to establish a Society for the Protection of Ghosts, with the Mayor as president and with the rest of you as directors.

TORII: But what if that old matter is brought up again?

MARUTAKE: That's right. We've been told there was a witness, and unless we know exactly who it is, we have no way of responding.

ŌBA: You're asking too much of me. I wasn't blessed with property, a distinguished family or anything like that—my

189

The Ghost is Here ▲

position is weak. But trust in my ability to deal with something of this sort. After all, I'm not trying to blackmail anybody or extort money. All I'm asking for is your cooperation in a project with a future. There's nothing to get nervous about. As for the ghost, maybe you can't believe in him right away. But don't forget even Mr. Ghost himself has said only a fool would believe in him right off the bat. You needn't worry. Our business has expanded steadily, regardless of such considerations. Soon it will spread throughout the whole country, and our Kitahama City will be the Grand Headquarters for the entire ghost population of Japan. What a blessing for us all! These days every bright idea gets taken over by Tokyo, and the rest of the country is going to seed. Isn't this the point for us all to gird our loins for combat? It is . . . (*Drinks the beer.*) Well, what do you say? (*Pause.*) Unless I hear some contrary view, may I take it that you have all agreed?

(*The others, avoiding one another's eyes, remain silent.*)

(*Abruptly.*) I take it, then, it's all right with you . . . I'm most obliged. I'm absolutely delighted. (*Laughs.*) But could somebody please tell me the time? (*He darts a glance at* MARUTAKE'S *wristwatch.*) Four o'clock, is it? . . . If any ghosts happen to be with us now, I would be grateful if one of you would please fly over to my office and inform Mr. Fukagawa that agreement has been reached in the negotiations. I'm sure he'll be just as delighted as myself . . . But . . . (*Looks around at the others.*) it's unfortunate we can't see them . . . No, it might be better to say that it's because we can't see them that we can be so relaxed. (*Looks around and lowers his voice.*) I've been informed that ever since we started the present enterprise the number of ghosts in this town has considerably increased. The place is positively swarming with them. Just think—in a house somewhere, a house where one might think just a husband and wife were living, there may be more than ten ghosts in residence. When the couple sits down to have a meal, the ghosts line up around the dinner table. When the husband opens a newspaper, they swarm up behind him to have a look. When the couple get into bed, the ghosts crawl in beside them . . .

190

▲ *The Ghost is Here*

As long as the people in question don't know about it, there's no harm done . . . but if they learn about it, there'll be hell to pay . . .

(*Telephone rings. They are all startled.*)

MARUTAKE (*taking the telephone*): Hello . . . just a minute. Mr. Ōba, it's for you.

(*They all show their tension.*)

ŌBA: Hello. This is Ōba . . . Ahh . . . I see . . . What? . . . That's right. Just now the Mayor has gladly accepted . . . No, it's all right . . . You see, there was a ghost here, whoever it was, and I thought I'd ask him to convey the message to you. I hope you're pleased. Everything went well. Oh, the Mayor asks you to send his best regards to Mr. Ghost . . . That's all right. Well, I'll be seeing you tonight and we' can discuss it further at that time. (*Hangs up.*)

(*The others look stunned.*)

MAYOR (*timidly*): Then, he really *was* here.

MARUTAKE: I don't suppose *his* ghost will appear.

ŌBA: Just supposing it does, now that you're an officer of the Society for the Protection of Ghosts, what harm can he do you?

MARUTAKE (*looks around him*): That's right, we're all like one family now . . . But, incidentally, if there's some way to ask, and one of them is living in my house now, as a special favor I'd like him not to pay us any attention . . .

ŌBA: Not to pay attention?

MARUTAKE: It's not that I wish to keep him away . . . No, that's not it . . . In the first place, I'm not very religious by nature . . . It's just a matter of—what shall I call it—privacy. I couldn't stand it if I thought I was being spied on all year round.

ŌBA: I see . . . Well, how would it be if I requested that special consideration be given to officers of the Society of Friends? . . . (*Gives a series of short, rapid nods. Fans himself with his handkerchief.*) But you know, Mr. Marutake, I have a feeling that one of these days we'll simply have to build a Ghost Convention Center.

MARUTAKE (*hastily*): That's a wonderful idea! Really, a splendid suggestion. It'll become the chief attraction of the city.

ŌBA: We'll be catering to the ghosts of the entire country . . . And, come to think of it, Mr. Mayor, you will have the backing of every last ghost in Japan. There'll be no problem about your being elected next to the Prefectural Assembly.

MAYOR: You think so? . . .

ŌBA: And if things go well, there's no reason why you can't become a member of the House of Representatives . . .

MAYOR (*not displeased by the possibility*): Not really.

TORII: It's strange, but the case fits exactly the second law of *Investment Economy*.

ŌBA: What's that?

TORII: According to the book, capital attracts everything, just like a magnet, and what it attracts becomes more capital, and that in turn attracts more things. Isn't that exactly what's happening now?

THE OTHERS (*nodding, variously*): That's right.

ŌBA: Then, how about a toast to the Society for the Protection of Ghosts?

(*They all raise their glasses. In the dark outside, far off, a voice calls.*)

HAKOYAMA'S VOICE: Somebody's been drowned!

(*A street somewhere.*)

CITIZEN F: They say someone's drowned!

CITIZEN G: A man? Or a woman?

CITIZEN F: A young man, they say. He had T.B. Seems he was a high school teacher.

CITIZEN G: A young man? What a waste!

(*Sound of knocking. They put down their glasses and turn toward the door.*)

TORII: Who is it?

HAKOYAMA'S VOICE: It's Hakoyama. (*Opens the door.*) Something's happened. A suicide by drowning.

TORII (*losing his temper*): What do you mean by creating an uproar over something like that? We're in the midst of an important conference.

HAKOYAMA: I think what I have to say is also important. (*Takes a piece of paper from his pocket.*) This is a copy of the suicide note.

ŌBA: What's so unusual about that?

192

▲   *The Ghost is Here*

HAKOYAMA: Please listen. (*Reads.*) "I decided to kill myself after reading the articles about ghosts in the *Kitahama News* . . . (*They all fall silent.*) One way or another, my decision was the result of despair, but this is not a simple case of suicide brought on by weariness of life. I thought I would make an experiment. I believe that anyone who has cursed life as much as myself will probably become a ghost and wander once again through the world. But they say that once you die you forget the past, and that would be a pity. I am going to put down on paper my distinguishing features, so I can be recognized. I am wearing a dark blue serge suit. In the left trouser pocket there is a small hole. I have attached a red ribbon, about half an inch wide, to the breast of the suit, and I have written on it the initial T. I am enclosing a photograph of myself together with this suicide note. Please forward it to Mr. Fukagawa at Sunbeam Electronics . . . 'Mr. Fukagawa, we have never met, but I hope you will please cooperate in my experiment. If a ghost wearing a dark blue serge suit and a ribbon marked with a T appears at your place, would you please inform him that he is myself? And please read to him the diary in which I have described my past and what I would like to do after becoming a ghost. I have sent you the diary separately, by registered mail. I have included with the diary a small amount of money for your expenses. One more request—I beg you not to open the envelope containing the diary until I appear as a ghost. Please forgive this imposition as the wishes of a dead man. Goodbye! I go to my death hoping that the experiment will succeed . . .' "

(*The men embarrassedly exchange glances.*)

ŌBA (*all of a sudden, in an excited voice*): Terrific! (*Looks from one man to another. Snaps his fingers.*) Do you get it? Another big enterprise has come our way . . . Mr. Torii, this is your bailiwick, but this is something big . . . Eh? . . . You don't understand? . . . Ghost Insurance! (*Rubs his hands frenziedly.*) I'm shaking all over! Ghost Insurance!

TORII (*anxiously attempts to reimpose his authority*): Insurance? . . . You mean . . . taking out insurance policies on ghosts?

ŌBA: We get people, while they're still alive, to lay aside money with us by way of fees in return for our looking after them

193

once they've become ghosts, so that they'll never have the lonely feeling of being nothing more than vagrants . . . Now you can understand, can't you? We'll issue badges as marks of identification for people who have taken out our insurance, and we'll ask them to wear them at all times—like the tags they put on kids so they won't get lost. We will carefully register the numbers and keep on file all materials concerning each registered person. This will make it possible to provide materials for any kind of investigation or consultation. Once someone takes out one of our insurance policies, they'll be completely covered even if they suddenly get killed in a traffic accident or whatever it might be. Then they can go back to their homes and keep a strict watch over them and make sure that their wives don't do anything peculiar. (*He licks his lips.*)

MAYOR: But won't the wives object?

TORII: No, they won't. If they raise any objections it will be immediately apparent that they have ulterior motives.

MAYOR: Hmm. That makes sense.

MARUTAKE: But in that case the wives won't want their husbands to be insured. (*Then, as if with a sudden flash of inspiration.*) Now I understand! There certainly will be cases when it's awkward, but it'll be hard for the wives to refuse to have their husbands insured . . . A very clever plan.

TORII: It's certainly developed into quite a project. Ghosts act as really strong magnets.

CHORUS:
Then the dead will return to life
And be led by blind dogs.
People will hear the voices of the dead
And kneel before their invisible shapes.

ŌBA: Mmm. That's right. But there's more still! . . . (*As if in a dream.*) I feel as if my mind has really started moving down the track . . . (*Swallows.*) Mr. Marutake, how would it be if you started manufacturing ghost clothes? . . . Ghosts have only the clothes they died in. It's bound to make even ghosts— particularly female ghosts—feel small if their clothes are behind the times . . . And that's why we should make a ghost uniform that'll never go out of fashion. We will guarantee that as long as they're wearing this uniform when they die,

194

there's absolutely no fear of their ever feeling dowdy . . . The plan is brilliant, I think you'll admit . . .

TORII: But how about people who die in unforeseen accidents? They won't have time to put on their uniforms, will they?

ŌBA: Providing the necessary care is given to the design, it may well become popular among living people as well.

MARUTAKE (*to the others*): I'm in complete agreement. I think it's a really splendid idea for people to be dressed for death all the time, so they'll be ready whenever it comes. I'll provide the capital.

TORII (*thinking*): While we're at it, how would it be if we made it the uniform of the Society for the Protection of Ghosts?

ŌBA: An excellent suggestion.

MARUTAKE: About how many ghosts should we figure on?

ŌBA: A lot. They say that three people die every minute, and if you calculate the number for the whole country, it's enormous. It'll take a big factory to keep up with the demand.

TORII: It's exactly like the rule set down in *Investment Economy*.

CHORUS:

Once the wise man has spoken,

Get ready a great big saucepan.

The season of the dead is approaching;

Gather the ghosts and make jam.

(*They all laugh.*)

HAKOYAMA: Please, all of you, calm yourselves a minute.

TORII: What—are you still here?

HAKOYAMA: If you don't cut short this nonsense, something disgraceful is bound to happen.

ŌBA: Mr. Torii, why do you allow such a man to keep chattering on?

HAKOYAMA (*with a wry smile*): That's just what I wanted to ask.

TORII: Enough is enough. Go lose yourself somewhere.

HAKOYAMA: It's crazy. Talking about ghosts when not one of you believes in them.

ŌBA: What do you mean, not believe in ghosts?

HAKOYAMA: It'd be all right if it was all just a joke, but now someone's killed himself, and people won't tolerate it as a joke any more.

ŌBA: Of all the cheek! (*Glaring at the* MAYOR *and the others.*)

Tell me, Mr. Mayor, do ghosts exist or don't they? (MAYOR *is speechless.*) How about it? Eh?

MAYOR: . . . They do . . . They seem to.

ŌBA (*to* MARUTAKE): How about you?

MARUTAKE: Uhh, they do, they do indeed.

ŌBA: Of course, you do, too . . . (*To* TORII. TORII *nods. To* HAKOYAMA.) Now what have you got to say for yourself? This is no time for a greenhorn like you to put in his two cents . . . Behind me 48,500,000 ghosts stand waiting!

HAKOYAMA: OK. I understand. But for the moment, it'd be a good idea to devote slightly more serious attention to the problem of what to do about the teacher who killed himself.

ŌBA: We'll issue him a certificate. We'll put it in a frame and hang it up at the entrance to the Ghost Convention Center.

HAKOYAMA: You make me sick. When somebody, out of goodwill, has tried to warn you . . .

ŌBA: What kind of goodwill is it when somebody insults the ghosts!

HAKOYAMA: But it's absolutely clear that there aren't any ghosts.

ŌBA: I say there are! I tell you there are!

HAKOYAMA: Yes, in the head of that poor deluded guy who killed himself. But there's no connection between the ghosts he believed in and yours.

ŌBA: Don't talk nonsense! Mr. Ghost is a friend of mine.

HAKOYAMA: Well, you can be sure you're going to have a fight and break with him very soon.

ŌBA: Shit! Mr. Torii, fire this guy!

HAKOYAMA: Why? All I did was follow orders and investigate.

ŌBA: Regardless, I can't stand him. Fire him at once!

TORII: . . . Is that so? . . . Well, you're fired.

HAKOYAMA: Fired?

TORII: Yes, fired.

(*Somewhere in the city. The body of the teacher who committed suicide is borne by on a stretcher.* CITIZENS *watch as it passes. Some run around it with cameras. Explosion of flash bulbs.*)

CHORUS (*Song of Farewell to Teacher's Corpse*):
Your ghost,
Where is it now?
It is searching the city for you.

▲ *The Ghost is Here*

Now that you are dead,
You are splendid.
Photographs of people who have just died
Are worth twenty percent more,
And for suicides
There is an additional five percent.
Now that you are dead
You are much in demand.

SCENE 6

MISAKO: What do you intend to do?

GHOST: . . .

FUKAGAWA (*nods confusedly*): He says that somebody dies every 41 seconds, and to make such a fuss simply because one or two people have committed suicide . . . Besides, a steady pace of suicides will increase the available research materials and make further study easier . . .

MISAKO (*pursuing the matter*): Then, there's no need for you to feel any special duty toward your ghost.

FUKAGAWA: He's different. He died for me. I should really have died, and he should really have lived, not me.

GHOST: . . .

FUKAGAWA: What's that? Of course, it should have happened that way.

(*Enter* CITIZEN H.)

CITIZEN H: Sorry to bother you, but I've brought some exchange coupons, eight of them altogether.

FUKAGAWA: Are you from an agency? Have you got your identification papers?

CITIZEN H: Yes, I have. (*She produces the papers.*)

FUKAGAWA: How much does it come to?

CITIZEN H: Five at 100 yen, two at 130 yen, and one at 210 yen.

(FUKAGAWA *takes the coupons and the photographs, examines them, and then hands over the money.*)

CITIZEN H: Thank you very much . . . Oh, while I'm at it, I'd also like to ask for some treatment.

FUKAGAWA: Treatment is given only in the morning.

CITIZEN H: Oh. I didn't know that. I was planning to come this morning, but there was a perfect downpour just before noon . . . I'll come again tomorrow.

FUKAGAWA: Yes, please do.

CITIZEN H: Give my best regards to Mr. Ghost. (*Exits.*)

(*Pause.*)

MISAKO: Could we get Mr. Ghost to take a stroll somewhere?

FUKAGAWA (*perplexed*): But I don't especially . . .

(*Pause.*)

MISAKO (*angrily, at the invisible* GHOST): If you're a ghost, how about acting a bit more ghostlike?

FUKAGAWA: What do you mean by "more ghostlike"?

MISAKO: Why ask me? I don't know about such things . . .

FUKAGAWA: He'd like to act more like a human being.

MISAKO: Pretty pleased with himself, isn't he? Mr. Fukagawa, I doubt if even a woman would comply so completely with whatever a man asks. You're sure to make a big laughingstock out of yourself.

FUKAGAWA: Excuse me, but is it true your father killed somebody?

(MISAKO *does not answer.*)

FUKAGAWA: *He* has the highest respect for your father. It's thanks to your father that people have become aware of his existence . . . He's really a man of action.

MISAKO: I can understand being nice to the ghost, but is it necessary to make money out of him this way?

FUKAGAWA: He had to do something in order to make him seem more human . . . When you do something, whatever it is, you're bound to influence other people, aren't you? . . . Everybody likes to see his own face reflected in a mirror—it's exactly the same sort of thing.

MISAKO: But you dislike mirrors, don't you, Mr. Fukagawa?

FUKAGAWA: That's because I'm not really myself . . . I'm only living in place of him, nothing more than a substitute.

MISAKO (*to* GHOST, *directly*): Mr. Ghost, are you absolutely determined not to leave Mr. Fukagawa?

FUKAGAWA: Excuse me, but he's over here . . .

MISAKO (*losing her temper*): It doesn't make any difference where he is! (*She goes off to the kitchen.*)

▲   *The Ghost is Here*

FUKAGAWA: Wait! He wants to know if there's anything you'd like him to buy for you.

(TOSHIE *returns home from somewhere.*)

TOSHIE: Mr. Fukagawa, I've found quite a treasure! Look, these are photographs taken at the scene of a traffic accident!

FUKAGAWA: Yes, they're terrific . . . And how about the identification?

TOSHIE: Do you suppose I'd forget that? Here.

(*She takes out an investigation report.*)

FUKAGAWA: You haven't overlooked anything . . .

TOSHIE: How much does it all come to?

FUKAGAWA: Let's see. If he buys them, it'll certainly come to 300 yen. In the case of traffic accidents, there's a fair percentage of people buying back the pictures, and that makes the price go up.

TOSHIE: If he buys them? I'll take whatever I'm offered.

FUKAGAWA: You will?

TOSHIE: Isn't that obvious? I have to look after the rest of you, and there are so many household expenses.

FUKAGAWA: There must be . . . (*Takes money from his pocket and gives it to her.*)

(MISAKO *enters.*)

MISAKO: Is that your money, Mother?

(TOSHIE *hastily puts away the money.*)

FUKAGAWA (*as if trying to mediate between the two women*): It's for some pictures taken at the scene of a traffic accident.

MISAKO (*pulls her mother off to one side*): Mother! Tell me! Who was the witness?

TOSHIE: What do you mean? Out of a clear blue sky . . .

MISAKO: If you don't want to go to the police, I'll go in your place.

FUKAGAWA: Excuse me, but he's asking me to find out what he can do to make Misako like him.

MISAKO: The only way is for the ghost to leave you.

TOSHIE: But if he does, there won't be anyone to interpret for him, and the ghost'll feel very lonely, won't he? You should be kinder to the dead . . .

FUKAGAWA: That's right. Don't you see . . .

MISAKO (*starts to leave*): I'm going to the police.

199

The Ghost is Here ▲

TOSHIE: Wait! (*Catches up to* MISAKO *at the door.*) Why are you so obstinate?

MISAKO: What else can I do?

TOSHIE (*stammering*): All right, then, I'll tell you. I take no further responsibility. Do what you please. I'll tell you. I'll come out with it.

MISAKO: Yes, tell me.

TOSHIE: It was me. Me.

MISAKO: You, Mother!

TOSHIE: That's right. In those days I used to go all around town, taking in laundry . . . The eyewitness was myself . . . You can go tell whoever you like. I'm sure I'll be killed. And if I'm killed, I'll become a ghost. You can make money out of it, selling my pictures . . . for as much as 300 yen!

CHORUS: When she's dead, give me the pictures! Three hundred yen!

(TOSHIE *and* MISAKO *leave.* FUKAGAWA *takes out an aspirin and swallows it.*)

ACT III, SCENE 1

(ŌBA *stands before the curtain. He is wearing even more splendid clothes than in the previous act. Licking his lips, he takes out a huge handkerchief and wipes his face.*)

ŌBA: Thank you for having gathered together today in such large numbers in spite of the rain. I should like, without further ado, to open the ceremonies marking the inauguration of the Society for the Protection of Ghosts, for which you have all been waiting.

(*Applause. When curtain goes up, a lectern, consisting of a frame only, is seen at stage center. Above, a placard reads: "Honoring the Inauguration of the Society for the Protection of Ghosts." At stage left, the four executives are seated. At stage right, FUKA-GAWA, and next to him, an empty chair.*)

The people on the stage are all well-known to you, so I shall not introduce them one by one. However, I'd like to point out that the empty chair is occupied by today's guest of honor, Mr. Ghost. First of all, we will have greetings from His Honor, Mayor Kubota.

▲   *The Ghost is Here*

(THE MAYOR *stands before the lectern. He bows his head and proceeds to deliver his greetings. The words have no particular meaning, but they are accompanied by an exaggerated panto-mime. In contrast to the pompousness of the gestures executed by the upper half of his body, the lower half, visible through the lectern though he is not aware of this, provides a most slovenly contrast: he repeatedly scratches his right shin with the heel of his left foot. At the conclusion of the speech,* MARUTAKE *reverently places an unpainted wooden box of some sort at* TORII'S *feet.* TORII *opens the box, and takes from it a badge. He steps forward and pins the badge on the* MAYOR'S *lapel. While this is going on, there is a short selection of music played by a brass band.*)

This is the Number One "Ghost Insurance Badge." You will find at the reception desk near the front entrance an applica-tion form together with a specimen completed form. On your way out, please be sure to examine them carefully.

(THE MAYOR *and* TORII *bow in unison and return to their seats.*)

MARUTAKE: Next, we would like you to see today's chief attrac-tion, the fashion show of "Ghost Clothes."

(TWO WOMEN, *wearing clothes that are at once rather grotesque and suggestive, enter mincingly. They pose.*)

ŌBA: We will be showing the rest of the collection one at a time, and we would like each of you to write in, on the card we have left at your seat, your favorites among the costumes displayed—one each for a man's and a woman's—and de-posit the card at the ballot box you will find by the reception desk at the entrance. The costumes that receive the most votes will be chosen as the first "ghost clothes" anywhere in the world. In addition, one man and one woman will be chosen by lot from among those who have elected the win-ners, and we will present each of them with a prize of ten thousand yen and a complimentary suit of ghost clothes.

(*Music.* MODELS *enter. Dance of models.*)

Next, we have our guest of honor, Mr. Ghost! (*Waves his handkerchief, then blows his nose.*)

(FUKAGAWA *steps forward to lectern, gesturing to* GHOST *to come with him.*)

FUKAGAWA (*bows and takes a slip of paper from his pocket*): I am truly happy that so many people have gathered together to-day. This hall now contains not only human beings but many, many ghosts. (*Glances at* GHOST.) Or, I might more accurately say, there are many times as many ghosts here as human beings, not only in the aisles but on your laps and on your shoulders. They are packed in solidly, all the way up to the ceiling . . . Ladies and gentlemen, what you are breathing now is not air but ghosts.

(*Music.* MODELS *enter then, striking poses, exit to stage right.*)

FUKAGAWA: The ghosts are extremely excited to be treated this way. He wishes he could communicate this to you directly, but unfortunately, this is not possible, and since it would be a great waste of time for me to interpret one by one what each ghost has to say, I will read instead the manuscript I prepared last night with his assistance. (*Reads.*) "Who am I? That's something I can't remember. But I do remember how once a certain woman was weeping for a man who was dead, and I thought, 'Maybe she's weeping for me.' Then I realized she was weeping for herself. Everybody looks the other way . . ."

(*Music.* MODELS *enter. They dance, then leave.*)

(*Continues reading.*) "But now is the season for ghosts. The season of ghosts has at last arrived! I want to die. I want to live. I want to live again so I can die again. Thank you, all of you." (*He bows and starts to return to his seat, but is called back by the* GHOST. *He turns in its direction.*) Eh?

GHOST: . . .

(*Music.* MODELS *enter. They perform the longest and most color-ful of their wild dances.* FUKAGAWA *continues to exchange whis-pers with the* GHOST. *Suddenly he motions for the dance to stop and stands.*)

FUKAGAWA: Quiet, please. (*Music stops.* MODELS *stand still.* ŌBA *leans forward in surprise.*) He has just now made an important decision! (*Firmly.*) He has made up his mind. He says he wants to be the president of the Society for the Protection of Ghosts, and he has now assumed office as its second president!

▲   *The Ghost is Here*

SCENE 2

(*The Sunbeam Electronics shop. Just before dusk. Preparations for moving are underway. The shop is empty.* MISAKO *stands under the steps.* LABORERS 1 AND 2 *are about to carry out the last of the boxes.*)

LABORER 1: Is this it, miss?

(MISAKO *turns around and nods.*)

LABORER 2: Then, we'll be pushing off.

MISAKO: That's fine.

(LABORERS *exit, pulling a bicycle trailer.* MISAKO *goes outside and takes down the sign. She places it next to the entrance, the writing facing away from the audience. She beats the dust from her hands and looks around.* HAKOYAMA *approaches from stage left, his hands thrust into his pockets. He spits out the cigarette in his mouth, and grinds it out. He goes to the entrance and peers in.*)

HAKOYAMA: Hello!

MISAKO: Ohh, have you found a job?

HAKOYAMA: Nothing great so far. (*Goes in.*) So, you're finally moving.

MISAKO (*not answering his question*): Have you finished your article attacking the Ghost Protection Society?

HAKOYAMA: Mmm. I've written it all right, and I've sent it to newspapers all over the place. They say they might use a piece saying ghosts exist, but saying ghosts don't exist isn't news. Maybe they're right. In the first place, divinities are protected by law.

MISAKO: That's right. You can't plainly say they don't exist.

HAKOYAMA: But this is different. The law doesn't say it believes in gods. All it does is to protect an established fact . . . The ghosts also seem to have become an established fact.

MISAKO: They're quite aggressive. They're not satisfied unless they get a daily accounting.

HAKOYAMA (*laughs and nods*): In other words, that proves ghosts exist?

MISAKO: You can't be absolutely sure they don't, can you?

HAKOYAMA: Yes, you can. It's simply an illusion on Fukagawa's part.

203

The Ghost is Here ▲

MISAKO: Can an illusion become the president of a society?

HAKOYAMA: I have to admit the connection with money shows a sense of reality.

MISAKO: Mr. Fukagawa and the ghost are not the same thing.

HAKOYAMA: To change the subject, where's your mother?

MISAKO (*unsociably*): I think she's gone to have a permanent. Lately she's out all the time.

HAKOYAMA: Good. We can have a quiet talk together. I don't know why it is, but your mother seems to be avoiding me . . . (*He sits at some appropriate place.*) The most interesting thing I've seen lately on the subject is an article by a certain psychologist. It's called "Interview with a Ghost." It gives a pretty clear idea of the nature of ghosts. For example, there's a far higher proportion of male ghosts than female ghosts. Their clothes date from the wartime or immediate postwar period. With respect to age, the heaviest concentration is of men in the prime of life. Next, the change in psychology after self-awakening as ghosts—to use Fukagawa's language—is marked first by a period of loneliness, next by a despair that makes them want to die again, and then thirdly by a period of active impatience when they want to live in order to die . . .

MISAKO (*laughs*): It's marvelous how well you remember it.

HAKOYAMA: There's a problem—not one ghost has been discovered who corresponds exactly with a photograph.

MISAKO: I thought there had been some.

HAKOYAMA: They were just decoys. If it had been the real thing, there would have been a much bigger fuss.

(MISAKO *is silent.*)

HAKOYAMA: Are you satisfied with the situation as is?

MISAKO: It's not bad having money.

HAKOYAMA: To tell the truth, I'm writing something like a novel now. No, it's less like a novel than a true story about the present events . . . I've sent articles to all kinds of places, and one magazine publisher asked me for a story. If it goes well, it may bring me seventy or eighty thousand yen. That's not much money, but I've been thinking with that as a start, I might go on to Tokyo . . .

MISAKO: I'm so glad.

▲   *The Ghost is Here*

HAKOYAMA: But there's one condition. The publisher says that unless there's some clear conclusion to the story, he can't use it.

MISAKO: There won't be any conclusion to ghosts.

HAKOYAMA: Do you *really* think so?

MISAKO: What do you mean?

HAKOYAMA: I toyed with the idea at one time that Fukagawa might be a police detective, or maybe a private detective . . .

MISAKO: That's inconceivable!

HAKOYAMA: You're right, it's inconceivable. If he had been a detective, there were any number of other means he could have used. For example, he could have got hold of a photograph of the old guy who got killed—Yoshino, was that his name?

MISAKO: That would be worth about 500 yen, wouldn't it?

HAKOYAMA: You mean you really don't know?

MISAKO: If I say I don't know, you'll probably say that's proof that I do know.

HAKOYAMA (*laughs*): What's happened? I thought you were angry about all the fuss that's been made.

MISAKO: It's just that I feel sorry for Mr. Fukagawa. He does exactly what the ghost tells him.

HAKOYAMA: Ah-hah . . . So you've become fond of the great Fukagawa after all.

MISAKO: It's nothing like that. It's just that it's all been my father's fault that things have turned out this way.

HAKOYAMA: That's proof that you've fallen for him.

MISAKO: Unfortunately, the ghost is extremely jealous.

HAKOYAMA: That makes things tough for me.

MISAKO: Why?

HAKOYAMA: I've written almost the whole story. Only the conclusion's left. And in this story you and I find affinities and in the end become very great friends.

MISAKO (*giggles*): I'm sorry for you.

HAKOYAMA: You're damned right . . . Well, how would this be—I'll give you fifty thousand yen, and you ask your mother the name of the witness. And if I must, I'm willing to give you the entire eighty thousand yen I'm supposed to receive. I desperately need some sort of foothold that'll enable me to move on to Tokyo. I beg you. I'm sure you agree with me that it's about time something was done to wind up this business.

MISAKO: I see—money's the name of the game!

HAKOYAMA: I only wish a ghost, no matter whose, would do me the favor of putting in an appearance at my place, too . . .

MISAKO (*laughs. Looks at her watch*): Oh dear, it's just the time when Mr. Fukagawa, the mayor and the others are supposed to be on the radio.

HAKOYAMA: What, again? Probably part of the election campaign.

(MISAKO *takes a small radio from her pocket. In the background,* FUKAGAWA, *the* MAYOR, TORII, *and* MARUTAKE *are visible through a screen, sitting around a microphone.* HAKOYAMA *and* MISAKO *listen to the radio, which she has placed on a shelf in the deserted room.*)

TORII: The recent prosperity of our city has been nothing short of astonishing . . . But I wonder, Mr. Ghost, what your thoughts are on the matter. There's to be an election for mayor shortly. I know it's peculiar to ask you, with the present mayor sitting before you, but if you had your choice, for which candidate would you vote?

MAYOR (*embarrassed*): Oh, come . . .

HAKOYAMA: That's putting it pretty baldly.

MISAKO: I wonder if it's not a violation of the electoral law.

(FUKAGAWA, *looking at* GHOST, *remains silent.*)

MARUTAKE: Just a casual comment is all we need.

FUKAGAWA: He . . . I mean, the president of the Society . . . is of the opinion . . . (*He hesitates, but is urged on by the* GHOST.) that he himself should be the mayor.

MISAKO: Heavens!

HAKOYAMA (*at the same time as* MISAKO): What did he say?

TORII (*his face shows no trace of amusement, but his voice is jolly*): Hee-hee-hee. That's a good one!

MARUTAKE: Yes, I'm sure the voters would be delighted if we could persuade him to run.

FUKAGAWA (*embarrassed*): He really wants to be the mayor.

MISAKO: He means it!

TORII: But how can he . . . (*Confused.*) Ha-ha-ha.

▲   *The Ghost is Here*

MARUTAKE: Why, he can't even do routine jobs like putting his seal to a paper.

FUKAGAWA: I can act as his substitute . . . Anyway, he says he intends to take over as the next mayor.

HAKOYAMA: It's a case of dilatation of the stomach. He doesn't feel secure unless he keeps eating one thing after another.

TORII: It's all very well for him to say he wants to be the next mayor, but there'll have to be an election.

MARUTAKE: That's right. You can never tell what'll happen in an election.

TORII: All kinds of stupid things are possible. For example, he may have trouble getting votes because he's not married.

HAKOYAMA: What an idiot! All he has to say is that ghosts are not eligible for election.

FUKAGAWA: Are you implying that it's all right for him to get married?

(*General consternation.*)

MARUTAKE (*with affected cheerfulness*): Well, that's a delightful prospect. It'll create quite a sensation.

FUKAGAWA: He says that getting married would be an interesting experience for him, too.

(MAYOR *gives a loud laugh.*)

MISAKO: He's making fun of us!

TORII (*starts to give the signal to break off the broadcast, but* FUKAGAWA *prevents him*): Yes, that really would be interesting.

FUKAGAWA: He says he'll get married and then be the mayor.

MARUTAKE: I'm sure there'll be so many requests pouring in from women who would like to be his bride that the clerical work will be something terrible.

FUKAGAWA: He says that, if he's going to get married, there's somebody he has in mind . . . (*Uneasily stares at* GHOST.)

(TORII *suddenly gets up and gives the signal for ending the broadcast. The radio gives forth incomprehensible noises.*)

FUKAGAWA (*his voice is clearly heard amidst the noises*): His choice is Miss Ōba Misako!

(*The radio abruptly stops and the figures behind the screen also disappear.* MISAKO *and* HAKOYAMA *stand rooted in their tracks.*)

VOICE OF ANNOUNCER: May we ask your kind indulgence?

207

The Ghost is Here ▲

Owing to circumstances beyond our control, we have had to cancel the remainder of the broadcast. In the meantime, until the beginning of our next broadcast, we will offer you some music.

(*Music.* MISAKO *switches off the radio.*)

HAKOYAMA: It beats me whether they're fattening off the ghost or if the ghost is fattening off them. (MISAKO *is silent.*) How about it? You can't remain a disinterested spectator any longer, can you? Why not make up your mind and cooperate in the ending of my story?

(MISAKO *trembles barely perceptibly. It is getting dark. The telephone rings.*)

MISAKO: Father? . . . Yes, I heard it. (*Bites lips.*) . . . All right, then, I'll tell you. I know who the witness was . . . Yes . . . But I'm not in the same position as Mother. There's nothing to keep me from telling! . . . No, I won't! (*Hangs up.*)

HAKOYAMA: What! You knew all along! (*He stands in* MISAKO'S *way.*) Tell me who it is. I'm begging you. If you won't tell for eighty thousand, I'll make it a hundred thousand, or even a hundred and fifty thousand . . . I'll tell you the whole truth. There's somebody who says that if I publish the story, he'll give me extra money. He's in the City Council, an influential member of the faction opposed to the mayor . . . If this succeeds, I guarantee to get him to look after you and your mother.

MISAKO: At last, you've come out with your real intentions. Let me pass!

HAKOYAMA: But sooner or later you'll have to do it anyway. So, why not now?

MISAKO: Let me pass!

HAKOYAMA (*steps aside*): I'm sorry . . . I thought I was making a reasonable proposition.

MISAKO: You're not. All you're thinking of is the ending of your story. (*Exits quickly.*)

(HAKOYAMA, *left to himself, glances at his watch. He takes out his notebook and writes something in it.*)

SCENE 3

(The infirmary of the Ghost Convention Center. At stage center a hospital bed. CITIZEN F *is being treated by the* GHOST.*)*

FUKAGAWA (*he wears a white smock. In a depressed voice*): Open wide now.

CITIZEN F: Ah, ah, eh . . .

FUKAGAWA: Are you ready? Mr. Ghost is about to put his hand in . . . It's in now, and he's pushing it all the way down to your throat . . . Ah—now his fingers are touching your bronchial tubes . . . He's pressing and massaging them.

CITIZEN F (*from the back of his throat*): Eh, eh, eh.

(Door opens and a bewildered-looking OLD WOMAN *with a senile air about her enters.)*

OLD WOMAN: Excuse me, please . . . (*A hand stretches out behind her and pulls her back.*)

ŌBA: Treatment is given in order of appointment. You can't break into the line.

OLD WOMAN: No, I just . . .

ŌBA: It's no use.

OLD WOMAN (*as she is being dragged off*): Erh, my name is Yoshida . . .

ŌBA: I don't care what your name is! On your way! . . . What a cheeky old dame! Wasn't even wearing a badge.

*(*FUKAGAWA *looks startled, but he shakes off whatever was bothering him, and returns his attention to* CITIZEN F.*)*

(Scene shifts to an office in City Hall. The big shots are sitting around a table. ŌBA *enters. He goes to the telephone and dials furiously.)*

TORII (*leafing through the Statute Book*): Even forgetting about his planned marriage, his intention of becoming the mayor is one big headache.

MAYOR: I'm at my wits' end, I tell you.

MARUTAKE: The marriage is also a headache. (*To* ŌBA.) Can't you try once more to convince your daughter? I think he'd make an unusually desirable husband. He doesn't drink, doesn't play around, and there's absolutely no danger of his ever keeping a mistress.

TORII: I've searched high and low, but there's no law saying a

209

The Ghost is Here ▲

ghost can't run for public office. It's all a question of what constitutes a citizen. What does it mean to be a Japanese citizen? . . . (*Leafs through the pages.*)

MARUTAKE (*tapping his forehead*): We've certainly got involved in a first-class mess. I never knew that ghosts were so obstinate. It's like trying to get a stud horse in heat to sit quietly on a cushion in the *tokonoma*. I suppose that if a horse could talk he'd be popular, and he might at some stage say he wanted to marry a human woman or become the mayor, but public opinion wouldn't allow it. But if we don't handle this just right, it might end up by proving ghosts don't exist.

TORII: That's exactly the problem! My investigation seems to show that the only qualification missing in the ghost is that he doesn't pay taxes. If he says he wants to pay taxes, what then? The only way we can prevent him from becoming mayor is to accept the arguments of people who deny the existence of ghosts.

ŌBA: Heaven forbid! Are we going to stand by quietly when people deny the existence of ghosts?

MARUTAKE: That's out of the question, of course.

MAYOR: It's not that I'm wedded to the office of mayor, but it's a complicated job that demands a good deal of persistence and brains, too.

(*The* OLD WOMAN *who calls herself Yoshida appears.*)

OLD WOMAN: Excuse me . . . I'm Mrs. Yoshida and . . .

MARUTAKE: Where did you sneak in from?

(*She points at the door behind her.*)

TORII: You can't come in here. This is the boardroom.

MARUTAKE: What's the matter with the people at the reception desk? Are they asleep? I thought I'd told them to be on the lookout for strange people who come wandering around here.

OLD WOMAN: I'm the mother of the man who calls himself Fukagawa Keisuke . . .

ŌBA (*clicks his tongue*): Another one! Every day we have two or three imposters visit us, claiming to be his uncle, his younger brother, his wife or something. I can't be bothered dealing with every single one of them.

OLD WOMAN: Erh. I've brought with me a certified copy of his birth certificate.

▲   *The Ghost is Here*

MARUTAKE (*calls to back room*): Isn't anyone there?

OLD WOMAN: My name is Yoshida, and to tell the truth . . .

(*Hands stretch out and grab the old woman.*)

VOICE: Are you still here? I thought I told you to clear out.

OLD WOMAN: I . . . I mean . . . (*She is dragged off.*)

ŌBA (*clicks his tongue in rapid succession*): Women certainly cause a lot of trouble.

TORII: And, on top of everything else, just supposing the ghost runs for office . . . what do you think would happen? We'll all get knocked down like ninepins.

MARUTAKE: If we could only get him to be content with just one thing—getting married.

ŌBA: Damnation! Isn't there something like a love potion on sale somewhere? The kind that if you take one sip you fall in love with the first thing you see, even a pair of chopsticks.

MARUTAKE: Don't you think we could persuade him to be satisfied with some other woman?

ŌBA: Would you like to try? For all we know, he may have quite a range of interests. If we can find a really good-looking woman and use her as bait, he may be so dazzled that he'll snap at the bait, and forget about becoming mayor and all the rest.

MAYOR: That would be very welcome.

MARUTAKE: Do you remember that girl we used as a model for ghost clothes—how would she be? She was quite something, wasn't she?

(FUKAGAWA *looks at his watch. A sound of chimes.*)

FUKAGAWA: Five minutes. The treatment's finished.

CITIZEN F: Ugh. (*Gets up.*) Ahh, it seems to have worked. (*Takes a deep breath.*) I'd always thought ghosts were frightening, but they're really kind, aren't they? (*To* GHOST.) I'll be coming again . . . (*Exits to the flop-flop of his slippers.*)

VOICE: The next patient, please.

(*Sound of a baby crying.*)

ŌBA (*entering the infirmary*): Wait! I have something to discuss with you for a minute.

(THE MAYOR *and the others follow in behind him.*)

ŌBA: You must be exhausted by all those patients. But we've at last come to an agreement.

211

The Ghost is Here ▲

FUKAGAWA: Has Misako accepted?

ŌBA: Not exactly . . .

FUKAGAWA (*hides his relief. Nods*): But he says he won't take anyone but Misako.

ŌBA (*waving his hand at the invisible* GHOST): That's exactly what we were discussing.

FUKAGAWA: He's here.

ŌBA (*hastily changes direction*): In other words, we are entirely in sympathy with Mr. Ghost's wish to get married . . . and, after a great deal of consideration of the possibilities, we've fortunately been able to find the right girl. One look at her and Mr. Ghost will lose all power to resist.

FUKAGAWA: But . . .

ŌBA: No, I tell you, my daughter, compared to this girl, is nothing but a very ordinary woman . . . the dregs of womanhood. (*He describes something in the air with his index finger.*) Anyway, we decided that this young lady was worthy of Mr. Ghost.

FUKAGAWA: And what about Misako herself? What does she say?

ŌBA: She's well aware of her limitations. At any rate, this girl's sex appeal . . . (*Throws a glance at the others.*) is quite something . . .

MARUTAKE: That's right. She's the number one beauty of the town.

TORII: We're sure that one look at her will be all that it takes to satisfy him.

MARUTAKE: Once he's seen the girl, he'll think it was plain crazy to have wanted to do anything as troublesome as become the mayor.

FUKAGAWA: No, becoming the mayor is an entirely different question.

GHOST: . . .

FUKAGAWA: He says that the reason he's getting married is in order to become the mayor. He's determined to become the mayor.

ŌBA: I see. But it's quite possible the girl may say she doesn't want anyone as bourgeois as a mayor. But, in any case, we'd like him to see her first.

212

▲ *The Ghost is Here*

MARUTAKE: That's right—she's Miss Kitahama.

GHOST: . . .

FUKAGAWA: Well, where is she? He says he's in a hurry.

ŌBA (*perplexed*): Hold your horses! He seems to be awfully impatient.

MARUTAKE: Heh-heh.

(*The infirmary door suddenly opens.*)

OLD WOMAN: Excuse me, please.

TORII: How did she get back here?

MARUTAKE: Scram! (*He raises his arm and makes a gesture of chasing her away.*)

OLD WOMAN: I'm going! (*Disappears.*)

FUKAGAWA: He says that unless he gets married and becomes the mayor right away, the only thing left for him to do will be to head out to sea.

TORII: Can he swim?

MARUTAKE: He's probably going fishing.

ŌBA: What do you mean? He'll be on his honeymoon!

(*They all try unsuccessfully to force a laugh.*)

FUKAGAWA: He says there's a place, far out at sea, where ghosts congregate and form a whirlpool. It's a favorite haunt of the ghosts, and they play at war there. That's where he says he's going.

ŌBA: And if Mr. Ghost goes there, what will you do?

FUKAGAWA (*in an expressionless voice*): I'll go with him.

(*Pause.*)

TORII: I've had all I can take. It's intimidation, that's what it is. (*Looks from one to another of his pals, as if imploring their help.*)

MARUTAKE: That's exactly what it is. We can't let him get away with it.

ŌBA: If you're absolutely set on going, I'll go along with you.

FUKAGAWA: No, the best thing is for him to get married as soon as possible . . .

MARUTAKE: That's right, to the number one beauty in Kitahama.

ŌBA: Look! Here's a picture of the girl. (*He takes out a photograph.*)

ALL: Yes, this is the one!

The Ghost is Here ▲

(*Pause.* FUKAGAWA *looks at* GHOST. *Shakes his head.*)

ŌBA: You can't tell just from a picture. We'll put the real thing before him and let him examine her at leisure.

MARUTAKE: Yes, it takes direct appreciation . . .

TORII: Once they've talked together about this and that . . .

MARUTAKE: And he's fondled her a bit . . .

FUKAGAWA: But still . . .

ŌBA (*stepping back*): No, we'll listen to complaints later on. First, he should please try her.

MARUTAKE (*stepping back*): I guarantee he'll like her.

TORII (*stepping back*): We'll have the ceremony right away, tomorrow even.

MAYOR: Or, if he prefers, tonight.

MARUTAKE: That's right. An abbreviated ceremony for the time being . . . But as for becoming mayor, there has to be an election first, and we'd appreciate it if he didn't insist on being unreasonable.

FUKAGAWA: But the date of the election *could* be moved up, couldn't it?

MAYOR (*confusedly*): I'll have to look into this.

(*The executives of the Society for the Protection of Ghosts return to the boardroom.*)

FUKAGAWA (*to* GHOST): It looks as if you'll be heading off to sea, after all . . . (*His tone is mournful, but as a matter of fact, he is secretly not without a little hope.*)

GHOST: . . .

FUKAGAWA (GHOST *hits him*): Owww! (*Hurriedly.*) Of course, I will. Surely you know I won't desert you.

(*The door of the infirmary opens. Sounds of a baby crying.*)

VOICE: Doctor, there are people waiting. Next . . .

SCENE 4

(*A street corner in the town. A telephone booth close to the middle of the stage. A man stands by the booth. He is neatly dressed, but his type always looks somehow casual. At his feet, a small suitcase. He looks at his watch, then peers off to stage right. He takes out a cigarette, starts to light it, stops, and frowns. He seems to*

▲ *The Ghost is Here*

be fairly irritated. The OLD WOMAN *who calls herself Yoshida enters from stage left.*)

MAN: Well, what happened?

OLD WOMAN (*breathing hard, shakes her head*): I got nowhere.

MAN: Then, what were you doing all this time?

OLD WOMAN: They're all such frightening people . . .

MAN: Now, what am I going to do?

(OLD WOMAN *does not answer.* MISAKO *enters from stage left. She walks directly into the telephone booth.*)

MAN: It can't be helped. I'll go back to the hotel for the time being, and go over the plans again. (*Picks up his suitcase.*)

MISAKO: Hello. Is this the Ghost Convention Center? . . . This is Miss Ōba. Would you mind asking Mr. Fukagawa to come to the phone?

(MAN, *surprised, stops in his tracks. He puts his finger over his mouth to silence* OLD WOMAN, *who has started to say something, and listens.*)

MISAKO: Mr. Fukagawa? What happened—I mean about the plans for the ghost's wedding? . . . (*Long pause.*) No! You mustn't let it happen, no matter what. It's ridiculous.

OLD WOMAN: What is it all about? Is she . . .

(MAN *puts his finger on his lips to silence her.*)

MISAKO (*continues*): Well, why don't you plainly refuse? . . . Why? . . . Why can't you say so? . . . (*Disappointed.*) I see . . .Well, that's all right . . . (*Sharply.*) No, I don't like it. Mr. Fukagawa, I've had enough, until you and the ghost separate!

(MISAKO *hangs up and leaves the booth.* MAN *calls her back.*)

MAN: You're Miss Ōba, I believe? And you're acquainted with Fukagawa, the ghost man, aren't you?

MISAKO: And with whom have I the pleasure . . .

MAN (*takes a calling card from an inside pocket and shows it to her*): This is who I am. I'm a lawyer by profession.

(MISAKO *looks at card, then at* MAN. *She shows extreme agitation.*)

MAN: This is Mrs. Yoshida. (*He pushes* OLD WOMAN *forward.*) To make a long story short, she's the mother of Fukagawa, the ghost man.

The Ghost is Here ▲

MISAKO (*greatly perturbed*): Not really!

OLD WOMAN: Yes. Here . . . (*She takes an envelope from her kimono and pulls out the contents.*) I've brought along a certified copy of his birth certificate. (MISAKO *takes it and reads it.*)

MAN: Would you be so good as to take me to Fukagawa?

MISAKO (*recovering from her confusion*): There's something that's still not clear.

MAN (*persuasively*): It's your duty. You want to rescue him from the ghost, don't you? (MISAKO *nods.*) Then, lead me to him.

(*All three leave, the man strongly urging* MISAKO *ahead. The boardroom.* ŌBA *and the executives of the Society sit around the table. Their expression is extremely serious.* TORII *frantically thumbs through the Statute Book.*)

TORII: Mmm. Mmm . . . Article 114. "When a vacancy occurs in the directorship of a regional public organization or the incumbent has announced his intention of retiring . . . however, see Article 112." (*Turns pages.*) Ah-hah. (*Turns pages again.*) "In such an event, a reelection, in conformance with Article 109 . . ." (*Turns pages.*) Hmm. Hmm . . .

MARUTAKE (*looks over his shoulder toward the door*): Why is that girl so late? (*He impatiently drums on the table with his fingers.*) She's our only hope.

ŌBA (*stares angrily at the ceiling. To himself*): I don't understand it . . . I've played one trump card after another, and nothing seems to work . . . Maybe there really are ghosts . . . (*Clicks tongue. Returns to the conversation.*) Shit! If only I could see ghosts myself . . .

TORII: If he runs away from us, we're the same as dead. It would almost be better to hang ourselves.

MARUTAKE (*seriously*): Mmm. It might not be a bad idea to include one ghost among the executives of the Society . . .

TORII (*his voice is shaking*): But I want it to be understood that, no matter what happens, I expect a clear accounting for the money I've invested.

ŌBA (*severely*): This is no time for joking. I've no intention of letting you forget how big an investment I made to seal the mouth of the witness of the incident you know about.

216

MARUTAKE: Come, come. We mustn't allow dissension to divide us. But look! Here she is!

(MODEL *enters.*)

MODEL: Have I kept you waiting? Forgive me, won't you?

MARUTAKE (*rubbing his hands*): Yes, that's exactly the tone we want.

MODEL: Ohh . . . I'll leave if you talk that way.

ŌBA (*holding out a suit of ghost clothes*): Come on, just put on these clothes, the way we agreed on the phone.

MODEL: I still don't understand what this is all about, in such a hurry.

ŌBA: Don't worry. It doesn't concern you. All you have to do is give Mr. Ghost a full dose of your charm. You understand, this is a crucial matter on which the fate of our city depends. It will be a great achievement if you manage to seduce Mr. Ghost, and get him to go through with at least the motions of a marriage.

MODEL: Just flattery isn't enough for me.

ŌBA: I understand, of course . . . Here's a down payment, ten thousand yen . . . If everything goes well afterward, you'll get the balance, ninety thousand yen. And from then on we'll pay you a monthly subsistence allowance.

MODEL (*holding up ghost clothes and turning them around*): How much?

TORII: Twenty thousand yen every month. Not bad, is it?

MODEL (*coquettishly*): But it's hard on me. I've already got a boyfriend. You know what I mean . . . I'd like a little consolation money . . .

ŌBA: OK, OK. We'll add fifty thousand yen.

MODEL: Goodness! I'm overwhelmed! . . . Every month, right? (*She winks and starts to remove her clothes.*)

MARUTAKE: Don't be silly!

MODEL: But I thought . . .

ŌBA: You'll get an allowance! Thirty thousand yen a month! (MODEL *quickly slips off her clothes.*)

The Ghost is Here ▲

SCENE 5

(*Infirmary of Ghost Convention Hall.* FUKAGAWA *is alone.*)

FUKAGAWA (*weakly*): You're asking too much. It's more than I can handle. Don't make me, please . . . (GHOST *hits him.*) Oww!

(MODEL *enters, propelled forward by* ŌBA *and the others.* FUKAGAWA *turns around in surprise.* MODEL *parades around the room, showing off her charms.*)

MODEL (*looking off into space*): Mr. Ghost—I've wanted so much to meet you!

FUKAGAWA: He's here.

MODEL: Oh, dear. I'm sorry.

(*She slinks around room, striking poses.*)

I love transparent men . . .

(*As she walks, she suddenly jumps up and begins a dance.*)

I'm crazy about
A transparent man.
I want to marry
A transparent man.
I go for ghosts—
He's wonderful!

(*Stops dancing. Poses.*)

(*To* FUKAGAWA.) What does he say about me? . . . No, not yet. It's still too soon . . .

(*She prances, then flings herself into a dance. At the very moment when* FUKAGAWA, *without realizing it, raises his hand to stop her, the door opens and* MISAKO *enters.* MODEL *turns around and stops her dance.* MISAKO *looks amazed.* OLD WOMAN *and* MAN *with the suitcase follow her in. The executives of the Society are thrown into confusion.*)

(*Looking from* FUKAGAWA *to* MISAKO *and the others.*) It's no good. They've destroyed the mood.

MISAKO (*to* FUKAGAWA): This visitor seems to have important business with you.

(FUKAGAWA *shifts his attention to* MAN *with the suitcase, starts in amazement, stands up, and swallows hard. He looks as if he turned to stone.*)

MAN (*puts down suitcase. Smiling*): Hi, my old friend!

218

(*Pause.*)

MODEL (*as if asking for help*): What am I supposed to do now?

ŌBA: What are all you . . .? Misako—what are you doing here?
. . . Get out, right away, yes, I mean right away . . . (*He goes up to her with his arms outstretched, as if drive her away.*)

MAN: It's me! . . .

(*Violent anguish and agitation cross* FUKAGAWA'S *face.*)

ŌBA (*this also upsets him*): We'll talk later on . . . There's a wedding ceremony coming up . . . (*To* FUKAGAWA.) Mr. Fukagawa, I've made up mind. It's all the same, no matter when it takes place, and everything is ready. All we're waiting for is Mr. Ghost's reply . . . What does Mr. Ghost say?

(FUKAGAWA *is silent.*)

(*To* MISAKO *and the others.*) Would you mind going over there, all of you? This is an important, a sacred moment. (*To* MISAKO.) Aren't you ashamed of yourself? After having just said something like that? . . . (*He becomes increasingly agitated.*) I'm asking you, over there, please. (*To* FUKAGAWA, *as if seeking confirmation.*) I'm sure Mr. Ghost must be annoyed over all this.

MARUTAKE: Yes, angry. Angry as can be. Steaming with rage.

MAN (*calmly. Pointing at himself*): The ghost is here . . . (*To* FUKAGAWA.) Yoshida—it's me, Fukagawa Keisuke.

(*Astonishment sweeps over them like an electric charge. Only the* OLD WOMAN *smiles and nods.*)

FUKAGAWA (*staring around him*): Ohh—he's not there!

MAN: It's all right, even if he isn't . . .

FUKAGAWA (*looks around him*): Where could he have gone?

ŌBA (*excitedly searches along with* FUKAGAWA. *He peers under the bed.*): He must be somewhere . . .

(MODEL *wrinkles her nose in disdain. The executives stiffen, as if turned to stone. They huddle together and seem to grow smaller.*)

THE REAL FUKAGAWA (*takes from his suitcase a box and a canteen with a peeling surface*): This is the canteen . . . (*Removes the lid from the box and shows the contents.*) This is the coin . . . Remember it? The one who won the bet was not me but you. And you were so tormented, you switched yourself and me in your head.

219

FUKAGAWA: Damnation! (*Hands on his head, he sits on the bed.*)

(ŌBA, *still searching for the* GHOST, *wanders around the room, staring up at the sky.*)

THE REAL FUKAGAWA: . . . After that, I walked a whole night, dragging you with me. As soon as we emerged from the jungle, we were taken prisoners . . . But you came with the ghost to what you thought was my house. In fact, it was your own house . . . At the hospital they mistakenly thought that I was the one who'd run away, and they came to get me, because you had used the alias of Fukagawa. (*Laughs.*) And now, for the first time, your identity has been cleared up.

(*The executives suddenly run off toward the boardroom.* MODEL *follows them.*)

FUKAGAWA: Will somebody let me see myself in a mirror?

(MISAKO *takes a mirror from her pocket and gives it to him.* FUKAGAWA *stares into it.*)

(*The board room, with the overwrought executives.*)

MAYOR: What shall we do?

TORII: Do? . . . The most important thing is not to let that bunch escape.

MARUTAKE: I'll get some guys with plenty of strength to keep watch over them.

(MARUTAKE *leaves.*)

FUKAGAWA (*staring into the mirror*): That's right . . . It's me!

THE REAL FUKAGAWA: That's obvious. You are you.

FUKAGAWA (*absorbed*): It's me, right? It's really me!

MISAKO: That's right. It's you.

OLD WOMAN (*nods repeatedly*): You're looking well. Yes, very well.

THE REAL FUKAGAWA: It's your mother. Do you understand?

(FUKAGAWA *nods.*)

THE REAL FUKAGAWA: Then, tell me who I am.

FUKAGAWA: I understand . . . You're the real Fukagawa.

(*The boardroom.* TOSHIE *bursts in.*)

TOSHIE: Excuse me. Hasn't Misako come? And where's my husband?

TORII: He's over there. (*Points toward the infirmary.*) He's watching over the gang.

TOSHIE: Gang?

TORII: The whole thing's turned into a terrible mess.

TOSHIE: I don't know what's going on, but the town's buzzing with rumors that Misako and Mr. Ghost are getting married.

MODEL: I'm the one getting married!

TORII: You stay out of this! It's nothing as simple as that. The ghost has disappeared.

TOSHIE: Disappeared?

TORII: The ghost proposed, but your daughter wouldn't cooperate. Instead she brought some crazy man who says he's the real Fukagawa. The ghost got so mad he ran away.

TOSHIE: What a waste of an opportunity! How can anyone be so ignorant of the world? (*She storms into the infirmary.*)

ŌBA (*still searching for the* GHOST, *also goes into the infirmary*): He's disappeared! (*He sits himself down.*)

TOSHIE: Misako, what *have* you done?

ŌBA: Shhh. Don't get so excited. Keep calm.

MISAKO: Isn't it wonderful, Mother, the ghost has disappeared!

TOSHIE: Isn't it wonderful? (*She looks around her suspiciously. To* ŌBA.) What are you doing there—dreaming? Can't anything be done? (*To* MISAKO.) Misako, call Mr. Ghost and tell him you'll marry him or do anything else he wants.

THE REAL FUKAGAWA: She doesn't have to call to him. He's here. The ghost is here.

TOSHIE (*pulling* ŌBA'S *arm*): You've got to go right away and talk this over with the others.

ŌBA (*in a low voice*): Don't lose your head! The best thing for me to do now is to make my escape . . . before I get saddled with the blame.

THE REAL FUKAGAWA: How about going to the hotel and having a drink there?

ŌBA: Say, Mr. Fukagawa . . .

THE REAL FUKAGAWA: *I'm* Fukagawa.

(ŌBA *does not answer.*)

FUKAGAWA (*looks around him*): Are you sure he won't come back?

MISAKO: Do you feel lonely without him?

FUKAGAWA: Why should I? My only wish all along was that I

221

The Ghost is Here ▲

be left to myself . . . You'll still be willing to see me, won't you?

MISAKO: I'm seeing you right now.

THE REAL FUKAGAWA (*to* MISAKO *and* OLD WOMAN): Anyway, let's get away from here.

(FUKAGAWA, OLD WOMAN, *and* REAL FUKAGAWA *begin to walk.*)

MISAKO: Father, won't you and Mother come along, too?

OLD WOMAN (*turns back*): That's right. Yes, we must have the parents come along with us . . . (*Bows, as if meeting for the first time.*) I don't know how to thank you for all the trouble you've taken for my son.

ŌBA (*flurried*): Not at all. I'm sorry I wasn't able to do enough for him. (*To* TOSHIE.) Aren't you going to say anything? (TOSHIE *also bows her head.*)

OLD WOMAN: Please come with us to the hotel and have something to eat together . . .

ŌBA: I know it's an imposition . . .

(MODEL, *angry over this turn in the developments, suddenly interposes herself between them and slaps* ŌBA *in the face. She demands money.*)

TOSHIE: What does she want?

ŌBA: Shut up, I tell you! (*He shakes off* MODEL.)

(*Just as they all start moving,* MARUTAKE *rushes in at them.*)

MARUTAKE (*shouting*): Don't move, any of you! Get me? Nobody makes a move. I've got a whole gang of strongarm boys keeping watch outside. If you try anything funny, you'll be sorry.

MISAKO: What do you mean? We're the strong ones now. You won't be so happy if the police learn about the witness.

(MARUTAKE *cringes. The others start walking again.* MODEL *peevishly throws herself onto the bed. She stretches her splendid legs toward the ceiling and begins her calisthenics.*)

MARUTAKE (*calls to* ŌBA *as he goes off with the others*): You're not thinking of running away, are you, Mr. Ōba?

ŌBA: I have no further business here. (*Leaves.*)

(*As the* MAYOR *and the others hesitantly come into the infirmary, they look outside.*)

MARUTAKE: Damn it! Of all the imposters!

▲　*The Ghost is Here*

TORII: It's bankruptcy! We'll have to call the priest and cancel the wedding ceremony . . . And then the radio station, too.

MODEL (*unruffled, raises her legs, continuing her calisthenics on the bed*): Why? I'm willing to marry him.

MARUTAKE: What?

MODEL: It'd be better to hold the wedding. It suits me better, too.

MARUTAKE (*irritated*): Shut up! . . . Can't you get it through your head that there's nobody now to marry?

MODEL: But isn't that the same as before? There wasn't anybody from the start, was there? . . . It doesn't bother me. (*She sits up and strikes a coquettish pose.*)

TORII: You're right.

MODEL (*starts to parade around the room*): As long as you decide he really is here, that's all you need. (*Facing an imaginary person.*) Oh, is that where you were hiding yourself, Mr. Ghost? We've been looking for you . . . (*Dances.*)

I'm crazy about

A transparent man.

I want to get married to

A transparent man.

I go for ghosts—

He's wonderful!

MAYOR: That's really good!

(*They all burst out laughing.*)

TORII: You've saved our lives!

MARUTAKE: We're saved! This time he won't make any trouble about wanting to become president of the society or mayor.

TORII (*takes out a cigarette*): Isn't this exactly the same as in that book on investment economics? The ghost has stuck to us and won't leave us. And he's become a lot more cheerful and obedient. (*He laughs.*)

MODEL (*with a sniff, grabs one of* TORII's *cigarettes*): Don't take him for granted. My sweetheart can be *very* difficult . . . (*To imaginary person.*) That's right, isn't it? What? (*She listens attentively, nods.*) . . . Eh? My husband says he wants to become mayor, after all . . . (*Playfully, to the frightened* MAYOR.) But if that's not possible, he says that he'd like for the time being at least to have a house built for him . . . (*Her voice hardens.*) But, of course, he intends to remain president of the society.

(*The* MAYOR *and the others are too dazed to move.* MODEL, *observing them from the corner of her eyes, smiles at her invisible partner, and poses seductively. She crosses her arms . . . From outside, the sound of a baby crying.*)

VOICE: Excuse me, is he still busy? The other patients . . .

TORII (*looks at* MODEL *and waits for her nod*): Very well, ask the next person to come in.

(CITIZEN E *comes into the infirmary with a baby in her arms.* MODEL *flutters her hand over the baby's head.*)

CITIZEN E (*joins her hands in prayer*): Hail Amida Buddha!

(*The* MAYOR *and the others also join their hands in prayer.*)

(*Somewhere in the city.* FUKAGAWA *and the others walk under umbrellas, each full of his own thoughts.*)

CHORUS OF CITIZENS (*Chorus of Broken Dreams*):
　　The dream is broken
　　And the ghost's bride
　　Who missed her chance to lick the jam,
　　Is returning through
　　A town where it is raining.

TOSHIE (*to* MISAKO. *Her voice suggests her feelings are too strong to suppress*): Well, well, a girl who's not greedy for anything.

MISAKO: I'm not sure about that . . . But, you know, I really did want something.

TOSHIE: I can't imagine what.

(HAKOYAMA *comes running after them.*)

HAKOYAMA: Wait up, everybody!

ŌBA: That bastard . . .

MISAKO: Congratulations! You've got the conclusion to your story you wanted.

HAKOYAMA: Not by a long shot! Haven't you heard? The farce is continuing, just as if nothing happened. That crazy girl is saying now she can see the ghost.

(ALL *show expressions of surprise.*)

FUKAGAWA: Is that really the truth?

HAKOYAMA: If you don't believe me, go and have a look for yourself.

ŌBA: Son of a bitch! It's a crazy swindle!

224

▲　*The Ghost is Here*

FUKAGAWA: Shall we go have a look?

THE REAL FUKAGAWA: Don't! It doesn't make any difference, does it?

HAKOYAMA: It doesn't make any difference? Why? Is it all right to keep silent about such a fraud?

MISAKO: I wonder. Aren't you hoping just to find a conclusion for your story so you can collect your pay?

HAKOYAMA: That's unfair. Wasn't it, rather that I had to look after myself while trying to find a way to make sense of the story?

FUKAGAWA: Would you like an aspirin?

HAKOYAMA: What for?

FUKAGAWA: It soothes the nerves.

HAKOYAMA: Hmph.

THE REAL FUKAGAWA: We've got to hurry. It looks as if it's started to rain in earnest.

(*The others start to go, leaving* HAKOYAMA *behind.* TOSHIE *stops on the way.*)

TOSHIE: Papa! Are you going to take this lying down?

HAKOYAMA (*catching her words*): That's right! How can you remain quiet when the project you conceived has been taken over?

TOSHIE: You keep out of this. Nobody's talking to you.

ŌBA: But, after all that's happened, there's nothing to be done now . . . It's because you were careless enough to blab to Misako about the witness.

HAKOYAMA: Then wouldn't it be a good idea to use this witness to blast those bastards?

TOSHIE: Blast them? Don't be silly. Not as long as he's the chairman of the board.

HAKOYAMA: You mean, you still consider yourself one of them?

ŌBA: No, that's not possible either . . . This new ghost won't pay any attention to me.

TOSHIE: In that case, how would it be if you claimed that you could also see ghosts? If it's capital you need, there's nothing to worry about. I've deposited in my savings account all the money you gave me to seal the lips of the witness.

ŌBA: What do you mean?

TOSHIE (*whispers*): The witness, to tell the truth, was me.

225

The Ghost is Here ▲

(*Pause.*)

ŌBA (*recovers his spirits at once. Claps his hands*): Is that so! You're really a model wife! (*Kisses her. Looks around.*) Ohh— I can see him. I can see Mr. Ghost!

TOSHIE: Of course you can.

ŌBA: Yes, I can see him plainly. He's got a bald head and he's wearing glasses with gold rims. This ghost looks like a sea monster.

TOSHIE: Everything's turned out well, hasn't it? . . . Now we must hurry and spread word around town . . . (*To* HAKO-YAMA.) He's visible! Even to my husband!

ŌBA: Ahh—I see him! I see him! I can see the ghost! What a nice ghost he is!

(*The two of them run about the stage, spreading the news in loud voices.* HAKOYAMA *looks up indignantly, but his expression quickly turns to a suspicious frown. His shoulders droop with disappointment. He looks at his watch and writes in his notebook. In the background, the* MAYOR *and the others, headed by* MODEL, *appear, together with a procession of* CITIZENS *under umbrellas. In the foreground,* ŌBA SANKICHI *and* TOSHIE *run about, patting the invisible* GHOST.)

FULL CHORUS OF CITIZENS:

Once the wise man has spoken,
Get ready a great big saucepan.
The season of the dead is approaching.
Gather the ghosts and make jam,
Gather the ghosts and make jam.

Curtain.

▲ *The Ghost is Here*

◆

Other
Works
in the
Columbia
Asian
Studies
Series

TRANSLATIONS FROM THE ASIAN CLASSICS

◆   *Other Works*

Courtier and Commoner in Ancient China: Selections from the History of the Former Han by Pan Ku, tr. Burton Watson. Also in paperback ed. 1974

Japanese Literature in Chinese, vol. 1: Poetry and Prose in Chinese by Japanese Writers of the Early Period, tr. Burton Watson 1975

Japanese Literature in Chinese, vol. 2; Poetry and Prose in Chinese by Japanese Writers of the Later Period, tr. Burton Watson 1976

Scripture of the Lotus Blossom of the Fine Dharma, tr. Leon Hurvitz. Also in paperback ed. 1976

Love Song of the Dark Lord: Jayadeva's Gītagovinda, tr. Barbara Stoler Miller. Also in paperback ed. Cloth ed. includes critical text of the Sanskrit. 1977

Ryōkan: Zen Monk-Poet of Japan, tr. Burton Watson 1977

Calming the Mind and Discerning the Real: From the Lam rim chen mo of Tson-kha-pa, tr. Alex Wayman 1978

The Hermit and the Love-Thief: Sanskrit Poems of Bhartrihari and Bilhaṇa, tr. Barbara Stoler Miller 1978

The Lute: Kao Ming's P'i-p'a chi, tr. Jean Mulligan. Also in paperback ed. 1980

A Chronicle of Gods and Sovereigns: Jinnō Shōtōki of Kitabatake-Chikafusa, tr. H. Paul Varley. 1980

Among the Flowers: The Hua-chien chi, tr. Lois Fusek 1982

Grass Hill: Poems and Prose by the Japanese Monk Gensei, tr. Burton Watson 1983

Doctors, Diviners, and Magicians of Ancient China: Biographies of Fang-shih, tr. Kenneth J. DeWoskin. Also in paperback ed. 1983

Theater of Memory: The Plays of Kālidāsa, ed. Barbara Stoler Miller. Also in paper ed. 1984

The Columbia Book of Chinese Poetry: From Early Times to the Thirteenth Century, ed. and tr. Burton Watson. Also in paperback ed. 1984

Poems of Love and War: From the Eight Anthologies and the Ten Songs of Classical Tamil, tr. A. K. Ramanujan. Also in paperback ed. 1985

The Columbia Book of Later Chinese Poetry, ed. and tr. Jonathan Chaves. Also in paperback ed. 1986

The Tso Chuan: Selections from China's Oldest Narrative History, tr. Burton Watson 1989

Other Works ◆

Selected Writings of Nichiren, ed. Philip B. Yampolsky   1990
Saigyō, Poems of a Mountain Home, tr. Burton Watson   1990
The Cilappatikāram of Iḷaṅkō Aṭikaḷ, tr. R. Parthasarathy   1992

STUDIES IN ASIAN CULTURE

1. *The Ōnin War: History of Its Origins and Background, with a Selective Translation of the Chronicle of Ōnin,* by H. Paul Varley   1967
2. *Chinese Government in Ming Times: Seven Studies,* ed. Charles O. Hucker   1969
3. *The Actors' Analects (Yakusha Rongo),* ed. and tr. by Charles J. Dunn and Bungō Torigoe   1969
4. *Self and Society in Ming Thought,* by Wm. Theodore de Bary and the Conference on Ming Thought. Also in paperback ed.   1970
5. *A History of Islamic Philosophy,* by Majid Fakhry, 2d ed.   1983
6. *Phantasies of a Love Thief: The Caurapañcāśikā Attributed to Bilhaṇa,* by Barbara Stoler Miller   1971
7. *Iqbal: Poet-Philosopher of Pakistan,* ed. Hafeez Malik   1971
8. *The Golden Tradition: An Anthology of Urdu Poetry,* ed. and tr. Ahmed Ali. Also in paperback ed.   1973
9. *Conquerors and Confucians: Aspects of Political Change in Late Yüan China,* by John W. Dardess   1973
10. *The Unfolding of Neo-Confucianism,* by Wm. Theodore de Bary and the Conference on Seventeenth-Century Chinese Thought. Also in paperback ed.   1975
11. *To Acquire Wisdom: The Way of Wang Yang-ming,* by Julia Ching   1976
12. *Gods, Priests, and Warriors: The Bhṛgus of the Mahābhārata,* by Robert P. Goldman   1977
13. *Mei Yao-ch'en and the Development of Early Sung Poetry,* by Jonathan Chaves   1976
14. *The Legend of Semimaru, Blind Musician of Japan,* by Susan Matisoff   1977
15. *Sir Sayyid Ahmad Khan and Muslim Modernization in India and Pakistan,* by Hafeez Malik   1980
16. *The Khilafat Movement: Religious Symbolism and Political Mobilization in India,* by Gail Minault   1982
17. *The World of K'ung Shang-jen: A Man of Letters in Early Ch'ing China,* by Richard Strassberg   1983

◆   *Other Works*

COMPANIONS TO ASIAN STUDIES

INTRODUCTION TO ASIAN CIVILIZATIONS

Wm. Theodore de Bary, Editor

Sources of Japanese Tradition, 1958; paperback ed., 2 vols., 1964

Sources of Indian Tradition, 1958; paperback ed., 2 vols., 1964; 2d ed., 1988

Sources of Chinese Tradition, 1960; paperback ed., 2 vols., 1964

NEO-CONFUCIAN STUDIES

Instructions for Practical Living and Other Neo-Confucian Writings by Wang Yang-ming, tr. Wing-tsit China 1963

Reflections on Things at Hand: The Neo-Confucian Anthology, comp. Chu Hsi and Lü Tsu-ch'ien, tr. Wing-tsit Chan 1967

Self and Society in Ming Thought, by Wm. Theodore de Bary and the Conference on Ming Thought: Also in paperback ed. 1970

The Unfolding of Neo-Confucianism, by Wm. Theodore de Bary and the Conference on Seventeenth-Century Chinese Thought. Also in paperback ed. 1975

Principle and Practicality: Essays in Neo-Confucianism and Practical Learning, ed. Wm. Theodore de Bary and Irene Bloom. Also in paperback ed. 1979

The Syncretic Religion of Lin Chao-en, by Judith A. Berling 1980

The Renewal of Buddhism in China: Chu-hung and the Late Ming Synthesis, by Chün-fang Yü 1981

Neo-Confucian Orthodoxy and the Learning of the Mind-and-Heart, by Wm. Theodore de Bary 1981

Yüan Thought: Chinese Thought and Religion Under the Mongols, ed. Hok-lam Chan and Wm. Theodore de Bary 1982

The Liberal Tradition in China, by Wm. Theodore de Bary 1983

The Development and Decline of Chinese Cosmology, by John B. Henderson 1984

The Rise of Neo-Confucianism in Korea, by Wm. Theodore de Bary and JaHyun Kim Haboush 1985

Chiao Hung and the Restructuring of Neo-Confucianism in Late Ming, by Edward T. Ch'ien 1985

Neo-Confucian Terms Explained: Pei-hsi tzu-i, by Ch'en Ch'un, ed. and trans. Wing-tsit Chan 1986

◆ *Other Works*

Knowledge Painfully Acquired: K'un-chih chi, by Lo Ch'in-
shun, ed. and trans. Irene Bloom   1987
To Become a Sage: The Ten Diagrams on Sage Learning, by Yi
T'oegye, ed. and trans. Michael C. Kalton   1988
The Message of the Mind in Neo-Confucian Thought, by Wm.
Theodore de Bary   1989

MODERN ASIAN LITERATURE SERIES

Modern Japanese Drama: An Anthology, ed. and tr. Ted Tak-
aya. Also in paperback ed.   1979
Mask and Sword: Two Plays for the Contemporary Japanese
Theater, Yamazaki Masakazu, tr. J. Thomas Rimer   1980
Yokomitsu Riichi, Modernist, Dennis Keene   1980
Nepali Visions, Nepali Dreams: The Poetry of Laxmiprasad
Devkota, tr. David Rubin   1980
Literature of the Hundred Flowers, vol. 1: Criticism and Polem-
ics, ed. Hualing Nieh   1981
Literature of the Hundred Flowers, vol. 2: Poetry and Fiction,
ed. Hualing Nieh   1981
Modern Chinese Stories and Novellas, 1919–1949, ed. Joseph
S. M. Lau, C. T. Hsia, and Leo Ou-fan Lee. Also in
paperback ed.   1984
A View of the Sea, by Yasuoka Shōtarō, tr. Kären Wigen Lewis   1984
Other Worlds, Arishima Takeo and the Bounds of Modern Jap-
anese Fiction, by Paul Anderer   1984
Selected Poems of Sō Chōngju, tr. with intro. by David R.
McCann   1989
The Sting of Life: Four Contemporary Japanese Novelists, by
Van C. Gessel   1989
Stories of Osaka Life, by Oda Sakunosuke, tr. Burton Watson   1990
The Bodhisattva, or Samantabhadra, by Ishikawa Jun, tr. with
intro. by William Jefferson Tyler   1990
Fictional Realism in 20th-Century China, by David Der-wei
Wang   1992

Designer:	Teresa Bonner
Text:	Electra
Compositor:	Maple Vail
Printer:	Maple Vail
Binder:	Maple Vail